MW00563408

A CATHOLIC ENGAGEMENT WITH LATTER-DAY SAINTS

A Catholic Engagement with Latter-day Saints

*Edited by Francis J. Beckwith
and Richard Sherlock*

IGNATIUS PRESS   SAN FRANCISCO

Cover photo of the Madeleine Cathedral
Salt Lake City, Utah
by Richard H. Hegg

Cover design by Enrique J. Aguilar

© 2024 by Ignatius Press, San Francisco
All rights reserved
ISBN 978-1-58617-925-0 (PB)
ISBN 978-1-64229-315-9 (eBook)
Library of Congress Control Number 2024944149
Printed in the United States of America ∞

CONTENTS

INTRODUCTION

What Does Salt Lake City Have to Do with Rome?

Francis J. Beckwith and Richard Sherlock

For a great many people, especially Catholics, Mormonism seems like a strange and exotic faith.[1] Although having its origin in nineteenth-century America, its prophets and adherents claim more ancient roots. Mormonism's founding prophet, Joseph Smith, Jr. (1805–1844), proclaimed that God had chosen him to restore the lost gospel of Jesus Christ that had vanished from the earth for over seventeen hundred years.

In 1830 he founded what he named the Church of Jesus Christ, which he eventually came to call the Church of Jesus Christ of Latter-day Saints (LDS), as we know it today. Smith's story begins in 1820 in upstate New York, where as a young man he was bewildered with the seemingly endless number of Christian sects he found

---

[1] In 2018, the Church of Jesus Christ of Latter-day Saints—the official name of the Mormon church—published in its style guide that "while the term 'Mormon Church' has long been publicly applied to the Church as a nickname, it is not an authorized title, and the Church discourages its use. Thus, please avoid using the abbreviation 'LDS' or the nickname 'Mormon' as substitutes for the name of the Church, as in 'Mormon Church,' 'LDS Church,' or 'Church of the Latter-day Saints.'" The church also asked "that the term 'Mormons' and 'LDS' not be used" in identifying church members. ("Style Guide—The Name of the Church", newsroom of the Church of Jesus Christ of Latter-day Saints, updated April 13, 2021, https://newsroom.churchofjesuschrist.org/style-guide?lang=pon.) See also Doug Criss, "Mormons Don't Want You Calling Them Mormons Anymore", CNN.com, August 17, 2018, https://www.cnn.com/2018/08/17/us/mormon-church-name-trnd/index.html.

Although we have tried our best to honor this request, there is simply too much literature—including a vast majority of LDS works—that uses these terms and phrases. In fact, when one of us did an internal search of the terms "Mormonism", "LDS Church", and "Mormons" on the LDS website in late July 2021, we found hundreds of pages in which these terms and phrases still appear.

7

among his fellow citizens. Not being able to discern which one was correct, he went alone into the woods to pray and ask God for wisdom, in accordance with what the Bible commands in the Book of James: "If any of you lacks wisdom, let him ask God, who gives to all men generously and without reproaching, and it will be given him" (1:5). According to Smith, this is what happened next:

> After I had retired to the place where I had previously designed to go, having looked around me, and finding myself alone, I kneeled down and began to offer up the desires of my heart to God. I had scarcely done so, when immediately I was seized upon by some power which entirely overcame me, and had such an astonishing influence over me as to bind my tongue so that I could not speak. Thick darkness gathered around me, and it seemed to me for a time as if I were doomed to sudden destruction.
>
> But, exerting all my powers to call upon God to deliver me out of the power of this enemy which had seized upon me, and at the very moment when I was ready to sink into despair and abandon myself to destruction—not to an imaginary ruin, but to the power of some actual being from the unseen world, who had such marvelous power as I had never before felt in any being—just at this moment of great alarm, I saw a pillar of light exactly over my head, above the brightness of the sun, which descended gradually until it fell upon me.
>
> It no sooner appeared than I found myself delivered from the enemy which held me bound. When the light rested upon me I saw two Personages, whose brightness and glory defy all description, standing above me in the air. One of them spake unto me, calling me by name and said, pointing to the other—*This is My Beloved Son. Hear Him!*[2]

When Smith asked the "Personages" which religious group he should join, one of them said that he "must join none of them, for they were all wrong; and ... that all their creeds were an abomination in his sight; that those professors were all corrupt."[3] According to Smith, in 1823 he was visited by an angel named Moroni, who told him about gold plates buried in the Hill Cumorah in Palmyra, New York. These

---

[2] Joseph Smith—History 1:15–17, in the Pearl of Great Price (PGP). The PGP is one of three books that the LDS consider to be Sacred Scripture in addition to the Protestant Bible. The other additional books are the Book of Mormon and the Doctrine and Covenants.

[3] Ibid., 1:19.

plates contained the story of an ancient people, descended from the Hebrews, that once inhabited America and that Jesus had visited soon after his Resurrection. Smith claimed that he had translated these plates into English with the assistance of seer stones (the Urim and Thummim). The product of this translation is known as the Book of Mormon, which its introduction says "contains the fulness of the everlasting gospel".[4] For this reason, the LDS church teaches that the Book of Mormon is as much Sacred Scripture as is the Protestant Bible.[5]

Smith claimed that he and his friend Oliver Cowdery were visited on May 15, 1829, by John the Baptist, who conferred upon them the Aaronic priesthood. Smith also claimed that sometime between that event and April 6, 1830 (the founding date of the LDS church), he and Cowdery were ordained to the priesthood of Melchizedek by the apostles Peter, James, and John. This, according to LDS church teaching, marks the restoration of the gospel to which Smith had been called. The church quickly established an early version of its now-sophisticated hierarchical structure and began to gain converts. Over time, as a consequence of severe persecution and hostile conditions, the early Mormons moved from New York to Ohio to Missouri to Illinois and eventually settled in Utah. After Smith was assassinated by an angry mob in Illinois in 1844, the church's leadership, after some struggle and schism,[6] was passed on to Brigham Young, who took the group to the Salt Lake Valley in the Great Basin. Prior to his death, Smith claimed to have received further divine revelation in addition to the Book of Mormon: the Doctrine and Covenants (DC) and the Pearl of Great Price (PGP).[7] These three volumes, as well as

[4] Book of Mormon, introduction.

[5] Like Protestants, Mormons do not accept the deuterocanonical books that Catholics include in their Bible.

[6] Schismatic groups that emerged during this struggle for leadership include the Reorganized Church of Jesus Christ of Latter-day Saints, which rejected Young as Smith's successor as well as several doctrines embraced by the Utah Mormons, including plural marriage and exaltation to godhood. Since 1890 the Utah church has abandoned the doctrine of plural marriage. In 2001, the Reorganized Church officially changed its name to the Community of Christ. See the Community of Christ's official website at www.cofchrist.org.

[7] It should be noted that since Smith's death, the LDS church has edited and made additions to both the DC and PGP. Given the LDS belief in continuing revelation—that God may reveal more Scripture and insight through his prophets over time—there is nothing untoward in the church making changes in its standard works that may illuminate the church's beliefs and better instruct its people.

the Protestant Bible, are called the standard works of the Mormon church. It is from them, as interpreted and supplemented by Smith, Young, and their successors, that the LDS church derives its doctrines and practices. From its modest beginnings in 1830, with six founding members, the church has grown as of December 31, 2023, to more than 17.25 million.[8]

Unlike the American Protestantism within which Smith found himself bewildered, Mormonism is not a *sola scriptura* faith, one committed to the belief that the Bible alone (or in the case of the LDS, the four books of Scripture alone) is (or are) the only authority to which all believers in Jesus Christ should subscribe. For this reason, Mormonism seems to many Catholics both different and familiar. Its hierarchical structure and reliance on a kind of living magisterium with the authority to issue doctrinal pronouncements and clarify theological questions seems "Catholic". On the other hand, its cultural ethos, its rejection of the physical accruements of traditional liturgies and practices, and its claim that the doctrinal and ecclesiastical developments of Catholicism are corruptions of "original Christianity" all seem very "Protestant". As one of us (Francis J. Beckwith) once noted:

> Even if one thinks that [Joseph] Smith was profoundly mistaken (as I do), one cannot help but marvel at the religious genius of this project: It has all the advantages of Reformation Protestantism and nineteenth-century Restorationism ("Let's get back to what Jesus and the apostles originally taught") with all the advantages of Catholicism and Orthodoxy, an apostolic magisterium within the confines of a visible church. Smith has both a priesthood of all believers and a priesthood managed by a church hierarchy. He offers a new gospel unconstrained by centuries of theological precedent, yet he could claim that it is as old as the apostles. He could, without contradiction, reject tradition while claiming to be the true guardian of an ancient message. It may be wrong, but it was brilliant.[9]

---

[8] Tad Walch, "Latter-day Saint Membership Passed 17.25 Million in 2023, according to a New Church Statistical Report", *Deseret News*, April 6, 2024, www.deseret.com/faith/2024/04/06/latter-day-saint-mormon-membership-increased-this-much-in-2023-church-statistical-report.

[9] Francis J. Beckwith, "When the Saint Goes Swearing In", *First Things Online*, May 24, 2007, www.firstthings.com/web-exclusives/2007/05/when-the-saints-goes-swearing.

Even with the impressive international growth of Mormonism and the Catholic Church's efforts to dialogue with numerous religious bodies after the Second Vatican Council (1962–1965), there has been little theological discussion between Catholics and Mormons.[10] This is the primary reason we have assembled in this book a collection of Catholic scholars—for the purpose of addressing, understanding, and engaging the differences between our faith and the beliefs embraced by our LDS friends. The inspiration for this project was the 2002 book entitled *The New Mormon Challenge*,[11] a finalist for the Gold Medallion Book Award in Theology and Doctrine. It was a turning point in the discussion of Mormonism by Evangelical Christians. It not only was free from the ad hominem attacks and lurid historical details on which popular Evangelical assessments often focused but also was a careful scholarly examination and analysis of Mormon beliefs. The book's contributors took Mormonism seriously, critically assessing the LDS view of God's nature, the moral law, metaphysics, and its beliefs about the Bible and the Book of Mormon. Even Mormon scholars who disagreed with the book's conclusions nevertheless praised the quality of the critique.

Although *The New Mormon Challenge* was an important contribution to LDS-Christian dialogue, the book did not cover several crucial philosophical and theological topics. Some were excluded for reasons of space, such as the doctrines of the Trinity, the Incarnation, and justification (that is, the relationship between faith and works). Other topics, which would be of particular interest for Catholics, were left out because they are matters over which Evangelicals and Mormons are not that far apart. These topics will be the focus of most of the chapters of this present volume, *A Catholic Engagement with Latter-day Saints*.

The LDS church rejects the doctrine of the Trinity as it is found in the earliest creeds of the Catholic Church (which are accepted by most Protestant groups as well). Because Latter-day Saints do not

[10] Some notable exceptions in the literature include Donald Westbrook, "Catholic-Mormon Relations", *Religious Educator* 13, no. 1 (2012): 35–53; Stephen H. Webb and Alonzo H. Gaskill, *Catholic and Mormon: A Theological Conversation* (New York: Oxford University Press, 2015). Westbrook's article is particularly good.

[11] Francis J. Beckwith, Carl Mosser, and Paul Owen, eds., *The New Mormon Challenge* (Grand Rapids, MI: Zondervan, 2002).

believe in one divine essence, they affirm some form of tritheism. They believe that "the Father has a body of flesh and bones as tangible as man's; the Son also; but the Holy Ghost has not a body of flesh and bones, but is a personage of Spirit."[12] United only in purpose and doctrine, the Father, the Son, and the Holy Spirit are separate *Beings*.[13] To guide us in better understanding a most difficult doctrine, in chapter 1 ("The Trinity"), theologian Matthew Levering explains the Catholic view and shows how the LDS view diverges from it.

When the LDS founder said that "God [the Father] is an exalted man",[14] he separated the LDS church from the Western religious tradition in a fundamental way. The fifth president of the Mormon church, Lorenzo Snow (1814–1901), reduced this to a couplet that many Latter-day Saints know by heart: "As man now is, God once was: As God now is, man may be."[15] Grant this and there is no existential gap between God and man. They are of the same species. Hence, there is no need for a true incarnation to bridge this gap, as understood by traditional Christians including Catholics. In chapter 2 ("Becoming like God: A Critique"), philosopher Richard Sherlock shows how this diminished view of the deity combined with an elevated view of human nature has important implications across a range of theological topics.

Chapter 3 ("Classical Theism, Latter-day Saint Theism, and a Long-Awaited, Though Modest, Rejoinder to the Roberts-Van der Donckt Debate") concerns a 1901 through 1902 published debate between Mormon theologian B. H. Roberts (1857–1933) and Jesuit priest Father Cyril Van der Donckt (1865–1939), a pastor in Pocatello, Idaho. After publishing Roberts' talk "The Mormon Doctrine of Deity", editors of the periodical *Improvement Era* published Father Cyril's rebuttal. That was followed by Roberts' extensive rejoinder.

---

[12] Doctrine and Covenants 130:22.

[13] "Although the members of the Godhead are distinct beings with distinct roles, they are one in purpose and doctrine. They are perfectly united in bringing to pass Heavenly Father's divine plan of salvation." ("Godhead", Church of Jesus Christ of Latter-day Saints website, accessed February 15, 2024, www.lds.org/topics/godhead?lang=eng.)

[14] Joseph Smith, Jr., "The King Follet Sermon" (April 7, 1844), *Ensign* 1, no. 4 (April 1971), www.lds.org/ensign/1971/04/the-king-follett-sermon?lang=eng.

[15] Quoted in *Teachings of the Presidents of the Church: Lorenzo Snow* (Salt Lake City: Church of Jesus Christ of Latter-day Saints, 2012), 83.

Father Cyril did not publish a reply to the rejoinder. However, in this chapter philosopher Francis J. Beckwith offers his own rejoinder on behalf of Father Cyril. In the process of doing this, he provides detailed presentations of both the LDS and Catholic doctrines of deity as well as responses to Roberts' rejection of the Catholic views of the Incarnation, the Trinity, and the value of Greek philosophy in the development of Christian doctrine.

Protestants have historically held that sometime in the Middle Ages the Church lost her way and needed to be reformed. The Latter-day Saints, on the other hand, doubled down on the idea. According to the LDS church, "After the deaths of the Savior and His Apostles, men corrupted the principles of the gospel and made unauthorized changes in Church organization and priesthood ordinances. Because of this widespread apostasy, the Lord withdrew the authority of the priesthood from the earth. This apostasy lasted until Heavenly Father and His Beloved Son appeared to Joseph Smith in 1820 and initiated the Restoration of the fulness of the gospel."[16] What Mormons call the Great Apostasy is said to have happened in the early patristic period and to have been so severe that it required a restoration. The difference between the traditional Protestant and Mormon narratives is one of degree, not kind. In chapter 4 ("James Barker's Case for the Great Apostasy"), historian James Hitchcock offers a critical assessment of this claim by evaluating one of the most popular LDS books to defend it: *The Apostasy from the Divine Church.*[17]

The LDS church teaches that the goal or purpose of human existence is to achieve exaltation, literally to become a God. As the renowned LDS thinker B. H. Roberts once put it: "We believe that somewhere and some time in the ages to come, through development, through enlargement, through purification until perfection is attained, man at last, may become like God—a God."[18] And to again quote from the LDS church's fifth president, Lorenzo Snow: "As man

---

[16] "Apostasy", Church of Jesus Christ of Latter-day Saints website, accessed February 16, 2024, www.lds.org/topics/apostasy?lang=eng.

[17] *The Apostasy from the Divine Church* is not considered an official LDS church publication. It was published two years after Barker's death in 1960 by Barker's widow, Kate Montgomery Barker, with no location given.

[18] B. H. Roberts, *The Mormon Doctrine of Deity: The Roberts-Van Der Donckt Discussion, to Which Is Added a Discourse; Jesus Christ, the Revelation of God* (Salt Lake City: Signature Books, 1998; originally published 1903 by Deseret News [Salt Lake City]), 11.

now is, God once was: As God now is, man may be."[19] Although there is some dispute among LDS scholars as to the meaning of the first part of Snow's couplet,[20] it is clear that because the Mormon church believes that God and human beings are of the same species, some form of real deification is central to LDS doctrine.

In Eastern Orthodoxy and those Eastern Rite churches in communion with Rome, there is a teaching called *theosis*.[21] Found deep in Christian history, it is sometimes called deification or divinization. Some LDS scholars, such as Robert L. Millet and Shon D. Hopkin,[22] argue that the LDS idea of exaltation is a full restoration of what the early Christians once believed, a residue of which can be found outside Mormonism in the Eastern Christian belief in *theosis*. In chapter 5 ("Deification in Two Traditions"), historian Glenn Olsen shows what *theosis* meant to the early Christians and how their idea is in continuity with contemporary Catholicism and Orthodoxy and how the Mormon idea of deification differs.

Chapter 6 ("Liturgy in Mormonism and Catholicism") addresses the differences and similarities between how Mormons and Catholics

---

[19] Quoted in *Teachings of the Presidents of the Church*, 83.

[20] For example, Brigham Young University theologian Robert Millet writes: "Joseph Smith taught that God is an Exalted Man, a Man of Holiness, and that while He is God and possesses every power, every divine quality, and every perfected attribute, He is not of a different species with mortal men and women. Now don't misunderstand me here: the chasm between man and God is immense, but we do not believe it is unbridgeable, nor do we hold the same Creator-creature dichotomy that most Christians do. For us God is a man, a person, an actual being with a glorified and exalted personality. It is true that Presidents Joseph Smith and Lorenzo Snow both spoke of God once being a man, but we know very little if anything beyond that idea itself. I am not aware of any official statement or declaration of doctrine that goes beyond what I have just stated. Anything you may hear or read beyond that is speculative." (Robert L. Millet and Gregory C. V. Johnson, *Bridging the Divide: The Continuing Conversation between a Mormon and an Evangelical* [Rhinebeck, NY: Monkfish Book Publishing, 2007], 58.)

[21] Latin Rite Catholics do not deny this teaching, since, after all, they are in communion with their Eastern Rite brethren. Rather, they will often use different language to express the same idea. So, for example, the Catholic Church affirms, "Our justification comes from the grace of God. Grace is *favor*, the *free and undeserved help* that God gives us to respond to his call to become children of God, adoptive sons, *partakers of the divine nature* and of eternal life." (*Catechism of the Catholic Church*, no. 1996; second emphasis added.) See David Meconi, S.J., and Carl E. Olson, eds., *Called to Be Children of God: The Catholic Theology of Human Deification* (San Francisco: Ignatius Press, 2016).

[22] Robert L. Millet and Shon D. Hopkin, *Mormonism: A Guide for the Perplexed* (New York: Bloomsbury, 2015), 196–98. Millet and Hopkin also cite the work of the great Anglican scholar C. S. Lewis.

worship. Authored by Catholic convert and former Mormon Rachel Lu, this chapter respectfully compares and contrasts liturgical practices in both traditions, showing, among other things, how each is shaped by deeper theological differences.

The Catholic Church teaches that the Eucharist is the "fount and apex of the whole Christian life".[23] The reason for this is that the Church believes that when the priest celebrating Mass says the words of Consecration, the bread and wine are transformed into the actual Body and Blood of Christ, with his soul and divinity being present as well. Latter-day Saints, like virtually all Protestants, deny this is true. In chapter 7 ("Catholicism, Mormonism, and Eucharistic Realism"), philosophers Francis J. Beckwith and Alexander Pruss explain the Protestant, Mormon, and Catholic views. They show how the latter is the most consistent with the depiction of Communion in the New Testament, the view held by the earliest Christians, and why it is philosophically defensible.

Protestants disagree with what Catholics believe is the plain meaning of Christ's words to Saint Peter in Matthew 16:13–19, where he tells Saint Peter that he will found the Church on him as a rock and "the gates of Hades shall not prevail against it" (16:18). According to the Catholic Church, by declaring Saint Peter to be the rock on which the Church is built, our Lord was saying that Saint Peter was to become the first pope. Mormons agree with Protestants that Catholics are wrong about the "plain meaning" of this passage. Both groups also reject the Catholic belief that the current bishops of the Catholic Church, including the pope, are the successors to the apostles. In chapter 8 ("The Papacy: The Most Real Institution in the World"), theologian Ronald Thomas provides an explanation of the Catholic view of the Petrine office.

One of Mormonism's most astute observers, the late University of Utah philosopher Sterling McMurrin (1914–1996), once wrote that "Mormon theology is a modern Pelagianism in a Puritan religion."[24] This is because the LDS church emphasizes good works as essential to salvation. Mormon apostle Bruce R. McConkie (1915–1985) makes

---

[23] Vatican Council II, Dogmatic Constitution on the Church *Lumen Gentium* (November 21, 1964), no. 11, www.vatican.va/archive/hist_councils/ii_vatican_council/documents/vat-ii_const_19641121_lumen-gentium_en.html.

[24] Sterling M. McMurrin, *The Theological Foundations of the Mormon Religion* (Salt Lake City: University of Utah Press, 1965), x.

this explicit when he writes in his seminal work, *Mormon Doctrine*: "By believing the truths of salvation, repenting of his sins, and being baptized in water and of the Spirit, the seeker after salvation places himself on the strait and narrow path which leads to eternal life. (2 Ne. 31.) Thereafter his progress up the path is achieved by the performance of *good works*."[25] Philosopher and Catholic priest Father Joel Barstad points out in chapter 9 ("Mormon Pelagianism") that Protestants, ironically, often accuse Catholics of believing the same thing, for the piety of many Catholics seems to confirm this accusation. Nevertheless, Father Barstad argues that traditional Christian Pelagianism, however heretical it may be, is of a different order in comparison to Latter-day Saint Pelagianism. As part of his case, Father Barstad explains the Pelagian heresy and why the Catholic Church has condemned it, even though it still remains a temptation that individual believers sometimes find difficult to resist.

This book concludes with an essay authored by the highly acclaimed Notre Dame historian and philosopher Brad S. Gregory. Professor Gregory earned his B.S. degree from Utah State University in Logan, Utah, in 1985, graduating first in his class from the College of Humanities and Social Sciences. For this honor, he was invited to give a valedictorian address at the college's commencement. Entitled "On Being a Catholic in Utah", it is published for the first time in this book as its afterword. It is a poignant reflection on how the primacy of love should guide one's conduct and inner life when one is striving to practice Catholicism authentically while living and studying among Latter-day Saint friends who do not share one's faith.

The contributions to this book are wide-ranging in the way they address issues in LDS and Catholic theology and practice. Some are more descriptive and dialogical, while others are more apologetic and critical. In essence, what we want to display in this book are the various kinds of engagement that may (and should) occur in interreligious discussions between ecclesial groups, each of which believes that its faith tradition is in fact true while wanting to understand the other better and to cultivate a spirit of friendship. In the case of Catholics and Latter-day Saints, we share many of the same beliefs about

---

[25] Bruce R. McConkie, *Mormon Doctrine*, 2nd ed. (Salt Lake City: Bookcraft, 1966), 328 (emphasis in original).

morality, social life, and the common good,[26] even while disagreeing strongly on many theological issues including the nature of God, the church, and the sacraments.

We should also note that there are topics in this book that are not given chapter-length treatments, such as the Blessed Virgin Mary, the relationship between Sacred Tradition and Sacred Scripture, the development of doctrine, and the nature of the Magisterium (though our contributors touch on these topics in various ways while addressing other issues). Such chapters are absent for two simple reasons: space constraints, and we can't cover everything. We simply made the judgment that the issues covered in this book are the most central to Catholic and LDS dialogue, though we certainly can see why others may disagree.

We as editors have a unique perspective on this project. One of us, Francis J. Beckwith, was one of the editors of *The New Mormon Challenge* when he was an Evangelical scholar. The fifty-eighth president of the Evangelical Theological Society, he resigned from that post in 2007 soon after he returned to the Catholic Church of his youth.[27] Richard Sherlock was a Latter-day Saint until he was baptized a Catholic at the Easter Vigil in 2012.[28] In fact, he served as the first president of the Society for Mormon Philosophy and Theology.

So, as a revert and a convert, coming to Catholicism from Evangelicalism and Mormonism, respectively, we offer this book in a spirit of dialogue for the sake of mutual understanding. It is our hope that this book will help forge a path to greater cooperation on those matters over which we agree while at the same time provide a Catholic resource from which both Latter-day Saints and Catholics can learn

---

[26] See, e.g., Francis J. Beckwith, "Moral Law, the Mormon Universe, and the Nature of the Right We Ought to Choose", in Beckwith, Mosser, and Owen, *New Mormon Challenge*, 219–41. In this chapter, Beckwith mentions the overlapping moral views of Evangelicals, Latter-day Saints, and Catholics.

[27] Francis J. Beckwith, *Return to Rome: Confessions of an Evangelical Catholic* (Grand Rapids, MI: Brazos Press, 2009); and Francis J. Beckwith, "A Journey to Catholicism" and "Catholicism Rejoinder", both in *Journeys of Faith: Evangelicalism, Eastern Orthodoxy, Catholicism, and Anglicanism*, ed. Robert L. Plumber (New York: HarperCollins; Grand Rapids, MI: Zondervan, 2012), 81–114; 129–34.

[28] Richard Sherlock, "A Mormon Scholar's Journey to Catholic Faith", *First Things Online*, August 30, 2012, www.firstthings.com/web-exclusives/2012/08/a-mormon-scholars-journey-to-catholic-faith.

about our differences. For this reason, we are publishing this book as a modest contribution to the Catholic Church's mission to share the gospel in conversation with those of other faith traditions. We are trying, however inadequately, to practice what Pope Saint John Paul II preached in his 1990 encyclical *Redemptoris Missio*:

> In the light of the economy of salvation, the Church sees no conflict between proclaiming Christ and engaging in interreligious dialogue....
>
> Those engaged in this dialogue must be consistent with their own religious traditions and convictions, and be open to understanding those of the other party without pretense or close-mindedness, but with truth, humility and frankness, knowing that dialogue can enrich each side....
>
> Dialogue is a path toward the kingdom and will certainly bear fruit, even if the times and seasons are known only to the Father (cf. Acts 1:7).[29]

---

[29] Pope John Paul II, Encyclical on the Permanent Validity of the Church's Missionary Mandate *Redemptoris Missio* (December 7, 1990), nos. 55–57, www.vatican.va/content/john-paul-ii/en/encyclicals/documents/hf_jp-ii_enc_07121990_redemptoris-missio.html.

The Trinity

Matthew Levering

I. Introduction

In *The Grammar of God: A Journey into the Words and Worlds of the Bible*, the Jewish writer Aviya Kushner reflects upon the difference between reading the Bible in Hebrew and reading it in English, and also upon the difference between reading the Bible as a newcomer and reading it within a multigenerational matrix. Kushner's family members were avid readers of the Bible, and they read it with Jewish readers from across the centuries, such as Maimonides, Rashbam, and Rashi. They debated the meaning of biblical texts at the dinner table, and they reflected upon the interpretations given by the various rabbinic authorities. Kushner points out that the most famous rabbinic authorities were generally the sons or grandsons of rabbinic scholars, so reading the Bible was not an individual work but a family enterprise. She also appreciates the experience of readers who enter into the biblical world only as adults. Such readers, too, can become great expositors of the Bible.[1]

Reflection on the Trinity also has this kind of depth. It requires reading in Jewish texts and in Christian texts, in Scripture and in ancient Greco-Roman philosophical texts, in the writings of those who spearheaded the formation of Trinitarian doctrine and in the extant writings of their opponents. In this chapter, therefore, I seek to contribute to Catholic-Mormon dialogue by entering, insofar as possible in

---

[1] Aviya Kushner, *The Grammar of God: A Journey into the Words and Worlds of the Bible* (New York: Random House, 2015).

a very brief space, into the ancient dialogues, or controversies, from which Trinitarian Christianity—and thus the meanings of "Trinity" and "Christian"—emerged.[2] In my view, Catholic-Mormon dialogue about the Trinity (and thus about the meaning of Christian worship) ultimately must first be a dialogue about earlier constitutive dialogues, reaching far back into the past in order to make progress in the present.

My chapter proceeds in two steps. First, I describe the Mormon position on the doctrine of the Trinity and related topics. Given that I lack competence to discuss the Book of Mormon and other authoritative Mormon texts (beyond the Bible), my description of the Mormon position on the Trinity relies upon the contemporary Mormon theologians Robert Millet and Alonzo Gaskill, both of whom have engaged in valuable theological dialogue on the Trinity (with Evangelical and Catholic interlocutors, respectively). Second, I examine the development of the doctrine of God in the Old and New Testaments, and I explore the Church Fathers' writings in light of challenges posed by Jewish and Muslim theologians. I hope thereby to anchor Catholic-Mormon dialogue in the constitutive dialogues that continue to inform Catholic Trinitarian theology.

II. Mormon Perspectives

Mormons believe that in a premortal existence, Jesus Christ was "the firstborn spirit child of God" the Father.[3] All other humans, too, existed as spirit sons or daughters of God in this premortal realm.

---

[2] I recognize that my use of the term "dialogue" is anachronistic and potentially misleading with regard to the controversies of the Christian past. I use the term to describe theological interchange. My intention is to underscore the fruitful aspect of polemical controversies as well as of intersections such as that between Second Temple Judaism and Hellenistic philosophy. Although premodern Christian theologians could and did cite positively the work of non-Christian theologians—as, for example, Thomas Aquinas did with Maimonides and Avicenna—Ellen T. Charry rightly comments with regard to Jewish-Christian "dialogue": "Interreligious dialogue is a modern notion. Perhaps its earliest appearance is in Lessing's comedy, *Nathan the Wise* (1779), that promotes respect, communication, and friendship among religions. Previously, the primary stance was contempt, the mode of communication between Judaism and Christianity was polemic." (Ellen T. Charry, "The Doctrine of God in Jewish-Christian Dialogue", in *The Oxford Handbook of the Trinity*, ed. Gilles Emery, O.P., and Matthew Levering [Oxford: Oxford University Press, 2011], 559.)

[3] Robert L. Millet, "Creator, God of the Ancients", in Robert L. Millet and Gerald R. McDermott, *Evangelicals and Mormons: Exploring the Boundaries* (Vancouver, BC: Regent College Publishing, 2010), 41.

Jesus Christ, however, was the Eternal God in a sense different from that of other spirit sons or daughters. In the Heavenly Council, God the Father asked for a volunteer to save all humans. Jesus Christ, the Firstborn, volunteered. He admitted that he could not save all, and he showed his absolute obedience to God the Father, to whom he gave all glory. The Grand Council voted that the Firstborn be sent, and so he was. But Satan was jealous of this, and so there was war in heaven. The Firstborn is also the One who, directed by God the Father, created worlds without number from preexistent matter.

The Mormon theologian Robert Millet affirms, therefore, that "Jesus Christ existed before the world and ... he was a member of the Godhead before this world was created. He was God for centuries and millennia prior to his birth in Bethlehem."[4] At the same time, Millet grants that Jesus Christ has not always been God. Instead, as Millet explains, Jesus grew into being God during his premortal existence. For Millet, the key point is that Mormons hold that Jesus Christ was God for premortal eons and is God now. He argues that it does not really matter "whether Jesus was always God or at a certain point in the pre-mortal realm he became God".[5] He is God now, and Mormons worship him as God. He was never a lesser God, subordinate to the Father. Rather, he was not God until he grew into God, and when he became God, he became "one with the Father in all things—in mind, in thought, in purpose".[6] Millet maintains that when Scripture refers to God as "eternal", this Greek word can mean a long time, but it does not mean a condition that transcends time or that is literally without beginning. Millet states, "My adoration or worship of him [Jesus] is not dependent on when or how or under what circumstances he became God."[7]

Millet differentiates the "Trinity", in which he professes belief, from classical Christian doctrines of the Trinity. One major difference is that he denies that "Father, Son, and Holy Spirit are somehow three persons but one Being."[8] Mormons believe that the Father, Son, and

---

[4] Robert L. Millet, "Rebuttal and Concluding Thoughts", in Millet and McDermott, *Evangelicals and Mormons*, 54.

[5] Ibid.

[6] Ibid.

[7] Ibid., 55.

[8] Robert Millet, "A Latter-Day Saint Response", in Millet and McDermott, *Evangelicals and Mormons*, 71.

Holy Spirit denote three distinct beings, even if their thoughts and wills are intimately united—"totally and completely one" and "infinitely more one than they are separate".[9] For Mormons, there is no doubt that Jesus Christ is the Son of God sent by the Father, and there is no doubt that Jesus is God. The Holy Spirit, too, has the fullness of the divine attributes. But Mormons "do not believe in an ontological oneness within the Trinity, that is, that our Heavenly Father, our divine Redeemer, and the Holy Spirit are in fact the same being".[10] Mormons do not see how one ontological Being can be three distinct Persons. Instead, Mormons embrace "the Trinity as that divine community made up of three holy persons".[11] Humorously but earnestly, Millet notes that his position is common sense: if we knew that the Father, Son, and Holy Spirit were coming over for dinner, should we not expect three Persons and therefore three place settings at the table?

Millet denies that this position means that Mormons are polytheistic. The Father, Son, and Holy Spirit are profoundly united; they enjoy a "magnificent and infinite oneness" even if not an "ontological merger".[12] Due to this oneness (though not an ontological oneness), Millet considers it mistaken to accuse the Mormons of polytheistic worship of multiple Gods.

Millet describes God as "the Infinite".[13] At the same time, he also affirms that Mormons "believe that God our Heavenly Father has a body of flesh and bones as tangible as a man's" and that Jesus Christ, the Son of God, does as well.[14] He recognizes that Joseph Smith taught that humans may become God. He explains, however, that Mormons "simply do not know which of God's attributes are or will be communicable and which are incommunicable"; in addition, he affirms that there will always be "a chasm" between God and humans.[15] Father, Son, and Holy Spirit—three united divine Beings— are and will be the sole object of worship for Mormons. Regarding

[9] Ibid.
[10] Ibid.
[11] Ibid., 70.
[12] Ibid., 72.
[13] Ibid., 73.
[14] Ibid., 76.
[15] Ibid., 73.

Joseph Smith's teaching that God began as a man, Millet argues that Mormons do not consider this a central teaching. Mormons accept Joseph Smith's teaching but understand it as a mystery, not as a necessary saving doctrine. Millet grants that for Mormons, there is continuity between Jesus Christ's origins and that of all humans (all of whom existed, as noted above, in the premortal realm). He affirms that "Jesus was a spiritual child of God, just as every other man or woman once was"; but he explains that it is important to clarify that "Jesus was the firstborn spirit child of our eternal Heavenly Father" and grew into his stature as God, becoming thereby the "Creator of worlds and the God of Abraham, Isaac, and Jacob".[16] Jesus differs from all other humans in that he was firstborn and he became God and acted as Creator and Savior. Jesus has been God for eons and will always be God.

Millet grants that, for Mormons, God and humans are of the same species. God the Father and God the Son have human bodies (in an exalted way). But Millet emphasizes that Mormons nevertheless believe in "God's majesty, magnificence, and infinity" as well as in the fact that God is "omnipotent, omniscient, and perfected".[17] No other humans can be described in this way, since we are "frail, weak, and imperfect".[18]

Mormons do not believe in the Christ of the early councils, because, in their view, the conciliar Christ is not the Christ of the Gospels. Regarding the councils, for Mormons the key problem is ontological oneness of the three divine Persons, but it is also a problem that the early councils have a Greek philosophical understanding of God, according to which God is not bodily. Mormons do not believe there are any nonphysical or nonmaterial realities. As the Mormon theologian Alonzo Gaskill states (drawing upon a May 1843 revelation received by Joseph Smith), "Mormons believe that spirit is material; man is material; angels are material; the earth is material; and God is material."[19] Gaskill goes on to differentiate God and humans, while also identifying the basis for the claim that God and humans do

---

[16] Ibid., 76.

[17] Ibid.

[18] Ibid.

[19] Alonzo L. Gaskill, "Matter", in *Catholic and Mormon: A Theological Conversation*, by Stephen H. Webb and Alonzo L. Gaskill (Oxford: Oxford University Press, 2015), 110.

not differ in species: "While the matter of which He is composed is unquestionably 'more fine and pure' than is the matter from which you and I are currently made, nevertheless, that does not negate the possibility that mankind was created in His 'image' and 'likeness.' "[20] Gaskill rejects the idea that "image" and "likeness" should here be taken metaphorically. Instead, Scripture means precisely that man is God's " 'offspring' and His species".[21] Gaskill holds that conceiving "of God in immaterial and wholly non-anthropomorphic terms is to confuse both what we are now (theomorphic humans), and what our divine potential holds (divinized children of the one true God)".[22]

When Gaskill sketches what Mormons believe about the Trinity, he begins by differentiating between Mormonism and Arianism. For Arianism, the Son of God is never fully God. For Mormons, by contrast, it is true that there was a time when Jesus was not yet a member of the Godhead, but once he became God, he was fully God. Indeed, as I have already indicated, Mormons believe that Jesus in the premortal state "was God—and part of the Godhead or Trinity—long before He was born as Mary's son".[23] When Jesus became God, was he subordinate to the Father? Mormons believe that the answer is yes in some sense, and they appeal to a number of New Testament texts in this regard. Jesus was and is subordinate to the Father, but this does not mean that Jesus is less than God. He became truly God, but God in a manner proper to the Son of God, obedient to the Father. For Gaskill, the Mormon position here makes Mormons "essentially what have been called 'social Trinitarians' ".[24]

For Mormons, as Gaskill explains, Jesus grew into his divine stature in part because of his uniqueness among God's offspring, that is, among humans (all of whom were created in a premortal state). His uniqueness consists in the fact that "Jesus is the only of God's children—His

---

[20] Ibid.

[21] Ibid.

[22] Ibid., 112.

[23] Alonzo L. Gaskill, "Jesus", in Webb and Gaskill, *Catholic and Mormon*, 128.

[24] Alonzo L. Gaskill, "Ritual", in Webb and Gaskill, *Catholic and Mormon*, 94. Gaskill does not cite any works, but on social Trinitarianism and the eternal subordination of the Son, respectively, see, for example, William Hasker, *Metaphysics and the Tri-Personal God* (Oxford: Oxford University Press, 2013), and Bruce A. Ware, *Father, Son, and Holy Spirit: Roles, Relationships, and Relevance* (Wheaton, IL: Crossway, 2005).

creations or offspring—which He fathered spiritually and physically."[25]
For all eternity, Jesus will be God, and he will always be greater than
any other human offspring of God. Gaskill states, "Jesus is a fully divine
being who is literally God's Son.... He is an eternal being who was
given by the Father a place in the Godhead and, thus, was God from the
'beginning' of this Holy Plan of Salvation instituted by the Father."[26]
God has the ability to make his firstborn spirit child to be God; God
the Father drew his Son into the Godhead. God the Son "is dependent
upon the Father for His existence" but is no less God.[27] Moreover,
Jesus was God for eons in the premortal state. Gaskill remarks that
"Mormons hold that each of us (as spirits) dwelt with God for millions,
if not billions of years, prior to being born as mortals here upon the
earth. There we learned, developed, grew, and gained an understanding of God, His great plan of salvation, and the role Jesus would play in
the salvation of all God's creations."[28]

III. A Catholic Perspective: Tracing Earlier Dialogues

Catholic theologians recognize that Mormons sincerely worship Jesus
Christ. It seems that if people who worship Christ are not Christians,
then the meaning of "Christian" has been narrowed in an implausible
way. From a Mormon perspective, therefore, it is clear that Catholics should identify Mormons as Christians. Catholics and Mormons
would then be left attempting to give an account of vast differences,
without being able to identify these differences as anything but differences within Christianity. Mormons suggest that Catholics in
the early centuries of the Church abandoned the New Testament's
understanding of Jesus and God and replaced it with a Greek philosophical understanding. For their part, Catholics can make it seem
as though if Mormons had only attended better to the Greek philosophical frameworks of person and nature, substance and relation, and
spirit and matter, then Mormons would be able to be full Christians.

[25] Gaskill, "Jesus", 129.
[26] Ibid., 130.
[27] Ibid.
[28] Alonzo L. Gaskill, "Soul", in Webb and Gaskill, *Catholic and Mormon*, 175–76.

Is there a better way forward for dialogue about the Trinity? I am not sure, but it does seem clear that Mormon-Catholic dialogue cannot (from the Catholic side) be artificially separated from earlier dialogues that have shaped Catholic faith. What "Christian" means was first developed within a particular Jewish and Hellenistic dialogue about God, in the light of Jesus Christ. In conversing with Mormons about the Trinity, Catholics cannot bracket these foundational dialogues between Jews (some of whom believed in Jesus as the Christ); between Jews and pagans; and between Christians, Jews, and pagans.

The remainder of my chapter will attempt to sketch these foundational dialogues, as part of supporting a Catholic-Mormon dialogue that goes to the roots of the debated terms ("Trinity", "Christian", and so forth). A dialogue between Catholics and Mormons will inevitably be a dialogue about these roots—or, to put it another way, a dialogue about earlier dialogues.

In the Second Temple period, Judaism and Hellenism entered into significant contact, and this shaped a number of late–Second Temple texts that belong to the Catholic Bible. These texts include the Wisdom of Solomon and certain later prophetic texts, but most importantly the letters of Paul and the Gospel of John. Speaking of the "rapprochement between Biblical faith and Greek inquiry", Pope Benedict XVI comments that within the Old Testament, this rapprochement took hold with respect to the interpretation of Exodus 3:14, "I AM WHO I AM."[29] New Testament authors employed the Septuagint Greek translation of Israel's Scriptures, in which Hellenistic Jewish translators rendered Exodus 3:14 as "I AM WHO AM." They intended to connect the God of Israel with an infinite, unbounded Being—God as sheer "AM", sheer "to be", not limited by any finite mode. Greek philosophers had been pushing in this direction for some centuries, as had Jewish teachers and prophets.

Aristotle's view that God can be nothing less than pure act (of being) is well known. In the world, we always see actuality in finite modes. Aristotle employs the term "potency" to name what limits actuality, or what makes for a finite mode of actuality. Every act/potency composite receives its actuality and is dependent upon another entity

---

[29] Pope Benedict XVI, "The Regensburg Lecture", in *The Regensburg Lecture*, by James V. Schall, S.J. (South Bend, IN: St. Augustine's Press, 2007), 135.

for its being. Only infinite actuality, pure act, can be the source of all finite being. Later Hellenistic philosophers brought together Aristotle's insights with Plato's broadly similar insights into God (especially his understanding of pure perfection, above all, "the Good") and Plato's account of participation in God.

In Israel's Scriptures, monotheistic statements began to appear—according to the historical-critical reconstruction shared by many scholars, among them Mark Smith and Baruch Halpern—shortly prior to the Babylonian Exile.[30] Smith directs attention to such statements as Deuteronomy 4:35, "The LORD is God; there is no other besides him"; Deuteronomy 4:39, "The LORD is God in heaven above and on the earth beneath; there is no other"; Jeremiah 16:20, "Can man make for himself gods? Such are no gods!"; and Psalm 96:5, "For all the gods of the peoples are idols [nothings]." Such statements arise within a context in which God had previously been supposed to be the most powerful God among all the gods. Isaiah 40:18–19 proclaims that only God is God, and there are no gods: "To whom then will you liken God, or what likeness compare with him? The idol! a workman casts it, and a goldsmith overlays it with gold." Many more such passages could be cited.

In John 8:58, "Before Abraham was, I am", Jesus takes the divine name of Exodus 3:14 upon himself. The biblical scholar Craig Keener comments on John 8:58: "When 'I am' lacks even an implied predicate ... it becomes unintelligible except as an allusion to God's name in the Hebrew Bible or LXX."[31] The name I AM was a recognizable Second Temple Jewish name for God. Keener notes that the Gospel of John likely had a Diaspora Jewish context, meaning that its original audience could be expected to include Hellenistic Jews and pagan converts.[32] Keener explains that it is not possible here to draw a sharp division between Judaism and Hellenism. He states, "The Hellenistic context of the Gospel is not ... to be understood apart

[30] Mark S. Smith, *The Origins of Biblical Monotheism: Israel's Polytheistic Background and the Ugaritic Texts* (Oxford: Oxford University Press, 2001), 153; Baruch Halpern, "The Names of Isaiah 62:4: Jeremiah's Reception in the Restoration and Politics of 'Third Isaiah'", *Journal of Biblical Literature* 117 (1998): 623–43.

[31] Craig S. Keener, *The Gospel of John: A Commentary*, vol. 1 (Grand Rapids, MI: Baker Academic, 2003), 769–70.

[32] Ibid., 175.

from Judaism, but as a broader context for Judaism (both Palestinian and, to a greater extent, Diaspora Judaism). Almost everything Hellenistic in this Gospel can be explained in terms of Hellenistic influence already known in early Judaism."[33]

The God who is "I am" is "the blessed and only Sovereign, the King of kings and Lord of lords, who alone has immortality and dwells in unapproachable light, whom no man has ever seen or can see" (1 Tim 6:15–16). Paul warns against worshipping anything less than such a God. He says of the Gentiles that "although they knew God they did not honor him as God or give thanks to him, but they became futile in their thinking and their senseless minds were darkened. Claiming to be wise, they became fools, and exchanged the glory of the immortal God for images resembling mortal man or birds or animals or reptiles" (Rom 1:21–23). According to Paul, God is not like anything that can be represented by physical images. God has an "invisible nature" (1:20). The relationship of God the Father to the Son is not like the relationship of a human father and son but rather may be conceived in terms of an infinite mind knowing himself in his "Word" (Jn 1:1). In this sense, Christ, in whom "all things were created, in heaven and on earth" (Col 1:16), is "the image of the invisible God" (1:15; cf. 2 Cor 4:4). Christ is the "first-born" (Col 1:15) because divine Wisdom is the firstborn of God. Christ is "in the form of God" (Phil 2:6) but in an invisible way in accord with God's invisible nature. Christ, as the Son, "reflects the glory of God and bears the very stamp of his nature, upholding the universe by his word of power" (Heb 1:3). There is no change in God, no becoming: "Every good endowment and every perfect gift is from above, coming down from the Father of lights with whom there is no variation or shadow due to change" (Jas 1:17). With regard to the divine unity, Jesus teaches that the greatest commandment is "Hear, O Israel: The Lord our God, the Lord is one; and you shall love the Lord your God with all your heart, and with all your soul, and with all your mind, and with all your strength" (Mk 12:29–30, quoting Deut 6:4).

It is this one God who is the simple "I am", infinite plenitude of being and power, capable of creating, sustaining, and redeeming finite

[33] Ibid., 155.

beings. No wonder, then, that Jesus' fellow Jews, hearing him declare his divine identity, treat him as a blasphemer who seeks to lead Israel away from the true God: "So they took up stones to throw at him" (Jn 8:59). Jesus does not cast doubt upon the ontological unity of God that we find in the name I AM, but he does include himself along with the Father (and the Spirit) within the unity of the infinite I AM. He states, "I and the Father are one" (Jn 10:30). Keener comments on John 10:30: "Greek thinkers could speak of the deity as a unity, but Jewish hearers would think even more immediately of the Shema, the basic confession of Judaism that affirmed God's unity. With such words, Jesus not only denies that his hearers are in right relation with God but claims a divine status that they could only understand as blasphemy."[34]

In the Hellenistic Jewish context, two finite beings, no matter how exalted, could not be the God of Israel. If there were two divine Beings, then there would be two Gods to worship, and this cannot be. Instead, the divine Son is related to the Father as his invisible Word or Image. There is a distinction, but not a separation into two Beings. The Son fully has and is all that the Father has and is, except for the Father's paternity.

These New Testament claims continued to be a matter of contention between Jews and Christians well after the first century. The medieval *Nizzahon Vetus*, written by Jewish critics of Christianity, carries on the intra–New Testament debate by observing: "If you say that he [Jesus] is God, then you have in effect denied God, for it is written in the Torah, 'See, then, that I, I am he; there is no god beside me' [Deut 32:39]. The counter-argument that they are one may be refuted by reference to Jesus' statement, 'It is I and he who sent me; he has not left me alone'; this implies that they are two."[35] In reply to such charges, Christians insisted that in fact the Father and Son are ontologically one while being distinct in an ineffable (relational) way.

This debate was also carried forward in Islam. In Sura 4:171 of the Qur'an, for instance, Muhammad reports the following revelation

---

[34] Ibid., 826.

[35] *The Jewish-Christian Debate in the High Middle Ages: A Critical Edition of the Nizzahon Vetus*, ed. and trans. David Berger (Northvale, NJ: Jason Aronson, 1979), 200.

directed toward Christians who, according to the revelation, have falsified the message of God's prophet Jesus: "O People of the Book! Do not exceed the bounds in your religion, and do not attribute any-thing to God except the truth. The Messiah, Jesus son of Mary, was only an apostle of God, and His Word that He cast toward Mary and a spirit from Him. So have faith in God and His Apostles, and do not say, '[God is] a trinity.'"[36] True faith, for Islam, rejects Trinitarian belief. The same Sura goes on to exhort Christians: "Relinquish [such a creed]! That is better for you. God is but the One God. He is far too immaculate to have any son."[37] There are further examples in the Qur'an of the same exhortation. Along the same lines, two centuries later the Muslim scholar Abū 'Īsā al-Warrāq wrote a treatise on the refutation of the Trinity. Al-Warrāq suggests that Christians should be confronted with the following question: "Tell us about the one substance. Why are its hypostases differenti-ated so that one is Father, the other Son and the third Spirit, although the substance, according to you, is one in its substantiality, eternal and undifferentiated in its being, not composed of distinct classes?"[38] Al-Warrāq puts forward many other similar questions, and of course many other Muslim scholars wrote similar treatises.

Writing around the same time as Muhammad began to report his visions and to obtain military victories, Saint Maximus the Confessor testifies to a fully biblical (and also Hellenistic) perspective when he explains: "God is in the proper sense always by nature one and unique, encompassing in himself in every way the totality of what being is in the proper sense, since indeed he is in the proper sense beyond being itself."[39] Maximus adds, along lines that accord fully with the biblical testimony, that nothing that began as a finite entity could ever become literally God or a member of the Godhead. This is because God is infinite actuality, and therefore nothing finite can become or be transformed into his infinite "substance". Maximus

---

[36] Gabriel Said Reynolds, *The Qur'an and the Bible: Text and Commentary* (New Haven, CT: Yale University Press, 2018), 185. Brackets in original.

[37] Ibid.

[38] *Anti-Christian Polemic in Early Islam: Abū 'Īsā al-Warrāq's "Against the Trinity"*, ed. and trans. David Thomas (Cambridge: Cambridge University Press, 1992), 113.

[39] Maximus the Confessor, *Two Hundred Chapters on Theology*, ed. and trans. Luis Joshua Salés (Yonkers, NY: St Vladimir's Seminary Press, 2015), 47.

distinguishes between the infinite God and everything else: "Nothing at all different in substance can simultaneously be contemplated with him coevally, neither eternity, nor time, nor any of those things living within these. For what being is in the proper sense [i.e., God] and what is not being in the proper sense do not ever coincide with each other."[40] Finite, material beings could not be God. They will always be dependent for their being upon a source of being, and the ultimate Source of their being is the true God.

In emphasizing the simplicity, unity, and pure actuality of the divine plenitude, Maximus is not undermining the Trinity. He knows that three divine Beings, unified by their bonds of intimacy, would be nothing new. Others have worshipped triads before. What is new are three Persons who are, in their essence, the indivisible God. How can the Father, Son, and Holy Spirit be truly distinct from one another while being utterly undivided in essence? Maximus does not suppose that there is a "one God" who could be met "outside" the Father, Son, and Holy Spirit. Neither does he suppose that there are three Persons who, like three-headed conjoined triplets who share the same bodily trunk, participate diversely in the one divine essence. On the contrary, there is no difference between the Father and God, because the Father *is* God. Likewise, the Son *is* God and the Spirit *is* God, and, together, the Father, Son, and Spirit are the one God. Maximus comments: "The same whole is in the Father and the whole Father is in the same whole; and the same whole is in the whole Son and the whole Son is in the same whole."[41] The point is that God (the divine essence) does not differ at all from the Person or Persons (Father, Son, Spirit). As Maximus says: "The substance, potentiality, and actuality of the Father, Son, and Holy Spirit are one and the same."[42] If this is so, however, is it possible to say along biblical lines that the Father, Son, and Spirit truly differ from one another?

Maximus allows his thought to be shaped by John 1:1: "In the beginning was the Word, and the Word was with God, and the Word was God." The difference between God the Father and the Word is not

[40] Ibid.
[41] Ibid., 105.
[42] Ibid., 107.

a difference in divinity, but it is instead a relational distinction found in the Father's eternal speaking of his Word. Maximus holds, therefore, that "the Word reveals the begetting Mind whom He knows as Father."[43] But stating this in words that explain the difference between the Father and the Son (and the Spirit) is not an easy task. Scripture teaches us that the human nature of Christ is united to the divine nature in the distinct Person of the Son. We know that we are caught up in Christ and through his Spirit into the unity of God, who is a tripersonal communion. But to articulate this further can be difficult.

Augustine devotes his *On the Trinity* to examining the biblical portraits of the Son and Holy Spirit in order to help us express both their real distinction and their ontological unity. He reflects upon the Old Testament theophanies, the missions of the Son and Spirit, the work of the Mediator (Christ), and the names applied in Scripture to distinguish the three divine Persons and to illuminate in what their difference consists. Although God, as infinite actuality, is not like finite and material things, rational creatures are made in his image. Contemporary biblical scholars argue that the "image of God" (Gen 1:27) is the human ability to exercise dominion over the other creatures.[44] Such dominion would require, above all, wisdom and love. This is not far from Augustine's view that the image of God consists preeminently in the highest of human powers, namely, our knowing and loving. For Augustine, we are properly in the image of God when our graced knowing and loving participate in the Trinitarian life by knowing and loving the Father, Son, and Holy Spirit. Following the promptings of Scripture, Augustine shows that the Persons of the Trinity reveal themselves in ways that enable us to express how the Three may be One. The Son is Word and Image; the Spirit is Gift and Love. The relational distinction of the three Persons characterizes both the economy of salvation and the intra-Trinitarian life.[45] The Trinitarian analogy (remembering, knowing, and loving) illuminates the work of Christ and the Spirit in salvation history, as Word, Image, Love, and Gift.[46]

---

[43] Ibid., 121.

[44] See, for example, J. Richard Middleton, *The Liberating Image: The* Imago Dei *in Genesis 1* (Grand Rapids, MI: Brazos, 2005).

[45] Augustine, *The Trinity*, trans. Edmund Hill, O.P. (Brooklyn, NY: New City Press, 1991).

[46] See Gilles Emery, O.P., *The Trinity: An Introduction to Catholic Doctrine of the Triune God*, trans. Matthew Levering (Washington, DC: Catholic University of America Press, 2011).

Basil of Caesarea and Gregory of Nazianzus composed replies to charges of tritheism—charges brought by other Christians but echoed by Jews. In his *Homily on Not Three Gods, Against Those Who Calumniate Us, Claiming That We Say That There Are Three Gods*, Basil rejects any notion that there is more than one God. He states that "if anyone who confesses the Trinity names three gods, he denigrates baptism and impugns the faith."[47] He insists: "Learn from Paul. He did not say 'two' or 'three'."[48] The Father and the Son are not different Beings; they are the one I AM. They do not divide the Godhead by sharing it among two (or three) finite beings. Nor do they divide the Godhead in any other way. If they did, then either the Father would not be identical to the whole deity (in which case the Father would not be God), or else the Father and Son would together be more "God" than they are as distinct from each other. Deity is not like a fount from which both the Father and the Son draw their water; rather, the Father *is* the Godhead, the simple and infinite plenitude of I AM, and so are the Son and Spirit. How, then, can we articulate the difference between the Father and his Word, if it is neither a difference in essence nor two distinct *participations* in the one essence? For Basil, the difference can be easily named: the Father eternally begets; the Son is eternally begotten. But what this means cannot be pinned down more fully, since our analogies are finite and temporal. We rely, therefore, upon faith, while avoiding dissolving the mystery of the ontological unity and simplicity of the Trinity.

In his *First Theological Oration*, Gregory of Nazianzus similarly warns that Christian language about God the Trinity can, if not carefully set forth, be appropriated by a pagan "to defend his own gods".[49] Gregory wrote this oration not many years after Emperor Julian's nearly successful attempt to restore classical paganism. Gregory also counted among his sharpest opponents those who held as

---

[47] Basil the Great, *Homily on Not Three Gods, Against Those Who Calumniate Us, Claiming That We Say That There Are Three Gods*, in *On Christian Doctrine and Practice*, trans. Mark Del-Cogliano (Yonkers, NY: St Vladimir's Seminary Press, 2012), 272.

[48] Ibid.

[49] Gregory of Nazianzus, *The First Theological Oration: An Introductory Sermon against the Eunomians*, trans. Frederick Williams, in Gregory of Nazianzus, *On God and Christ: The Five Theological Orations and Two Letters to Cledonius*, trans. Frederick Williams and Lionel Wickham (Crestwood, NY: St Vladimir's Seminary Press, 2002), 29.

"a matter of principle that the difference of substance, or being, between Father and Son should be maintained".[50] Thus for Gregory, worshipping multiple Gods is not something that seems far away, impossible for believers in Christ. Both he and his opponents know people who do worship multiple Gods or divine beings. They agree that this is something to be avoided at all costs, because God is ontologically one.

IV. Conclusion

Robert Millet remarks with gladness that Mormons and Evangelicals are beginning to have positive exchanges, rather than merely issuing mutual condemnations. Through his scholarship and friendships, he has contributed much "toward better understanding on the part of two faith traditions who have a history of confrontation, two faith groups who have often been eager to point up doctrinal differences but less enthusiastic about acknowledging doctrinal similarities".[51] I agree with Millet that criticizing others' beliefs gets tiresome quickly. When one is constantly critical of those who are outside the circle of fellow believers, one can have difficulty maintaining charity and humility outside this circle. A focus on disagreement can turn into a corrosive outlook that insists the other's glass is always half-empty or that takes God's place by consigning outsiders to everlasting punishment (as distinct from inviting others to share in the fullness of God's revelation). Millet is well aware that "there are ... doctrinal differences between the Mormon and evangelical communities."[52] Without denying these differences, he seeks to explore and accentuate the commonalities.

In 2015, the Catholic theologian Stephen Webb teamed with Alonzo Gaskill to write an important book of Catholic-Mormon dialogue. As Webb and Gaskill observe: "While Latter-day Saints and Catholics have worked together well for many years on social issues and on humanitarian initiatives, they have kept their distance—theologically

---

[50] Lionel Wickham, "Gregory of Nazianzus: An Introduction for the Reader", in Gregory of Nazianzus, *On God and Christ*, 15.

[51] Robert Millet, "Introduction", in Millet and McDermott, *Evangelicals and Mormons*, 10–11.

[52] Ibid., 11.

speaking—from each other."[53] Webb and Gaskill do not conceal the reason for this. They explain: "Catholicism is a continuous tradition, committed to the conservation of the earliest, ecumenical creeds, while Mormonism teaches that the landscape of Christian history is riddled with sin and apostasy and is in need of radical revision and spiritual healing."[54] Mormons do not accept Catholic (or Protestant) baptism as valid, and Mormons criticize the early ecumenical councils and reject almost all Catholic dogma. In turn, Catholics deny the truth and authority of the Book of Mormon as well as the other works the Latter-day Saints believe are Sacred Scripture: the Doctrine and Covenants and the Pearl of Great Price.

Regarding the nature and worship of God, Catholics are beneficiaries of earlier dialogues. Of course, these dialogues were deeply confrontational and sometimes violent, but they were dialogues in the sense that they shaped and sharpened Christian thinking (and did the same for Christianity's opponents). Second Temple Hellenistic Jews, pagan philosophers, Jews who followed Christ and Jews who did not, rabbinic Jews, Muslims, Christians who denied Christ's full divinity—all these groups stand behind the development of Christian worship of the Trinity and thus the development of what "Christianity" means.

A new arena of dialogue is opening today between Catholics and Mormons. Gaskill objects to the 2001 decision of the Congregation for the Doctrine of the Faith (CDF, then headed by Joseph Ratzinger) to reject the validity of Mormon baptism on the grounds that Mormons do not understand the Trinity in an adequate way and therefore are unable to baptize someone in the Trinitarian name. But it seems to me that the CDF was correct to make this decision and that, far from closing matters, it invites a richer Catholic-Mormon exploration of Trinitarian faith. This dialogue, however, will first have to be a dialogue about the earlier dialogues, in which the teachings and concerns of ancient pagan philosophers, the first Jewish "monotheists", Second Temple Judaism, the New Testament, rabbinic Judaism, Christians who rejected the Trinity, early Christian defenders of the Trinity, and Islam will receive a place at the table. Only in this

[53] Stephen H. Webb and Alonzo L. Gaskill, "Introduction", in *Catholic and Mormon*, ix.
[54] Ibid., viii.

way will Mormons and Catholics together be able to appreciate what the Catholic theologian Gilles Emery calls the " 'Trinitarian Christian culture' that was formed at the end of antiquity, as much in the East as in the West", rooted in the gospel of God.[55]

[55] Emery, *Trinity*, xvi.

2

Becoming like God: A Critique

Richard Sherlock

At the core of Western monotheistic faiths is a conviction of the oneness and absolute transcendence of God.[1] God is not merely an organizer of preexisting matter or a manager of what he has crafted out of this material; he is the Creator of all that exists. This is known as the concept of *creatio ex nihilo* (that is, creation out of nothing), an essential belief of early Christianity.[2] Some current theoretical physicists are thinking in terms of many universes, what is called the multiverse hypothesis. This view is not relevant here. However many universes there may be, God created them all.

This truth has been argued for by great philosophers and theologians past and present. Even Aristotle, not known for his overt religiosity, has a brilliant version of the prime mover argument for an agent creating the world,[3] even though he did not embrace *creatio ex nihilo* as his later Muslim, Jewish, and Christian followers would.

Once this conclusion is granted as a truth of reason and faith, many further questions follow. For Christians, a foundational question is how the Christian conviction about the divine Trinity can be

---

[1] The essential oneness of God is emphasized in the central conviction of Judaism, the Shema, found in Deuteronomy 6:4: "Hear, O Israel: The LORD our God is one LORD."

[2] For analysis of the idea in both theology and patristics, see Markus Bockmeuhl, "*Creatio ex Nihilo* in Palestinian Judaism and Early Christianity", *Scottish Journal of Theology* 65, no. 3 (August 2012): 253–70; Menahem Kister, "*Tohu wa-Bohu*, Primordial Elements and *Creatio ex Nihilo*", *Jewish Studies Quarterly* 14, no. 3 (2007): 229–56; Paul Copan, "Is *Creatio ex Nihilo* a Post–Biblical Invention?", *Trinity Journal* 17 (1996): 77–93.

[3] Aristotle, *Physics*, trans. Hugh Lawson-Tancred (New York: Penguin, 1999).

understood in a manner compatible with this absolute monotheism.[4] Perhaps equally important is this question: Since God is a Creator beyond his creation, thus outside of time and space, how can his eternal nature connect to human beings, his most precious creation?

Humans are finite embodied beings whose deepest longing is for permanent and final rest and happiness, which even ancient philosophers like Plato understood as a divine transcendent realm of wisdom, beauty, and goodness, that is, God.[5] If God is infinitely perfect in every way, how can this connection with creation be established?

I. Monotheism

The great monotheisms of the West have addressed this fundamental metaphysical problem in a variety of ways. Islam, for example, holds that God (Allah) has provided to people his eternal Word in the form of a text, the Qur'an, which is given in a specific form and language, Arabic.

The Christian tradition, in all its forms, has bridged this existential gap with a conviction that is at the core of the Christian faith: God's Incarnation as an embodied human Person, Jesus of Nazareth. The Christian tradition from the New Testament on has generally held that Jesus Christ is one divine Person with two natures. He is at once fully divine and fully human.[6]

In thinking about God, whose nature we know only "in a mirror dimly" (1 Cor 13:12), we must employ analogies to things in the created world that we know much better. While remembering that any

---

[4] For crucial works articulating and defending the concept of the Trinity, see Saint Augustine, *De Trinitate (On the Trinity)*, trans. Edmund Hill, O.P., 2nd ed. (New York: New City Press, 2012); Richard of St. Victor, *On the Trinity*, trans. Ruben Angelici (Portland: Cascade Books, 2011); Saint Thomas Aquinas, *Summa Theologica* I, qq. 27–43, trans. Fathers of the English Dominican Province, 2nd and rev. ed. (London: Burns, Oates & Washbourne, 1920), www.newadvent.org/summa/1027.htm (hereafter cited as *ST*).

[5] Joseph Pieper, *Divine Madness: Plato's Case against Secular Humanism* (San Francisco: Ignatius Press, 1995).

[6] Technically, this is the problem of Christology. For recent defenses, see Thomas V. Morris, *The Logic of God Incarnate* (Ithaca, NY: Cornell University Press, 1986); C. F. D Moule, *The Origins of Christology* (London: Cambridge University Press, 1979); James Papandrea, *The Earliest Christologies* (Chicago: IVP Academic, 2016).

analogy is deeply imperfect, we should also remember Aquinas' sage argument that some important knowledge can be gained through analogical reasoning. We employ analogies in common reasoning and speech regularly. For example, when we refer to a boss as a "tyrant", we analogize his behavior to real tyrants (e.g., Stalin, Hitler, and Mao). When someone eats in a sloppy manner, we say they "eat like a pig". When Luther referred to the "Babylonian Captivity of the Church", he was analogizing the state of the Catholic Church in his day to the actual Babylonian Captivity of ancient Israel in the sixth century B.C.

The difficulty in using analogies in thinking about God is that he is metaphysically separate from any part of his creation. Yet we must use analogies to speak meaningfully about God. This is the point made by Thomas Aquinas in the *Summa Theologica*. He argues that when we speak of God, our language cannot be univocal because that would mean that God is just like us with feet, hands, a face, etc.[7] For example, when, in Exodus 33:11, we read that "the LORD used to speak to Moses face to face, as a man speaks to his friend", a univocal understanding would mean that God has a face like Moses. Neither can our language about God be equivocal, for this would mean we could say nothing about God that is true. The result would be that all rational arguments for the existence of God and some of his qualities are false. As Aquinas writes: "Such a view is against the philosophers, who proved many things about God, and also against what the Apostle says: 'The invisible things of God are clearly seen being understood by the things that are made (Romans 1:20). Therefore it must be said that these names are said of God and creatures in an analogous sense, i.e. according to proportion."[8] Acknowledging that analogies are imperfect does not mean that we should not use them, only that we should use them with care.

We shall examine the metaphysical fittingness of the Incarnation shortly. First, however, it is important to distinguish the concept and necessity of the Incarnation and issues associated with this belief from two closely related beliefs: (1) the nature of Christ as one Person with two natures, human and divine, and (2) beliefs about Christ's

[7] *ST* I, q. 13, www.newadvent.org/summa/1013.htm.
[8] *ST* I, q. 13, art. 5.

Crucifixion on the cross and his Resurrection on Easter. Of course, these are all closely connected. Salvation on the cross and Christ's Resurrection are possible only because of his two natures. He is sinless, so he can carry the weight of human sin. He is mortal, so he can actually die. He is God, so he cannot be limited by or be afraid of death. Most Christian churches accept the formula adopted by the early Church at the Council of Chalcedon (A.D. 451):

> We all with one accord teach men to acknowledge one and the same Son, our Lord Jesus Christ, at once complete in Godhead and complete in manhood, truly God and truly man, consisting also of a reasonable soul and body; of one substance with the Father as regards his Godhead, and at the same time of one substance with us as regards his manhood; like us in all respects, apart from sin; as regards his Godhead, begotten of the Father before the ages, but yet as regards his manhood begotten, for us men and for our salvation, of Mary the Virgin.[9]

There are many complex theological and philosophical issues related to salvation on the cross and Christ's two natures. But these issues come precisely because Jesus Christ is the incarnate God, the Son. Many eminent Catholic thinkers of the medieval period thought deeply about these issues: Augustine, Anselm, Abelard, Bonaventure, and Aquinas.[10]

These problems associated with salvation on the cross and Christology are possible only because we have first understood the nature and necessity of the Incarnation. Let us now turn to the Incarnation as such before we turn to the Latter-day Saint alternatives.

II. God, Creation, and Reason

Christians, including but not limited to Catholics, begin with a truth that can be clearly argued for by reason. God is a Creator outside his creation. If he were in creation, he would be limited by the matter he

---

[9] *Documents of the Christian Church*, ed. Henry Bettenson (London: Oxford University Press, 1947), 72.

[10] See, e.g., *ST* III, q. 1, www.newadvent.org/summa/4001.htm; Saint Anselm, "On Faith in the Trinity and on the Incarnation of the Word against the Blasphemies of Rocelin", in *The Complete Philosophical and Theological Treatises of Anselm of Canterbury*, ed. and trans. Jasper Hopkins and Herbert Richardson (Minneapolis: Arthur Banning, 2006).

must work with to create the world. This limitation would mean that God is not all-powerful. To use a human analogy, of the sort Mormons are fond of, consider an artist who does sculpture. The artist is limited by whatever he is using. There are things he can do with clay that he cannot do with marble or metal. There are things he can do with metal that he could not have done before the development of welding. Furthermore, if God were said to have a material body, constituted by any sort of material, his ability would be limited by the properties of the material of which he is made. Thus, God cannot either use preexisting material or be himself made of some sort of material.

Thus, if we are to believe in a God with power enough to save us, this God must have all possible power. Since we have little knowledge of the barriers to our salvation, we must trust that he has complete power. Anything less would be insufficient for complete confidence in God, such as the confidence Abraham had in taking his son up Mount Moriah.

According to Aquinas, if God cannot have worked with already existing "stuff" in creation, God must be the ultimate cause of all that exists. His necessary existence grounds the actual, contingent existence of all that exists apart from God.[11]

All contingent things, for example, human beings, must be caused to exist by some cause apart from them. When we ask the fundamental human question about entities or events in the world, "Why?", we responsibly reply that it is because something, A, caused this entity or event, B, to happen or exist.

This causal principle, known as the principle of sufficient reason (PSR), is simply fundamental to any human person's rational grasp of the world. Whenever any event happens, such as the appearance of the Hale-Bopp comet, we ask: Why this comet? Why here? Why now? The first question we ask about a major disaster such as an airplane crash that killed hundreds is "Why?" In short, what caused these events?[12]

In thinking through the why, we begin with a set of contingent causes. People built the plane. Other people flew the plane. Weather

[11] ST I, q. 44, www.newadvent.org/summa/1044.htm; q. 45, www.newadvent.org/summa/1045.htm.
[12] On the principle of sufficient reason, see Alexander Pruss, The Principle of Sufficient Reason (London: Cambridge University Press, 2009).

affected the flight plan or flight path. This set of contingent causes ultimately ends in a necessary first cause. This conviction that all that exists had a creative first cause is a truth of each of the great Western monotheisms.

There are a number of eminent philosophers who, while not being theists, admit that PSR is simply basic to the way human beings understand the world. Once this is granted, there we must posit a cause for the existence of the world and things in the world. In a volume that preceded this one, *The New Mormon Challenge*, William Lane Craig (along with Paul Copan) offered a brilliant defense of this view of God as a Creator, as distinguished from the Latter-day Saint view of God as a manager.[13]

This view of the universe as a created reality distinguished Christianity at its beginning from Greek thought, with which it came into contact in the first century of its existence. The Christians adopted many beliefs from the philosophical world of their founding—for example, the rational conviction of an immaterial substance that most early Christian thinkers, especially Augustine, took from Platonism. The eternity of the world they could not adopt. Nor should they, since Scripture shows that the universe had a beginning.

The principle of sufficient reason, that is, the "why" principle that grounds the rational belief in a first cause, is, as we said earlier, basic to human reason's grasp of the world. Even "friendly atheist" William Rowe has shown this foundational character of PSR. Rowe has also admitted that once PSR is granted, the belief in a first cause must be accepted.[14]

---

[13] William Lane Craig and Paul Copan, "Craftsman or Creator: An Examination of the Mormon Doctrine of Creation and a Defense of *Creatio ex Nihilo*", in *The New Mormon Challenge*, ed. Francis Beckwith, Carl Mosser, and Paul Owen (New York: HarperCollins; Grand Rapids, MI: Zondervan, 2002), 95–152. It should be noted, however, that because Craig denies the doctrine of divine simplicity and that God is essentially timeless, he is not a defender of "classical theism", the view embraced by the Catholic Church as a *de fide* dogma. Nevertheless, his (and Copan's) defense of God as Creator can be employed to defend classical theism. For example, David Oderberg, a classical theist, is a proponent of Craig's *Kalām* cosmological argument. See David Oderberg, "No Beginning, No Explanation: The Kalām Cosmological Argument and the Principle of Sufficient Reason", in *The Kalām Cosmological Argument: Philosophical Arguments for the Finitude of the Past*, ed. Paul Copan and William Lane Craig (London: Bloomsbury, 2018), 120–34.

[14] William L. Rowe, *Philosophy of Religion: An Introduction* (Belmont, CA: Wadsworth, 1978). By "friendly atheist", I mean someone who believes that theism is rationally defensible even though he is not convinced of the truth of theism.

A second set of reasons why theists must hold that God necessarily has the qualities of aesthetic, moral, and intellectual perfection has to do with the core of religious belief: a conviction that human life has a purpose even in the face of the worst evils and tragedies. Human beings have always sought a meaning to their lives and to life itself that can withstand challenges from those consumed by the problem of evil and tragedy in the world. Western monotheism has answered this search for meaning by holding that human beings can be in communion with God eternally in the Beatific Vision.[15]

As an example, let us think of God's perfect knowledge. If we are to have absolute confidence in God's saving grace, we must have confidence that nothing can thwart God's salvation. Yet, if God does not have perfect knowledge, especially knowledge of the future, how can we have complete faith that he can overcome any obstacle to our salvation? We cannot. Unfortunately, many Latter-day Saint thinkers have recently become enamored of what is called open theism, a view among some Protestants that God does not have complete knowledge of the future.

Two questions follow from this necessity of confidence in God's salvation: (1) the need for purpose in our lives, and (2) the theodicy problem.

First, only intelligent agents can give a purpose to any object or event. Human lives cannot have an ultimate purpose if the universe in which they exist has no purpose. Human beings may engage in purposeful acts for limited times and events. But such actions do not show that we have ultimate or transcendent purpose.

Consider, for example, a baseball game. In the context of the game, every game-related action has a purpose: to help one team or the other win the game. The pitcher may throw a certain way to a certain batter or in a certain situation, for example, to get the batter to hit into a double play. The runner may try to get to third from first on a single given the team's need, his speed, where the ball is hit, etc.

These actions have a purpose in the game. But what is the purpose of the game? If this game is part of a series of league games, the

---

[15] "Because of his transcendence, God cannot be seen as he is, unless he himself opens up his mystery to man's immediate contemplation and gives him the capacity for it. The Church calls this contemplation of God in his heavenly glory 'the beatific vision.'" (*Catechism of the Catholic Church*, no. 1028.)

purpose of this game will be to help the team win the league title. But this observation only pushes the question of meaning back a step.

Every action in existence may have a purpose, but what is the purpose of existence itself? The ultimate meaninglessness of the universe as such will eventually undermine any supposed purpose for these limited moments. Without God as a perfect Creator and the telos of our existence as people created by God, Macbeth wins. Life is a "tale / Told by an idiot, full of sound and fury, / Signifying nothing."[16]

Closely connected to the question of the meaningfulness of existence is the question that is generally regarded as the most difficult problem faced by sincere theists: the problem of evil, that is, the theodicy problem. Mormons and many other Christians believe that the best answer to the theodicy question is found in the concept of character building, an argument brilliantly put forth by John Hick in his classic *Evil and the God of Love*.[17] We are often told that "challenges build moral character." Since character building requires freedom, theists seemingly have the right combination of claims to offer a serious answer to the problems raised by atheist critics, such as the following: If there is a God, why is there so much pain and suffering? Could God not have prevented the actions of Stalin, Hitler, and Mao, to name three recent scourges of mankind? Could he not have created a world in which the Black Death would not have killed a third of the population of Europe in the 1340s?

The problems with this theodicy are legion and do not require extensive treatment here. But consider just one example: Think about children whose lives are destroyed by sexual abuse. Broadly, their character has been compromised. These children may never grow and develop. It is sometimes argued, however, that those caring for such heavily damaged children will develop their character in virtuous ways. The problem here is with the idea of a God who would sacrifice one character to build another. One wonders how anyone could worship or pray to such a God.

This character-building idea contradicts Scripture at its core. The central text of the biblical tradition dealing with the problem of evil

[16] William Shakespeare, *Macbeth*, Ignatius Critical Editions, ed. Joseph Pearce (San Francisco: Ignatius Press, 2010), act 5, scene 5, lines 26–28.
[17] John Hick, *Evil and the God of Love* (London: Palgrave MacMillan, 1966).

is the Book of Job. Job is said to be "blameless", not sinless (1:1). He does not merit and cannot understand the horrendous evils that have befallen him. His three friends and then Elihu believe that bad things happen only to bad people. Hence, they try to get Job to confess the grave sins he is either hiding or forgetting. Yet Job cannot admit as true what is false. The Book of Job specifically rejects the idea that evils are a punishment for sin or merely human free action. Interestingly, Job and his friends agree on the same principle: bad things happen only to bad people. The friends believe that Job must have done something horrible. Job denies that he has done something so horrible as to deserve what has befallen him.

The suffering of Job is not the result of human sin or thoughtlessness, like building a house in a flood plain and believing the house is sturdy enough to withstand any flood. Nor, we might add, does the character-building argument make any appearance in Job. At the end, when God speaks to Job, he does not say "Job, you stood the test" or "You have developed a great character, Job; it will serve you well in the future." God's answer to Job is essentially what Job himself says in a "light bulb" moment: "Though He slay me, I will hope in Him" (13:15, NASB).

What God tells Job is essentially this: "I, God, have a plan for you, Job, that you cannot fully understand. Your reason cannot wrap itself around my love for you or the direction I have for your life. But if you place your absolute trust in me, you can face anything."[18]

This sort of trust in God's power and goodness, even in the face of the worst evils, makes sense only with a specific concept of God. This is the perfectly wise, powerful, and good God that Christians have proclaimed for two millennia. Anything less is not the God of Job, nor can a lesser God be our safe harbor in the face of massive suffering.

Some Latter-day Saint thinkers hold that all we need to believe is that God has power sufficient to achieve his purposes. This, too, will not suffice. Even granting that from revelation we know what God's purposes are in a precise manner (a claim I doubt), there remains a major problem. Since we do not know the extent of the forces

---

[18] This is not a direct quote from Scripture but simply my summary of what most readers think God is trying to communicate to Job.

attempting to thwart the achievement of God's purposes, anything less than complete or absolute power will not provide a ground for absolute trust such as displayed by Job (see chapters 38–41).

Can we, however, reach this final rest and complete happiness by our own effort? One would think that after millennia of effort by our wisest minds, we might have succeeded. But human beings are no closer to finding the path to eternal happiness on their own than they ever were. If being with God forever brings about our ultimate joy and fulfillment, then relying on our coming to God by our own effort means that this fulfillment will always be frustrated. As Christians, we cannot find any answers to our deepest longings until we say yes to Christ.

Since reason and Scripture teach of one Creator God who is infinitely good, wise, and powerful, how can human beings come to know and approach this God? From our position in time and space, we cannot fully know God's nature as *the* necessary Being outside of time and space. We know that he exists, and we know some of his qualities. However, the full nature of God's love, grace, and forgiveness must be known from God. Innumerable other truths, for example, the Real Presence in the Eucharist, must also be revealed to us by God. That is, God must come to us rather than vice versa. We must open our hearts to his Word in person, text, and tradition. But God must fill the open heart of the person.

We can understand the existential gap between God and human beings. We can also grasp the longing for fulfillment that all human beings have deep within their souls. A complete phenomenology of the human person such as found in Dietrich von Hildebrand and Pope Saint John Paul II will reveal this longing and its necessary completion in God. This completion, however, cannot be ours to achieve. It must be God's to give.

III. Bridging the Gap

Having seen the rationally and scripturally required nature of God, and thus the existential gap between God and mankind, we can now turn to how Christian, especially Catholic, thought argues that this gap is bridged.

For Christians the central text in this regard is the first eighteen verses of the Gospel of John,[19] often referred to as the prologue to the Gospel. This text begins with a teaching that Greek philosophers would have understood well: "In the beginning was the Word, and the Word was with God, and the Word was God" (1:1). When we restate this with the Greek equivalent for "Word" we read: "In the beginning was the Logos, and the Logos was with God, and the Logos was God." This framework of a Divine Logos that rules the world is largely a restatement of Neoplatonism of the period in which John wrote, that is, the first century of the Christian era. The structure of this first sentence is also found in works of the Jewish diaspora that are in the Septuagint, that is, the Bible of the early apostles and the Church until Luther removed some of its books. (Protestants refer to these books as the Apocrypha, while Catholics refer to them as the deuterocanonical books). Mormons, like Protestants, generally do not include these books.

This is odd. The LDS believe there was a general breakdown of the early Church, which they refer to as the Great Apostasy. This happened soon after the early apostles died. Yet the official Latter-day Saint Bible is not the Bible the early apostles used to spread Christianity around the eastern Mediterranean, which was the Septuagint.

Chief among these books, for our purposes, is Wisdom. It is often called the Wisdom of Solomon, but it has no relation to the actual Solomon. It is likely to have been written in the first or second century before the Christian era.[20]

In Wisdom 7:22—8:1, Wisdom, that is, the Divine Logos, is personified. Interestingly, Wisdom is described with female pronouns, her and she. Wisdom is said to have a fullness of divine qualities, for example, "she is more beautiful than the sun, and excels every constellation of the stars" (7:29). She is said to be a "spotless mirror of the working of God" (7:26). Yet she is distinct from God. She is "all-powerful" (7:23) and penetrates all creation. But wisdom as here personified is distinguished from God.

Wisdom is said to have been existent from the beginning and to be "the fashioner of all things" (7:22). As in the Book of Job, "against

---

[19] The best commentary on John is by Raymond Brown, S.S., *The Gospel According to John*, 2 vols. (Garden City, NY: Doubleday, 1966–1970).

[20] On the Wisdom of Solomon, see *The Wisdom of Solomon*, trans., intro, and commentary David Winston (New York: Doubleday, 1979).

wisdom evil does not prevail" (Wis 7:30). Thus, wisdom is divine and yet distinct from "the Almighty" (7:25). Further, wisdom "reaches mightily from one end of the earth to the other, and she orders all things well" (8:1).

This framework from a biblical text perhaps written only two centuries before the Gospel of John teaches a metaphysical structure that was certainly familiar to the patristic Church. This structure connects very closely to the prologue to the Gospel of John.

Of all the background sources of the beginning of John's Gospel, the most important and obvious are writings of Philo of Alexandria, a Jewish thinker steeped in Neoplatonism of the beginning of the Christian era. Though the dates of Philo's life are uncertain, most scholars hold that he was born c. 20 B.C. and died c. A.D. 50. Thus, he is a slightly older contemporary of the early apostles, especially, for our purposes, John.[21]

Philo's writings are extremely significant for showing that the marriage of ancient Platonism and revealed religion predates any of the writings of the New Testament. Many Latter-day Saint authors claim that a primary source of what they refer to as the Great Apostasy of the early Church was the mixing of the "simple truths of the gospel" with Greek philosophy. Two examples make this point. In the first decade of the twentieth century, LDS apostle James E. Talmage wrote the first comprehensive treatment of what Mormons refer to as the Great Apostasy, that is, the complete breakdown of the early Church. He wrote about external causes such as the bitter persecution faced by Christians. His attention then turned to internal causes. The first internal cause he cited was "the corrupting of simple principles of the gospel by the admixture of the so-called philosophic systems of the times".[22]

A second official example is very recent. Over the last couple of years, the LDS church has put out a number of "gospel topics" essays to provide an approved version of controversial topics related to Mormonism, for example, the Book of Abraham. One of the essays is entitled "Are 'Mormons' Christian?" In this essay we read a restatement of the view set forth by Talmage, that one of the main causes of

---

[21] The best comprehensive study of Philo is still Harry Austryn Wolfson, *Philo*, 2 vols. (Cambridge: Harvard University Press, 1949). See also D. T. Runia, *Philo in Early Christian Literature* (Minneapolis: Fortress, 1993).

[22] James E. Talmage, *The Great Apostasy* (Salt Lake City: Deseret News, 1909), 90.

the loss of truth in the early Church was the attempt to bring Greek philosophy into Christianity.[23]

Reading carefully the first eighteen verses of John shows the error of this claim. The patristic Church did not *add* Neoplatonism *to* Scripture. They *found* Neoplatonism *in* Scripture (or Neoplatonic philosophy, which illuminated their understanding of what Scripture is trying to teach us about the divine nature).

Philo's work is much too wide-ranging and complex to treat in detail here. Neither would it serve our purposes to do so. We can, however, note several similarities. First, we call attention to the symbolism of light that is pervasive in Philo. As John says of Christ, "The true light that enlightens every man was coming into the world" (Jn 1:9). Second, Philo speaks often of the Logos as "life giving water". This symbolism is pervasive in the New Testament, especially in John—for example, the Samaritan woman at the well (see 4:7–42). Third, an even more pervasive symbolism in the New Testament is to see Christ as the Good Shepherd. This, too, is a pervasive symbolism in Philo[24] (as well as an Old Testament motif—Psalm 23:1, for example).

Perhaps most foundationally, Philo's allegorical method of interpreting the Jewish Scriptures gave impetus to the patristic tradition of allegorical interpretation that finds its apex in Saint Augustine.

For our purposes here, it is Philo's teaching about the Divine Logos that connects directly to John and to the necessity of an Incarnation to bridge the gulf between God and man.[25]

Philo sees God as Wisdom (Logos). This Logos is the governor of the universe: "The divine reason is the helmsman and governor of the universe."[26] This Logos that governs all of creation including "the nature of the heaven and the periodical revolution of the sun and the moon and the variations and harmonious movements of the other stars" is the Divine Logos, "his own right reason, his first born son".[27] Finally, in his

[23] "Are 'Mormons' Christian?", Church of Jesus Christ of Latter-day Saints website, accessed May 30, 2024, www.lds.org/topics/christians?lang=eng.
[24] Philo of Alexandria, *The Works of Philo: Complete and Unabridged*, trans. C.D. Yonge (New York: Hendrickson Publishers, 1993).
[25] See C.H. Dodd, *An Interpretation of the Fourth Gospel* (London: Cambridge University Press, 1952). This work is an excellent treatment of Philo's thought as it relates to the prologue of John.
[26] Philo, *On the Cherubim* 11, 35, in *Works of Philo*, 84.
[27] Philo, *On Husbandry* 12, 45, in *Works of Philo*, 178.

discussion of the unchangeable nature of God, he writes: "For in addition to the fact of his wanting nothing he actually has everything and when he gives he employs reason (i.e. logos) as the minister of his gifts by whose agency he also created the world."[28]

What Philo argues is that the God whom he sees, not without reason, as the platonic absolute requires a mediator between his eternal and perfect world and our temporal and imperfect world. Philo argues that Divine Reason, that is, the Logos, is the mediator between God and man. The Divine Logos is the agent through which God created the world, by which he governs it, and with which he brings or gives gifts to the world. The Christian appropriation of this framework in John is obvious.

To sum up, we can quote one of the most eminent scholars of the Gospel of John in the twentieth century: "In all respects the Logos is the medium of intercourse between God and this world. As some of the later Old Testament writers sought to avoid saying that the transcendent God had direct dealing with men and spoke of his angel or his name so Philo calls the logos by such biblical terms as 'angel' and 'head angel'.... By Logos Philo means the Platonic world of ideas conceived not as self-existent but as expressing the mind of the one God. It is this that mediates between God and our world."[29] For those who are seeking, God is known in and through his Logos.

Most scholars seriously doubt that John actually read Philo. The intellectual air of the first century, however, was so permeated by this general structure that missing it would be akin to a contemporary study of genetic inheritance without mentioning DNA. Philo's God who is perfect is John's God. Further, the Logos who is with God, yet distinct, and becomes the necessary mediator between the Divine and the human is common to both John and Philo.

What John teaches that Philo misses is that the Divine Logos "became flesh and dwelt among us, full of grace and truth" (Jn 1:14). Furthermore, "no one has ever seen God; the only-begotten Son ... has made him known" (1:18). Christ, the only-begotten Son, is the preexistent Logos, who connects time and eternity not in a text or in a law but in a Person. This, of course, is fundamentally different

---

[28] Philo, *On the Unchangeableness of God* 12, in *Works of Philo*, 162.
[29] Dodd, *Interpretation of the Fourth Gospel*, 68.

from Philo's logos, the Platonic eidetic structure that, in a true Neo-platonic manner, is available only to the wise.

Philo's Platonism leads him to argue that, as the Divine Logos comes down toward humanity, the few wise persons, that is, true philosophers, rise up to meet the descending Logos and are brought to an eternal realm.

Christianity had to reject this elitism. John appropriates Philo's "logos theology" and transforms his elitism into a universal structure of salvation when in verse 14 he states: "The Word [Logos] became flesh and dwelt among us." In becoming a fully embodied Person, this Logos (Christ) makes salvation available to all humanity. As a Person, Christ opens the way to God for all, not just the few. Jesus called as his apostles ordinary people, for example, fishermen and tax collectors.

The point of treating Philo is to show that at the time of the birth of the Christian era, other thinkers rooted in monotheism were also wrestling with the need for an incarnational connection between time and eternity, between the necessarily existent and the contingently existent.

IV. Mormonism and the Incarnation

Mormonism has no serious concept of the Incarnation because it denies at the outset the nature of God and the metaphysical structure that makes the Incarnation necessary for human salvation, whether that salvation is the specifically Christian sort set forth in the New Testament or the Neoplatonic version found in Philo.

In short, at the outset, Mormons reject the picture of God found in much of the Bible, a perfectly wise, good, and powerful Creator, as seen at the end of Job and in the Book of Wisdom. They also reject the teaching about the Divine Logos found in John 1.

The core text where the Latter-day Saint view is presented is Joseph Smith's King Follett Discourse (also known as the King Follett Sermon), a work readily accessible on the website of the Latter-day Saint church.[30] The title comes from it being a funeral sermon

---

[30] Joseph Smith, Jr., "The King Follett Sermon" (April 7, 1844), *Ensign* 1, no. 4 (April 1971), www.churchofjesuschrist.org/study/ensign/1971/04/the-king-follett-sermon. Here, in the official magazine of the LDS church, this sermon is said to be "one of the classics of Church literature".

for King Follett, a Latter-day Saint who died in an accident in Nauvoo, Illinois. He was a close friend of Joseph Smith. The sermon was delivered in Nauvoo on April 7, 1844. It was given extemporaneously and recorded completely by four different people. By collating their texts, scholars can arrive at a reasonably accurate transcript.[31]

The central belief found in the picture of God in this text is that God and man are not different in kind or essence. They are different only in degree. Joseph Smith states confidently near the beginning that he is going to reveal the nature of God that the world has not known. This, of course, is wrong. Much of his picture of God as limited in power, not a creator, and made of a special kind of "spiritual matter" can be found in Manichean doctrine from the third and fourth centuries of the Christian era.[32] The Latter-day Saint view of the Trinity as three Persons not united in substance but only in will is largely a restatement of fourth-century Anomoeanism, promoted especially by Eunomius.[33]

Joseph Smith does, however, describe a deeply non-Christian picture of God and human beings. "The great secret", according to Smith, is that "God himself was once as we are now, and is an exalted man, and sits enthroned in yonder heavens!" God the Father "was once a man like us; yea, ... God himself, the Father of us all, dwelt on an earth, the same as Jesus Christ Himself did."[34] Another way of putting it is that God and man are of the same species.

Latter-day Saint church presidents and apostles continue to teach that, in the words of former church president Lorenzo Snow, "as man

[31] See Stan Larsen, "The King Follett Discourse: A Newly Amalgamated Text", *BYU Studies* 18.2 (1978): 193–208. A very helpful collection of several listeners' records of the sermon can be found on the website of the LDS church's Joseph Smith Papers Project: "Accounts of the 'King Follett Sermon'", accessed May 30, 2024, www.josephsmithpapers.org/site /accounts-of-the-king-follett-sermon.

[32] On Manicheanism, see Michael Tardieu, *Manichaeism*, trans. Malcolm DeBevoise (Chicago: University of Illinois Press, 2009); Samuel N. C. Lieu, *Manichaeism in the Later Roman Empire and Medieval China* (Tubingen: Mohr Siebeck, 1992).

[33] For the Eunomians, see Richard Vaggione, *Eunomius of Cyzicus and the Nicene Revolution* (London: Oxford University Press, 2007); Eunomius, *The Extant Works*, ed. and trans. Richard Vaggione (New York: Oxford, 2005); Lewis Ayres, *Nicaea and Its Legacy* (London: Oxford University Press, 2004); Aloys Grillmeier, S.J., *Christ in Christian Tradition*, vol. 1, *From the Apostolic Age to Chalcedon (451)*, 2nd ed. (Atlanta: John Knox Press, 1975).

[34] Smith, "King Follett Sermon".

now is, God once was: As God now is, man may be."[35] Two examples make this point. President Brigham Young stated: "He is our father—the Father of our spirits, and was once a man in mortal flesh as we are."[36] About a century later, Joseph Fielding Smith, the tenth president of the church, affirmed the same thing when he discussed the King Follett Discourse and how it could be that "our Father in Heaven at one time passed through a life and death and is an exalted man."[37]

According to LDS, since God is merely an exalted man, our goal is to become gods ourselves and rule our own worlds. "You have got to learn how to be gods yourselves, and to be kings and priests to God, the same as all gods have done before you." What does it mean to become a "joint heir" with Christ? "To inherit the same power, the same glory and the same exaltation, until you arrive at the station of a god, and ascend the throne of eternal power."[38]

If God is an "exalted man",[39] then he cannot be infinite or eternal. Infinity is not just one step ahead of the largest number or greatest quantity of which we can conceive. Infinity is qualitatively different. It is not simply the largest number that can be computed by the largest computer, plus one.

Eternity is also not simply a long stretch of time. Eternity is outside of time. This idea of eternity is central to the Christian idea of God and God's knowledge of future contingents. From patristic writers like Saint Augustine to the great early medieval thinker Boethius down to the present, Christians have generally held that the question of how God can know an event before it happens is misplaced.[40] With God there is no before and after. Physically embodied people

---

[35] Quoted in *Teachings of the Presidents of the Church: Lorenzo Snow* (Salt Lake City: Church of Jesus Christ of Latter-day Saints, 2012), 83.

[36] Brigham Young, "Progress in Knowledge, Etc." (remarks delivered in the Tabernacle, Great Salt Lake City, October 8, 1859, reported by G.D. Watt), in *Journal of Discourses* (Liverpool: Amasa Lyman, 1860), 7:333, https://archive.org/details/JoDV07/page/n339/mode/2up.

[37] Joseph Fielding Smith, *Doctrines of Salvation*, vol. 1, comp. Bruce McConkie (Salt Lake City: Bookcraft, 1954), 10. (See especially Fielding Smith's explanation on pages 10–12.)

[38] Smith, "King Follet Sermon".

[39] Ibid.

[40] See Augustine, *Confessions* 11, trans. F.J. Sheed, intro and notes Peter Brown, ed. with notes Michael P. Foley, 2nd ed. (Indianapolis: Hackett Publishing, 2006); Boethius, *The Consolation of Philosophy* 5, trans. Victor Watts (New York: Penguin, 1999); and Norman Kretzman and Elenore Stumpf, "Eternity", *Journal of Philosophy* 78 (1981): 429–58.

such as all of us, however, must be somewhere at some time. The Latter-day Saint sacred text Pearl of Great Price tells us that God is located somewhere near a "great" star called "Kolob".[41]

Furthermore, if many gods govern many individual worlds ("kingdoms" in Joseph Smith's language), then no one God can be the creator of everything. For Mormonism there is no fundamental gap between God and human beings. Hence, there does not need to be a true incarnation. There is only one nature. Our God, that is, the God of this world, is a fully developed human being, and we are infants headed in the same direction. If there is, as Smith claims, only one nature, then Christ does not need to be one Person with two natures in hypostatic union, as the Council of Chalcedon declared. There is, ultimately, only one nature.

Let us think a little more deeply about the implications of the framework presented in the King Follett Discourse. God the Father, seemingly as all gods before him, started out on a world like ours. He grew into divinity just as he had seen his father do. Joseph Smith is clear that Christ was doing only what he saw his Father do. Following this logic, it seems that the barrier of death would already have been shattered by some earlier god. Why, then, would it be so crucial that Christ destroy death at his Resurrection? It would not, unless the concept of death means something fundamentally different on various "worlds" or various "kingdoms".

Of course, Jesus would need to be resurrected like all of us. But the foundational significance of Easter that Christians have proclaimed for two millennia would be lost. The Christian proclamation that "he lives" would be reduced to a statement of something that has been going on almost forever.

Following this logic, we must ask about the classic Christian understanding of Christ's death on the cross, an understanding shared by Catholics and Protestants. In this view, the Son bears the weight of all human sin and thus reconciles humanity to God. But in Smith's framework, would not the Father have already paid the price for sin? Are not the cross and Resurrection then only reenactments of earlier events? Is not this the scenario exemplified in a famous movie entitled *Groundhog Day*, in which a newscaster is sent to cover the Groundhog

---

[41] Abraham 3:3, in Pearl of Great Price.

Day festivities in Punxsutawney, Pennsylvania (home of the famous
Punxsutawney Phil), and is caught in a time vortex where, according
to the tag line, "he's having the day of his life over and over again."

Mormonism does not have a serious theology or philosophy of
the divine Incarnation, for in their metaphysical scenario, they do
not need such a theology. But with the Latter-day Saint metaphysics,
they must also give up the classical Christian concept of God. As only
an organizer, their God cannot be the creator of all, a position most
Mormons readily admit they hold. God, for Mormons, is an organizer, not a creator in the sense that Christians have understood since
the beginning. Their God is in time and, thus, cannot know precisely
what the future for individuals holds. His power must be somewhat
limited. This, too, is admitted by thoughtful Mormons who hold
that God must have power only to achieve his purposes. Since we do
not know what the barriers are that he must overcome to achieve his
purposes, how can we have confidence that he can overcome them
if he is not all-powerful?

Ultimately, the absence of an incarnational understanding of the
relation between the divine and the human in Mormonism points to
far deeper problems. The Christian commitment to an Incarnation
follows from the conviction that God is the perfectly wise, good, and
powerful Creator. Human beings are creatures. Our ultimate telos as
persons is to unite with God. The restless striving of humans finds its
ultimate rest in God. As Saint Augustine tells in a memorable line:
"For Thou has made us for Thyself and our hearts are restless till they
rest in Thee."[42]

But we cannot reach this perfect rest and peace on our own or by
our own effort. We cannot reach God without God coming to us.
Christ alone, who is both fully man and fully God, can bridge the
gulf between God and persons, between time and eternity, between
perfection and imperfection.

Lacking an incarnational theism, Mormons give up a belief in the
perfect God of classic Christianity. They must hold that their God
is not the God of either Sacred Scripture or the Christian tradition.
Their God is not the God in whom we can trust that "though He slay
me, I will hope in Him" (Jn 13:14, NASB).

---

[42] Augustine, *Confessions* I, I.

3

Classical Theism, Latter-day Saint Theism, and a Long-Awaited, Though Modest, Rejoinder to the Roberts-Van der Donckt Debate

Francis J. Beckwith

The Latter-day Saint prophet Joseph Smith (1805–1844) proclaimed, "It is the first principle of the Gospel to know for a certainty the Character of God."[1] The great Catholic medieval philosopher and theologian Saint Thomas Aquinas (1225–1274) said something similar: "The chief aim of sacred doctrine is to teach the knowledge of God."[2] Both traditions, however, teach radically different understandings of God's nature. The Catholic view—often called classical theism—was, until very recently, also embraced by virtually all other Christian traditions, including the Orthodox churches as well as those communions that are rooted in the Protestant Reformation. Although classical theism is still the dominant view among non-Catholic Christians, in recent decades, especially among Evangelical Protestants, certain philosophers and theologians have suggested alternative theisms that Brian Davies, O.P., puts under the general heading "theistic personalism".[3] In this

---

[1] *Scriptural Teachings of the Prophet Joseph Smith*, selected and arranged by Joseph Fielding Smith with scriptural annotations and introduction by Richard C. Galbraith (Salt Lake City: Deseret Book, 1993), 345.

[2] Saint Thomas Aquinas, *Summa Theologica* I, q. 2, trans. Fathers of the English Dominican Province (New York: Benziger Brothers, 1947), https://dhspriory.org/kenny/CDtexts/summa/FP/FP002.html#FPQ2OUTP1.

[3] Brian Davies, *An Introduction to the Philosophy of Religion*, 4th ed. (New York: Oxford University Press, 2020), 1–22.

chapter, however, our focus will be on contrasting and comparing the philosophical theology of the Latter-day Saints (LDS) with that of the Catholic Church (and, by default, the view that still predominates in the wider Christian world). Theistic personalism, though a worthy subject of discussion, is outside the scope of this chapter.[4]

In the early development and articulation of LDS doctrine, there is no more an impressive figure than B. H. Roberts (1857–1933). Having emigrated from England as a young boy, Roberts arrived in the United States penniless and illiterate. According to LDS historians Leonard J. Arrington and Davis Bitton, Roberts "walked across the plains to Utah at the age of nine. He had little opportunity for formal education, but he became a voracious reader, devouring books of history, science, philosophy, and religion. Possibly no other LDS leader before or since has mastered such a range of scholarly works or published more prodigiously."[5] Although largely self-taught and working within an ecclesial body that had reached its centennial only three years before his death, Roberts, "by the end of his life", writes LDS philosopher David Lamont Paulsen, "had published over thirty books, more than three hundred articles, and more than a thousand sermons and discourses".[6]

In a 1901 address to the LDS church's Mutual Improvement Association (MIA), Roberts offered a presentation and defense of the LDS view of God in reply to several critiques that had been publicly delivered by two local Protestant ministers, Alfred H. Henry (Methodist Episcopalian) and William Paden (Presbyterian).[7] Entitled "The Mormon Doctrine of Deity", Roberts' "address was published in the

---

[4] Among the most important contemporary theistic personalists are Alvin Plantinga, Richard Swinburne, and William Lane Craig. For many years, I considered theistic personalism a species of classical theism. (See, e.g., Francis J. Beckwith, "Mormon Theism, the Traditional Christian Concept of God, and Greek Philosophy: A Critical Analysis", *Journal of the Evangelical Theological Society* 44, no. 4 [December 2001]: 671–95.) However, since having read Davies on this matter, I am convinced that theistic personalism and classical theism are two different theisms, though they have a family resemblance. Nevertheless, it is clear that neither is consistent with LDS theism, as I argue in my 2001 article.

[5] Leonard J. Arrington and Davis Bitton, *The Mormon Experience: A History of the Latter-Day Saints*, 2nd ed. (New York: Alfred E. Knopf, 1992), 257.

[6] David Lamont Paulsen, foreword to *The Mormon Doctrine of Deity: The Roberts-Van Der Donckt Discussion, to Which Is Added a Discourse; Jesus Christ, the Revelation of God*, by B.H. Roberts (Salt Lake City: Signature Books, 1998; originally published 1903 by Deseret News [Salt Lake City]), vi.

[7] Ibid., xvii–xix.

Deseret News and subsequently in two installments in the *Improvement Era*".[8] It elicited a response from Father Cyril Van der Donckt, a Jesuit priest in Pocatello, Idaho, who submitted to the *Improvement Era* a twenty-one-page essay, which was published in two installments in August and September 1902.[9] Beginning in the December 1902 issue, Roberts published a seventy-three-page rebuttal to Father Cyril that appeared in four consecutive issues.[10]

The entire exchange, along with an additional discourse by Roberts and selections from authoritative LDS writings, was published as a book later that year (1903). What makes this book so important is that it is the first real work of philosophical theology in LDS history that interacts with classical theism at a level of sophistication that, at the time, had no precedent in LDS writings.[11] Because both Elder Roberts and Father Cyril fully grasped the deep metaphysical divide between the LDS worldview and the one embraced by virtually all Christian communities, their interaction is an important milestone in the history of LDS-Catholic dialogue. For this reason, I want to reenter that dialogue in this chapter.

In what follows I first explain the differences between classical and LDS theism, paying particular attention to the doctrinal and scriptural concerns that gave rise to the former. I then move on to discuss some of the concerns raised by Elder Roberts in his dialogue with

---

[8] Ibid., xix.

[9] C. Van der Donckt, "Reply to Roberts' View of Deity I", *Improvement Era* 5, no. 10 (August 1902): 759–67; C. Van der Donckt, "Reply to Roberts' View of Deity II", *Improvement Era* 5, no. 11 (September 1902): 856–67.

[10] B.H. Roberts, "The 'Mormon' Doctrine of God: A Rejoinder to Rev. C. Van der Donckt's 'Reply' to Elder B.H. Roberts' Discourse on the Above Subject", *Improvement Era* 6, no. 2 (December 1902): 81–102; B.H. Roberts, "The 'Mormon' Doctrine of God: A Rejoinder to Rev. C. Van der Donckt's 'Reply' to Elder B.H. Roberts' Discourse on the Above Subject", *Improvement Era* 6, no. 3 (January 1903): 161–86; B.H. Roberts, "The 'Mormon' Doctrine of God: A Rejoinder to Rev. C. Van der Donckt's 'Reply' to Elder B.H. Roberts' Discourse on the Above Subject", *Improvement Era* 6, no. 4 (February 1903): 241–55; B.H. Roberts, "The 'Mormon' Doctrine of God: A Rejoinder to Rev. C. Van der Donckt's 'Reply' to Elder B.H. Roberts' Discourse on the Above Subject", *Improvement Era* 6, no. 5 (February 1903): 341–60.

[11] There have been, of course, numerous LDS authors since the time of Roberts who have built on his work. Among them are David Lamont Paulsen, Blake Ostler, Robert Millet, and Kent E. Robson. For a sympathetic treatment of LDS philosophical theology by a Catholic theologian, see Stephen H. Webb, *Mormon Christianity* (New York: Oxford University Press, 2013). For a critical analysis of Webb's work, see Richard Sherlock, "Stephen H. Webb's *Mormon Christianity*: A Critique", *Cultural Encounters* 11, no. 1 (December 2015): 88–92.

Father Cyril. My purpose is not to rebut LDS theism directly; rather, it is to offer our LDS friends an account of classical theism that may help them better grasp its logic and its connection to the Catholic Church's understanding of doctrinal development.

I. Theisms, Classical and Latter-day Saint

Unlike most contemporary Protestant communions, the Catholic Church's doctrine of God is a *de fide* dogma, which means that classical theism is an essential belief of the Church. What precisely, then, does the Church teach about the nature of God, and how does it differ from the LDS view?

I.A. Classical Theism

Classical theism is clearly affirmed in several of the Catholic Church's ecumenical councils (i.e., meetings at which nearly all the Church's bishops are present and as a group issue pronouncements on doctrine and/or practice):

> We firmly believe and unreservedly confess that there is only one true God, eternal and immeasurable, almighty, unchangeable, incomprehensible and ineffable, Father, Son and Holy Spirit, three persons but one absolutely simple essence, substance or nature.[12]

> The Holy, Catholic, Apostolic and Roman Church believes and acknowledges that there is one true and living God, creator and lord of heaven and earth, almighty, eternal, immeasurable, incomprehensible, infinite in will, understanding and every perfection. Since he is one, singular, completely simple and unchangeable spiritual substance, he must be declared to be in reality and in essence, distinct from the world, supremely happy in himself and from himself, and inexpressibly loftier than anything besides himself which either exists or can be imagined.[13]

---

[12] Profession of Faith, Fourth Lateran Council, 1215, www.ewtn.com/catholicism/teachings/god-and-his-creation-3.

[13] First Vatican Council, Dogmatic Constitution on the Catholic Faith (April 24, 1870), chap. 1, 1–2, www.ewtn.com/catholicism/library/first-vatican-council-1505.

It is called the *classical* concept of God because it is ancient, having its roots deep in Christian history. It is not an innovation forced on God's people by a small group of enterprising prelates[14] but an understanding of the divine nature that the Church had come to recognize and affirm as a consequence of its theological and philosophical reflection upon what God had revealed about himself in Scripture. It is neither the result of biblical proof texting nor the mere appropriation of Greek philosophical categories—as Elder Roberts asserts in his debate with Father Cyril[15]—but rather it is the doctrine of God that developed within the Church while that same Church was still in the process of settling the scope of the biblical canon. (The canon refers to those books that made it into the Bible.) Thus, the development and fixing of the Christian canon occurred alongside and in concert with the Church's development of her philosophical theology. This is important, because it means that one cannot easily pit the "God of the Bible" against the "God of the philosophers", since the same Church that settled the biblical canon[16]—the same canon that Elder Roberts embraces and in which he believes classical theism is *not found*[17]—reads that canon to teach classical theism. Thus, it should

[14] Take, for example, the comments made by Brigham Young University professor of ancient Scripture Stephen E. Robinson: "In order to satisfy the Gentiles steeped in Greek philosophy, Christianity had to throw out the doctrines of an anthropomorphic God and the resurrection of the dead, or reinterpret them drastically." (Stephen E. Robinson, "Warring against the Saints of God", *Ensign*, January 1988, www.lds.org/ensign/1988/01/warring-against-the-saints-of-god.)

[15] Elder Roberts writes: "And what the word of God in plainness teaches—so plain that he who 'runs may read,' so plain that 'wayfaring men though fools need not err therein'—'is not to be set aside by the gratuitous assertions' of 'religious innovators' of early Christian centuries who corrupted the plain meaning of God's word by their vain philosophies, and oppositions of science, falsely so called." (Roberts, *Mormon Doctrine of Deity*, 78.) (Quoted phrases are from Father Cyril's contribution. Elder Roberts is using Father Cyril's words against him.)

[16] See Craig A. Allert, *A High View of Scripture: The Authority of the Bible and the Formation of the New Testament* (Grand Rapids, MI: Baker Academic, 2007), 48–66. As my Protestant Baylor colleague, Dan Williams, notes: "The means by which the biblical books were regarded as inspired and divinely given for Christian doctrine and practice took place in the postapostolic centuries of the early church. This process was a gradual and untidy one that emerged out of the worship and liturgical practices of the early churches." (D.H. Williams, *Evangelicals and Tradition: The Formative Influence of the Early Church* [Grand Rapids, MI: Baker Academic, 2005], 55.)

[17] Because the LDS church holds to the Protestant biblical canon, which excludes the seven deuterocanonical books that are in the Catholic Old Testament, my implied claim that Elder Roberts had embraced the Catholic canon is not *technically* correct. However, those missing

not surprise us that even before the Church had a settled canon,[18] what would later become known as classical theism was an integral part of the early Church's doctrinal edifice, though it was sometimes presented in rudimentary form. For instance, the belief that God is the Source of all contingent reality, that he created the entire universe out of nothing (*creatio ex nihilo*)—a belief rejected by the LDS though fundamental to classical theism, as Elder Roberts correctly notes[19]— was ubiquitous in the Church's first centuries. One finds, for example, this belief in the writings of Hermas of Rome (c. A.D. 80–140),[20] Saint Aristides of Athens (c. A.D. 140),[21] Saint Theophilus of Antioch

---

books made no difference in the Protestant Reformers' belief in classical theism. Take, for example, this brief summary of God's nature from the Westminster Confession of Faith (1646): "There is but one only, living, and true God, who is infinite in being and perfection, a most pure spirit, invisible, without body, parts, or passions; immutable, immense, eternal, incomprehensible, almighty, most wise, most holy, most free, most absolute; working all things according to the counsel of His own immutable and most righteous will, for His own glory." (Westminster Confession, chapter 2, 1, Westminster Theological Seminary [website], https://students.wts .edu/resources/creeds/westminsterconfession.html.) On the attribute of divine simplicity, Barry D. Smith writes: "The simplicity doctrine is assumed by Protestantism in spite of its biblicism and critical stance towards the overly speculative tendencies of medieval scholasticism. Lutheran and Reformed theologians are indistinguishable from their medieval predecessors in this regard." (Barry D. Smith, *The Oneness of God and Divine Simplicity* [Eugene, OR: Pickwick, 2014], 34.)

[18] As Anglican historian J. N. D. Kelly notes concerning the New Testament canon, "The first official document which prescribes twenty-seven books of our New Testament as alone canonical is Athanasius's Easter Letter for the year 367, but the process was not everywhere complete until at least a century and a half later." (J. N. D. Kelly, *Early Christian Doctrines*, rev. ed. [San Francisco: HarperOne, 1978], 56.)

[19] Elder Roberts writes: "In this, the orthodox Christians and Mr. V. [regarding Father Cyril] may find their God of pure 'being,' that never is 'becoming,' but always is; also the creation of the universe out of nothing. The fact is that orthodox Christian views of God are Pagan rather than Christian.... So far as it is possible for the human intellect to conceive the infinite, the material universe is infinite, eternal, without beginning and without end. It is inconceivable that the universe could have had a beginning, could have been produced from nothing." (Roberts, *Mormon Doctrine of Deity*, 116, 123.)

[20] "First of all, believe there is one God who created and finished all things, and all things out of nothing. He alone is able to contain the whole, but he cannot be contained." (Hermas of Rome, *The Shepherd* 2, 1, 1 [c. A.D. 80], in *The Fathers Know Best: Your Essential Guide to the Teachings of the Early Church*, ed. Jimmy Akin [San Diego: Catholic Answers, 2010], 144.) Although Akin dates *The Shepherd* at c. A.D. 80, there is disagreement among scholars. For this reason, I have included in the text a broader range of possible dates consistent with present scholarship.

[21] "Let us proceed then, O King, to the elements themselves that we may show in regard to them that they are not gods, but perishable and mutable, produced out of that which did not exist at the command of the true God, who is indestructible and immutable and invisible; yet He sees all things and as He wills, modifies and changes things. What then shall I say concerning the elements?" (Saint Aristides of Athens, *Apology* 4 [c. A.D. 140], in Akin, *Fathers Know Best*, 144.)

(c. A.D. 181),[22] Saint Irenaeus of Lyons (c. A.D. 189),[23] Tertullian of Carthage (A.D. 197),[24] Saint Hippolytus of Rome (A.D. 217),[25] Origen of Alexandria (c. A.D. 225),[26] and Saint Cyprian of Carthage (c. A.D. 254).[27] (Interestingly, Saint Cyprian cites 2 Maccabees [7:27–29], a

[22] "And first, [the prophets of God] taught us with one consent that God made all things out of nothing; for nothing was coeval with God: but He being His own place, and wanting nothing, and existing before the ages, willed to make man by whom He might be known; for [man], therefore, He prepared the world. For he that is created is also needy; but he that is uncreated stands in need of nothing." (Saint Theophilus of Antioch, To Autolycus 2, 10 [c. A.D. 181], in Akin, Fathers Know Best, 145.)

[23] "While men, indeed, cannot make anything out of nothing, but only out of matter already existing, yet God is in this point pre-eminently superior to men, that He Himself called into being the substance of His creation, when previously it had no existence. But the assertion that matter was produced from the Enthymesis of an Æon going astray, and that the Æon [referred to] was far separated from her Enthymesis, and that, again, her passion and feeling, apart from herself, became matter—is incredible, infatuated, impossible, and untenable." (Saint Irenaeus of Lyons, Against Heresies 2, 10, 4 [c. A.D. 189], trans. Alexander Roberts and William Rambaut, in Ante-Nicene Fathers, vol. 1, ed. Alexander Roberts, James Donaldson, and A. Cleveland Coxe [Buffalo: Christian Literature Publishing, 1885], revised and edited for New Advent by Kevin Knight, www.newadvent.org/fathers/0103210.htm.)

[24] "The object of our worship is the One God, He who by His commanding word, His arranging wisdom, His mighty power, brought forth from nothing this entire mass of our world, with all its array of elements, bodies, spirits, for the glory of His majesty; whence also the Greeks have bestowed on it the name of Κόσμος. The eye cannot see Him, though He is (spiritually) visible. He is incomprehensible, though in grace He is manifested. He is beyond our utmost thought, though our human faculties conceive of Him. He is therefore equally real and great." (Tertullian of Carthage, Apology 17 [A.D. 197], trans. S. Thelwall, in Ante-Nicene Fathers, vol. 3, www.newadvent.org/fathers/0301.htm.)

[25] "On the first day God made what He made out of nothing. But on the other days He did not make out of nothing, but out of what He had made on the first day, by moulding it according to His pleasure." (Saint Hippolytus of Rome, fragment from On Genesis [A.D. 217], in Akin, Fathers Know Best, 146.)

[26] "The particular points clearly delivered in the teaching of the apostles are as follow: First, that there is one God, who created and arranged all things, and who, when nothing existed, called all things into being—God from the first creation and foundation of the world, the God of all just men, of Adam, Abel, Seth, Enos, Enoch, Noe, Sere, Abraham, Isaac, Jacob, the twelve patriarchs, Moses, and the prophets; and that this God in the last days, as He had announced beforehand by His prophets, sent our Lord Jesus Christ to call in the first place Israel to Himself, and in the second place the Gentiles, after the unfaithfulness of the people of Israel. This just and good God, the Father of our Lord Jesus Christ, Himself gave the law and the prophets, and the Gospels, being also the God of the apostles and of the Old and New Testaments." (Origen of Alexandria, Fundamental Doctrines, Preface 4 [c. A.D. 225], in Akin, Fathers Know Best, 146–47.)

[27] "[The mother of the seven Maccabean martyrs said:] 'O son, pity me that bare you ten months in the womb, and gave you milk for three years, and nourished you and brought you up to this age; I pray you, O son, look upon the heaven and the earth; and having considered all the things which are in them, understand that out of nothing God made these things and

pre-Christian Jewish book that concerns events of the mid-second century B.C., which affirms *creatio ex nihilo*. Second Maccabees is part of the Catholic Bible but rejected by LDS and Protestants.)

Consequently, in order to understand the Catholic Church's doctrine of God, one cannot treat the Bible that the Church gave to the Christian world—including the Protestant and LDS communities—as if it were something not organically connected to the same Church that affirmed classical theism. This, of course, does not mean that the Church's reading of Scripture is necessarily correct (though, of course, the contributors of this volume believe it is). It does mean, however, that those who challenge that reading on the grounds that the Church's embracing of classical theism is proof of its apostasy—as Elder Roberts maintains[28]—have the burden to show how it is possible that an apostate body can be trusted to give us the Bible while its reading of that very Bible (at least on the doctrine of God) should be distrusted and accorded no deference whatsoever.

---

the human race. Therefore, O son, do not fear that executioner; but being made worthy of your brethren, receive death, that in the same mercy I may receive you with your brethren.' The mother's praise was great in her exhortation to virtue, but greater in the fear of God and in the truth of faith, that she promised nothing to herself or her son from the honour of the six martyrs, nor believed that the prayer of the brothers would avail for the salvation of one who should deny, but rather persuaded him to become a sharer in their suffering, that in the day of judgment he might be found with his brethren." (Saint Cyprian of Carthage, *Exhortation to Martyrdom* 11 [c. A.D. 254], in Akin, *Fathers Know Best*, 147.)

[28] Writes Elder Roberts: "All this [i.e., that there are a plurality of finite and corporeal gods], coming so sharply in conflict with the ideas of an apostate Christendom which had rejected the plain anthropomorphism of the Old and New Testament revelations of God; also the scriptural doctrine of a plurality of Gods, for a false philosophy-created God, immaterial and passionless—all this, I say, could not fail to provoke controversy; for the revelation given to Joseph Smith challenged the truth of the conception of God held by the modern world-pagan, Jew, Mohammedan and Christian alike.... For a long time the paganization of the Christian religion had been going on. The men who esteemed themselves to be philosophers must needs corrupt the simple truth of the 'Apostles' Creed' respecting the three persons of the Godhead, by the false philosophies of the orient, and the idle speculations of the Greeks; until this simple expression of Christian faith in God was changed from what we find it in the 'Apostle's Creed' to the 'Athanasian Creed,' and those vain philosophizings and definitions which have grown out of it, and which reduce the dignity of the Godhead to a mere vacuum—to a 'being' impersonal, incorporeal, without body, without parts, without passions; and I might add also, without sense or reason or any attribute—an absolute nonentity, which they placed in the seat of God, and attempted to confer upon this conception divine powers, clothe it with divine attributes, and give it title, knee and adoration—in a word, divine honors!" (Roberts, *Mormon Doctrine of Deity*, 18.)

I.A.1. God as Creator

Classical theism, as with Scripture, starts with creation. God is Creator of all that exists: "In the beginning God created the heavens and the earth" (Gen 1:1). As the psalmist states: "Let all the earth fear the LORD, let all the inhabitants of the world stand in awe of him! For he spoke, and it came to be; he commanded, and it stood forth" (33:8–9); "Our help is in the name of the LORD, who made heaven and earth" (124:8); "Happy is he whose help is the God of Jacob, whose hope is in the LORD his God, who made heaven and earth, the sea, and all that is in them" (146:5–6).

Yet for the classical theist, God is not merely a Divine Craftsman who works with preexistent eternal matter but is the Source on which all contingent reality, including matter, depends for its existence. Saint Paul, for example, states in his famous address at the Areopagus: "Nor is he served by human hands, as though he needed anything, since he himself gives to all men life and breath and everything" (Acts 17:25). Elsewhere, in his epistles, Saint Paul is more explicit in conveying the radical dependency of everything on God: "For in him all things were created, in heaven and on earth, visible and invisible, whether thrones or dominions or principalities or authorities—all things were created through him and for him. He is before all things, and in him all things hold together" (Col 1:16–17). "For from him and through him and to him are all things. To him be glory for ever. Amen" (Rom 11:36).

Because God is the Source of all contingent reality, and thus not himself a contingent reality, he must by nature be self-existent, meaning that he has the attribute of *aseity*. In short, God exists necessarily. Unlike the universe and everything in it, nothing is required for God to exist. He simply is. Thus, when Moses encountered God in the burning bush and asked him to identify himself, "God said to Moses, 'I AM WHO I AM.' And he said, 'Say this to the sons of Israel, "I AM has sent me to you"'" (Ex 3:14). He is, in other words, the self-existent one. This is clearly implied not only in passages in which we are told God is unlimited in his power (Job 42:2; Jer 32:17; Mt 19:26) but also when the Scripture tells us that God's nature is to always be: "Who has performed and done this, calling the generations from the beginning? I, the LORD, the first, and with the last.... Before me no god was formed, nor shall there be any after me.... I am the first and I am the last; besides me there is no god" (Is 41:4; 43:10; 44:6). As Creator and Sustainer of all that exists, God is the First Cause. By "First Cause" we do not mean that God is "first" in a temporal series of causes. Rather, we mean that he is the First Cause metaphysically. That is, God is first in a sort of *foundational* sense. The world's causal activity is contingent and conditioned; it cannot contain within itself an explanation for its own existence. For this reason, the causal activity we observe must be caused by—or grounded in—that which itself is necessary and unconditioned. Some may insist that we need not explain the causal activity we observe by appealing to anything other than the proximate causal forces that precede that activity. For example, one need not explain my coming into being by appealing to anything other than the procreative act of my parents. Any other explanation is at best superfluous. This response, however, confuses two ways of conceiving causes and the causal series in which they occur.

It is the difference between whether there must exist a First Cause (or uncaused cause) of a causal series *per accidens* (i.e., can the present be the result of an infinite past series of events?) and whether there must exist a First Cause (or uncaused cause) of a causal series *per se* (i.e., can a present event, X, be the result of an infinite series of causes *right now*?).[29] For the classical theist, God keeps the universe in existence at every moment of its existence, since a universe, even an infinitely large one, consisting of contingent beings in causal relationships with one another, could no more exist without some sustaining First Cause than could an alleged perpetual motion machine exist

---

[29] The following are the two examples used by Saint Thomas Aquinas. He writes: "In efficient causes it is impossible to proceed to infinity 'per se'—thus, there cannot be an infinite number of causes that are 'per se' required for a certain effect; for instance, that a stone be moved by a stick, the stick by the hand, and so on to infinity. But it is not impossible to proceed to infinity 'accidentally' as regards efficient causes; for instance, if all the causes thus infinitely multiplied should have the order of only one cause, their multiplication being accidental, as an artificer acts by means of many hammers accidentally, because one after the other may be broken. It is accidental, therefore, that one particular hammer acts after the action of another; and likewise it is accidental to this particular man as generator to be generated by another man; for he generates as a man, and not as the son of another man. For all men generating hold one grade in efficient causes—viz. the grade of a particular generator. Hence it is not impossible for a man to be generated by man to infinity; but such a thing would be impossible if the generation of this man depended upon this man, and on an elementary body, and on the sun, and so on to infinity." (Saint Thomas Aquinas, *Summa Theologica* I, q. 46, art. 2, trans. Fathers of the English Dominican Province, 2nd and rev. ed. [London: Burns, Oates & Washbourne, 1920], www.newadvent.org/summa/1046.htm.)

without an Unmoved Mover keeping its motion perpetual. To offer an illustration adapted from an example employed by one of my former professors, the late James Sadowsky, S.J.,[30] imagine the universe consisted entirely and exclusively of people who could not act without first asking permission from another person, and suppose that this universe had always existed. Imagine further that everyone is acting. Unless there is a First Giver of permission (who by nature does not have to ask permission in order to act) outside the causal series of permitters and actors, no one would ever act, since asking permission is itself an act for which one would need permission.

For these reasons, the classical theist maintains that it is wrong to think of God as if he were one incredibly great Being (or the greatest Being) within a universe that contains a hierarchy of beings—as LDS theology teaches[31]—but rather, we should think of God as the Being on which everything that exists depends. This is what Saint Paul seems to have had in mind when he debated Stoic and Epicurean philosophers at the Areopagus:

> *The God who made the world and everything in it, being Lord of heaven and earth*, does not live in shrines made by man, nor is he served by human hands, as though he needed anything, since he himself gives to all men life and breath and everything. And he made from one every nation of men to live on all the face of the earth, having determined allotted periods and the boundaries of their habitation, that they should seek

[30] James Sadowsky, S.J., "The Cosmological Argument and the Endless Regress", *International Philosophical Quarterly* 20, no. 4 (December 1980): 465–67. Here is Father Sadowsky's illustration from which I borrow: "If we reject the principle of the Cosmological Argument, we have to agree that nothing (including causes) can exist without a cause. But if that makes sense, is not the following equally intelligible: 'No one may do anything (including asking for permission) without asking for permission.' Clearly there is no way in which this precept can be observed because there is no legitimate way of asking for permission. The problem in both cases is that no condition can ever be met without the fulfillment of a preceding condition. No permission may be asked for because each asking for permission requires a prior asking for permission. Likewise, no causation can take place because each act of causation requires a prior act of causation." (Ibid., 466.)

[31] Elder Roberts, for example, writes: "I take it that we may classify under three heads the complaints here made against us with reference to the doctrine of Deity. First, we believe that God is a being with a body in form like man's; that he possesses body, parts and passions; that in a word, God is an exalted, perfected man. Second, we believe in a plurality of Gods. Third, we believe that somewhere and some time in the ages to come, through development, through enlargement, through purification until perfection is attained, man at last, may become like God—a God." (Roberts, *Mormon Doctrine of Deity*, 11.)

God, in the hope that they might feel after him and find him. Yet he is not far from each one of us, for "*In him we live and move and have our being*"; as even some of your poets have said, "For we are indeed his offspring." (Acts 17:24–28; emphasis added)

What one finds in this passage is extraordinary. You have Saint Paul making a *philosophical* claim about God as the sustaining and transcendent, though ontologically imminent, First Cause of all that exists—"the God who made the world and everything in it", and "in him we live and move and have our being"—while quickly adapting this philosophical claim to anthropomorphic poetic language that his philosophical audience would understand: "For we are indeed his offspring." That is, the anthropomorphism is employed *to illustrate* a deep philosophical truth about God's ontological relationship to creation.

I.A.2. God as Perfect

For the classical theist, God is perfect, from which it follows that God has no potential to become "better", since perfection implies that the one possessing it has no need for change or improvement. In Scripture, God's perfection is often presented in the language of his intrinsic holiness (or goodness), indicating that the highest Good is identical to the divine (Lev 11:44–45; 19:2; Deut 32:4; Ps 92:5; Mt 5:48; Mk 10:18; Lk 18:9; 1 Pet 1:16). But if God cannot get better, he cannot increase in knowledge and power. Thus, tightly tethered to his perfection is his omniscience (Job 28:24; Ps 139:17–18; 147:5; Is 41:21–24, 46:10; Rom 8:29; 1 Pet 1:1–2) as well as his omnipotence (Job 42:2; Jer 32:17; Mt 19:26).

If, of course, God is perfect and self-existent, then he has always been perfect and cannot change. He is, as the biblical authors put it, unchanging, holy, and eternally God:

I the LORD do not change. (Mal 3:6)

When God desired to show more convincingly to the heirs of the promise the unchangeable character of his purpose, he interposed with an oath. (Heb 6:17)

Before the mountains were brought forth,
  or ever you had formed the earth and the world,
  from everlasting to everlasting you are God. (Ps 90:2)

Have you not known? Have you not heard?
The LORD is the everlasting God,
  the Creator of the ends of the earth.
He does not faint or grow weary,
  his understanding is unsearchable. (Is 40:28)

For thus says the high and lofty One
  who inhabits eternity, whose name is Holy:
I dwell in the high and holy place. (Is 57:15)

Ever since the creation of the world his invisible nature, namely, his eternal power and deity, has been clearly perceived in the things that have been made. So they are without excuse. (Rom 1:20)

To the King of ages, immortal, invisible, the only God, be honor and glory for ever and ever. Amen. (1 Tim 1:17)

Every good endowment and every perfect gift is from above, coming down from the Father of lights with whom there is no variation or shadow due to change. (Jas 1:17)

When we reflect philosophically on the matter of change, it is clear that change involves the movement from potential to actual. When, for example, my niece Darby was a teenager and we looked back at her infancy, we marveled at how the intellectual and artistic potentials inherent in her were actualized by her hard work and persistence. God, on the other hand, because he is eternally perfect and unchanging, could not have ever had unrealized potentials. Moreover, the actualizing of Darby's unrealized potentials requires a massive collection of interdependent causes—for example, her nature, her parents, the exercise of her will, a civilization, and a livable planet—none of which is self-existent, and all of which, like Darby, is composed of potentiality and actuality and cannot move from the former to the latter without a cause. But since, as I have already noted, there cannot exist an infinite series of *per se* causes, there must exist a Being that is not an effect and in which there is no potency, that is, an Immutable Being that is Pure Act and thus the First Cause.

I.A.3. God as Simple

From the considerations we've glossed so far, it follows that God is also simple. What could this possibly mean? First off, it does not mean that God is stupid or easy to understand. Rather, it means that God is not a composite or composed of parts. Take, for example, a typical human being. He is material, which means he has physical parts. He also consists of actuality and potentiality; that is, as long as he exists, he has the potential to change and actualize some unrealized potential. We know what these unrealized potentials could be because we know the sort of thing a human being is: a rational animal. So, for example, my niece Riley has the unrealized potential to master the Italian language, a potential not shared by the family cat. When Riley was a fetus, she had even more unrealized potentials. We make these judgments about individual human beings because we know their essence or nature—rational animal—which we could still know even if the individual about which we are making our judgment had never existed. Here is another way to put it: a "whatness" of a human being, its essence, is distinct from its existence. For it is not part of any human being's essence that it *must* exist. Human beings arise and perish, as we know all too well from our experience. So, human beings, as with everything else in the universe, are composed of essence and existence. But this is not true of God. God, because he is Pure Act, must be identical to his essence, since what is self-existent and eternal cannot not exist. Unlike any created thing that by its nature need not exist, it is of God's essence that he exists.

Nor could God be anything other than what he is. To deny this would suggest that he has the potential to be different from what he is, and thus he could not be Pure Act. If God were not simple—if he were like us, composite beings, as the LDS church teaches[32]—then his existence would depend on causes outside himself, and thus he would be just another contingent being in the infinite series of *per se*

[32] See note 31.

causes within the universe. But, as we have seen, such a series is impossible, even if the universe had always existed.

Moreover, if God is Pure Act, there cannot be more than one God, since any two alleged Gods would have to differ in some way. But any difference between them means that each lacks what the other has, and for a being to have a lack is for it to have a potential for change. Although much of what we have covered scripturally on the matters of God's self-existence and role as Creator should be sufficient to show that the Bible teaches that the divine nature belongs to only one, there are many passages of Scripture that specifically discuss God's uniqueness, that there is only one God (e.g., Is 43:10; 44:6–8; 45:5, 18, 21–22; Jer 10:10; Jn 17:3; 1 Cor 8:4–6; 1 Thess 1:9; 1 Tim 2:5).

It follows from the fact that God is Immutable, Source of all contingent reality, Simple and Pure Act that he is not a physical being like one of us, as the LDS church teaches. For to have a body means that one is contingent, composite, and subject to change. That God is incorporeal seems to be the teaching of Scripture. In John 4:24 Jesus says that "God is spirit, and those who worship him must worship in spirit and truth", while in Luke 24:39, he draws a contrast between his own body and that of an incorporeal spirit: "See my hands and my feet, that it is I myself; handle me, and see; for a spirit *has not flesh and bones as you see that I have*" (emphasis added). The Bible also teaches that God is invisible (Col 1:15; 1 Tim 1:17; Heb 11:27) and not a man (Num 23:19), both of which would follow from God's incorporeality.

As previously cited, the Catholic Church in her Profession of Faith at the 1215 Fourth Lateran Council also teaches that God is "incomprehensible and ineffable". And in her 1870 Dogmatic Constitution on the Catholic Faith, she teaches that God is "inexpressibly loftier than anything besides himself which either exists or can be imagined". What the Church is teaching here is that because God is so wholly other—so unlike anything we have experienced in the material world—we are incapable of fully or perfectly expressing what he is like in his essence or nature. To use an illustration outside of theology, most of us have struggled to describe to others a particular experience of beauty or loveliness, eventually confessing in exasperation that our language cannot fully express the experience. We may offer analogies or metaphors that succeed in providing an approximate account of the experience, but they invariably fall short of capturing it perfectly. I can, for example, try to describe to friends and family the sense of wonder and awe, and immediate awareness of intrinsic beauty, I felt when I first encountered the Pietà in St. Peter's Basilica in June of 2013, but no composition of words could fully capture the experience. I could say that it was "like watching a total eclipse of the sun at the edge of the Grand Canyon", but that would not communicate the essence of my encounter with Michelangelo's masterpiece, even though it would not be false.

Both Scripture and the Catholic Church teach that God, though knowable, is beyond our understanding: "Can you find out the deep things of God? Can you find out the limit of the Almighty? It is higher than heaven—what can you do? Deeper than Sheol—what can you know? Its measure is longer than the earth, and broader than the sea" (Job 11:7–9); "He has made everything beautiful in its time; also he has put eternity into man's minds, yet so that he cannot find out what God has done from the beginning to the end" (Eccles 3:11); "For my thoughts are not your thoughts, neither are your ways my ways, says the LORD. For as the heavens are higher than the earth, so are my ways higher than your ways and my thoughts than your thoughts" (Is 55:8–9); "O the depth of the riches and wisdom and knowledge of God! How unsearchable are his judgments and how inscrutable his ways!" (Rom 11:33); "For now we see in a mirror dimly, but then face to face. Now I know in part; then I shall understand fully, even as I have been fully understood" (1 Cor 13:12).

A few references to God's character can help illustrate this point. Scripture teaches that "God is love" (1 Jn 4:8), but it also says that the "love of Christ ... surpasses knowledge" (Eph 3:19). We are told that God is wise (Rom 16:27), yet we are also told that his wisdom is inscrutable (Rom 11:33) and "his understanding ... unsearchable" (Is 40:28). Jesus says that whoever "has seen me has seen the Father" (Jn 14:9), though Saint Paul tells us that "we see in a mirror dimly" (1 Cor 13:12), and Saint John affirms that "no man has ever seen God" (1 Jn 4:12). Saint Paul encourages his fellow Christians by telling them that "the peace of God, which *passes all understanding*, will keep your hearts and your minds in Christ Jesus" (Phil 4:7; emphasis added).

There is, of course, much more that can be said about the Catholic Church's affirmation that "there is one true and living God, creator and lord of heaven and earth, almighty, eternal, immeasurable, incomprehensible, infinite in will, understanding and every perfection" and that because "he is one, singular, completely simple and unchangeable spiritual substance, he must be declared to be in reality and in essence, distinct from the world, supremely happy in himself and from himself, and inexpressibly loftier than anything besides himself which either exists or can be imagined."[33] For example, the Catholic Church also teaches that God is triune; that he is Father, Son, and Holy Spirit; and that the second Person of the Trinity took on human nature. Although I will address those doctrinal beliefs when I assess Elder Roberts' critique of Father Cyril in section II below, what I hope I have adequately communicated to my LDS friends in this brief summary of the Catholic Church's doctrine of God is how the Church—with the resources of *both* Scripture *and* philosophical reflection—arrived at her beliefs about the nature of the divine.

I.B. Latter-day Saint Theism

The Mormon doctrine of deity, as Elder Roberts calls it, is radically different from classical theism. However, LDS theism is like classical theism insofar as it is tightly tethered to a metaphysical narrative about the order and nature of things. Given the complexities and nuances of the LDS worldview, I can only hope to offer a general sketch of this metaphysical narrative and the place of the deity in it.

For Latter-day Saints, the universe has always existed and thus is not in need of a creator. Moreover, everything in the universe is entirely made up of matter. "The elements are eternal", writes Joseph Smith.[34] Although, as we have seen, an eternal universe is not inconsistent with *creatio ex nihilo*, LDS doctrine explicitly denies it.[35] Even what we think of as "spirit" is really just a form of matter, according

---

[33] First Vatican Council, Dogmatic Constitution on the Catholic Faith, chap. 1, 1–2.

[34] Doctrine and Covenants (DC) 93:33.

[35] Joseph Smith writes: "Now, the word *create* came from the word *baurau*, which does not mean to create out of nothing; it means to organize; the same as a man would organize materials and build a ship. Hence, we infer that God had materials to organize the world out of chaos-chaotic matter, which is element, and in which dwells all the glory. Element had an existence from the time He had. The pure principles of element are principles which can never be destroyed; they may be organized and reorganized, but not destroyed. They had no beginning and can have no end." (Joseph Smith, Jr., *History of the Church of Jesus Christ of Latter-day Saints*, 7 vols., intro and notes B. H. Roberts [Salt Lake City: Deseret Book, 1978], 6:308–9.)

to Smith.[36] The spirits of human beings have preexisted in some form from all eternity and are thus uncreated intelligences: "The spirit of man is not a created being; it existed from eternity, and will exist to eternity. Anything created cannot be eternal; and earth, water, etc., had their existence in an elementary state, from eternity."[37] There is in LDS thought some mystery about personal identity and intelligences,[38] but solving that mystery is not relevant to this chapter. Suffice it to say, "what has been revealed ... is that there is something called intelligence that is an eternal part of man's nature."[39]

For the LDS, God the Father, in cooperation with "the Gods", organized our world out of preexistent eternal matter and produced spirit children from the reservoir of eternal intelligences who subsequently enter our mortal realm through ordinary human conception and birth.[40] God the Father is not only not the Source of the universe's being, as is the God of classical theism, but he is a "Man of Holiness"[41] who "has a body of flesh and bone as tangible as man's."[42]

It should be noted that one stream of LDS thought, which has been dominant for quite some time, holds that God the Father was once a man like us, living in a distant world, who eventually progressed to Godhood and became our Heavenly Father. Advocates for this perspective—which include Elder Roberts[43]—typically cite

---

[36] Smith writes: "There is no such thing as immaterial matter. All spirit is matter, but it is more fine or pure, and can only be discerned by purer eyes; we cannot see it; but when our bodies are purified we shall see that it is all matter." (DC 131:7–8.)

[37] Smith, *History of Latter-day Saints*, 3:387.

[38] "There are two main schools of thought on the subject: (1) Before spirit-birth, there is an eternal entity known as 'an intelligence' that possesses identity, agency and individuality; (2) There is a primal spirit matter that is eternal from which the spirit body was organized. Although statements from leaders of the Church can be found to support both of these points of view, there is no official doctrine of the Church on the matter." (Brent L. Top, "Intelligence(s)", in *LDS Beliefs: A Doctrinal Reference*, by Robert L Millet et al. [Salt Lake City: Deseret Book, 2011], 325.)

[39] Ibid.

[40] Abraham 3:21—4:31; Moses 3:5, in Pearl of Great Price (PGP).

[41] Moses 6:57, in PGP.

[42] DC 130:22a.

[43] Elder Roberts writes: "What think ye of Christ? Is he God? Yes. Is he man? Yes. Will that resurrected, immortal, glorified man ever be distilled into some bodiless, formless essence, to be diffused as the perfume of a rose is diffused throughout the circumambient air? Will he become an impersonal, incorporeal, immaterial God, without body, without parts, without passions? Will it be? Can it be? What think ye of Christ? Is he God? Yes. Is he an exalted man?

portions of Joseph Smith's King Follett Sermon (April 7, 1844), which he delivered three months before his death. What follows is a passage from that sermon:

> I am going to tell you how God came to be God. We have imagined and supposed that God was God from all eternity. I will refute that idea, and take away the veil, so that you may see. These ideas are incomprehensible to some, but they are simple. It is the first principle of the gospel to know for a certainty the character of God, and to know that we may converse with Him as one man converses with another, and that He was once a man like us....
>
> Here, then, is eternal life—to know the only wise and true God; and you have got to learn how to be gods yourselves, and to be kings and priests to God, the same as all gods have done before you, namely, by going from one small degree to another, and from a small capacity to a great one; from grace to grace, from exaltation to exaltation, until you attain to the resurrection of the dead, and are able to dwell in everlasting burnings, and to sit in glory, as do those who sit enthroned in everlasting power.[44]

As the fifth president of the LDS church, Lorenzo Snow (1814–1901), once put it: "As man now is, God once was: As God now is, man may be."[45] In this way, President Snow was connecting God's path to exaltation (which is the technical term in LDS theology) with the promise of our own exaltation if we live exemplary lives consistent with LDS practice and teachings. After becoming gods themselves, faithful Latter-day Saints will become gods of their own worlds, just like God the Father became the God of ours.

Yes; in the name of all the Gods, he is. Then why do sectarian ministers arraign the faith of the members of the Church of Jesus Christ of Latter-day Saints because they believe and affirm that God is an exalted man, and that he has a body, tangible, immortal, indestructible, and will so remain embodied throughout the countless ages of eternity? And since the Son is in the form and likeness of the Father, being, as Paul tells, 'in the express image of his [the Father's] person'—so, too, the Father God is a man of immortal tabernacle, glorified and exalted: for as the Son is, so also is the Father, a personage of tabernacle, of flesh and of bone as tangible as man's, as tangible as Christ's most glorious, resurrected body." (Roberts, *Mormon Doctrine of Deity*, 25–26.)

[44] Joseph Smith, Jr., "The King Follett Sermon" (April 7, 1844), *Ensign* 1, no. 4 (April 1971), www.lds.org/ensign/1971/04/the-king-follett-sermon.

[45] Quoted in *Teachings of the Presidents of the Church: Lorenzo Snow* (Salt Lake City: Church of Jesus Christ of Latter-day Saints, 2012), 83.

However, some LDS intellectuals have raised questions about aspects of this exaltation narrative that do not seem to be explicitly stated anywhere in the LDS canon of Scripture.[46] Take, for example, the comments of Brigham Young University ancient Scripture professor, Robert L. Millet:

> Joseph Smith taught that God is an Exalted Man, a Man of Holiness, and that while He is God and possesses every power, every divine quality, and every perfected attribute, He is not of a different species with mortal men and women. Now don't misunderstand me here: the chasm between man and God is immense, but we do not believe it is unbridgeable, nor do we hold the same Creature-creator dichotomy that most Christians do. For us God is a man, a person, an actual being with a glorified and exalted personality.
>
> It is true that Presidents Joseph Smith and Lorenzo Snow both spoke of God once being a man, but we know very little if anything beyond the idea itself. I am not aware of any official statement or declaration of doctrine that goes beyond what I have just stated. Anything you may hear or read beyond that is speculative.[47]

Elsewhere, in the reference work *LDS Beliefs*, Millet states:

> Because the King Follett sermon is not part of the canon of scripture and is not found within the standard works [of the LDS church], it does not carry the same weight in determining and explaining doctrine.... Also, because Joseph Smith died a short time after delivering the discourse, we do not have his singular, supplementary, prophetic insights into some of its more difficult doctrinal matters. For example, we have no problem as a people accepting the fact God is an exalted man. But we do not know the doctrinal details beyond what the Prophet taught. In addition, it remains for Joseph's apostolic and prophetic successors to set forth with greater clarity than we now possess how our Father in Heaven can be a man who became exalted (which

---

[46] The LDS church accepts four sources of scriptural revelation that it calls *the standard works*: the King James Version of the Protestant Bible, the Book of Mormon, the Doctrine and Covenants, and the Pearl of Great Price. See Top, "Standard Works", in Millet et al., *LDS Beliefs*, 602–3.

[47] Robert L. Millet, in *Bridging the Divide: The Continuing Conversation between a Mormon and an Evangelical* by Robert L. Millet and Gregory C. V. Johnson (Rhinebeck, NY: Monkfish Book Publishing, 2007), 58.

we accept) *and* eternally God (which we also accept). In addition, we do not know specifically what it means to become as God, beyond gaining exaltation and eternal life, which entails receiving a fullness of the glory and power of the Father as well as enjoying the continuation of the family unit in eternity. (D & C 132: 19–20)[48]

Catholics, of all people, can appreciate Millet's reasoning. Within our own tradition, we hold that doctrine can develop and that certain beliefs held by the Catholic Church are infallible teachings while other magisterial pronouncements have differing degrees of certainty and thus may in fact be subject to further elaboration, clarification, or even repudiation.[49] Thus, I think it is wise for Millet to suggest that his brethren withhold speculation and judgment until the LDS magisterium has offered a plausible account of two apparently disparate aspects of LDS thought—God's progression to Godhood and God's eternality.[50] However, it is important to note that Millet's suggestion implies that the Scriptures alone—special revelation without the assistance of theological reflection and magisterial authority—are inadequate to resolve doctrinal questions that arise from a "plain reading" of those writings, since the "plain reading" seems to result in an inconsistency, at least superficially. Interestingly, this very "Catholic" way to approach special revelation and the theologian's craft is, as I implied above and will argue below, the proper lens by which we should assess the development of classical theism.

So far I have mentioned only God the Father and the prospect of observant Latter-day Saints achieving exaltation to Godhood at some future state. But there are other beings in the LDS worldview to which the term "God" is attributed. Among them are God the Son (Jesus Christ) and God the Holy Ghost, both of whom, along with our Heavenly Father, are members of the Trinity. For the Catholic Church, as

---

[48] Robert L. Millet, "King Follett Sermon", in Millet et al., *LDS Beliefs*, 365. "D & C" refers to DC. See also James E. Faulconer and Susannah Morrison, "The King Follett Discourse: Pinnacle or Peripheral?", *BYU Studies Quarterly* 60, no. 3 (2021): 85–104.

[49] See Ludwig Ott, *Fundamentals of Catholic Dogma*, trans. Patrick Lynch, ed. (in English) James Canon Bastible (Rockford, IL: TAN Books, 1974; originally published 1955 by Mercier Press [Cork, Ireland]), 9–10.

[50] In LDS thought, God is eternal insofar as having everlasting existence in time and space. In classical theism, God's eternality refers to God's nontemporal everlasting existence, since he is the Creator of time and space and thus is not subject to it.

well as for the Orthodox churches and most Protestant groups, the triune God is one substance in three Persons, with the term "Person" referring to a real distinction within the one true God, and "because it does not divide the divine unity, the real distinction of the persons from one another resides solely in the relationships which relate them to one another".[51] In LDS theism, however, the Trinity consists of three separate Gods—Father, Son, and Holy Ghost—who together make up the Godhead. (Perhaps these are the "Gods" to which the LDS Book of Abraham refers when it discusses the organization of the earth and its first inhabitants, though the text does not specifically mention the triune Godhead by name.)[52] As the LDS prophet Smith put it: "I have always declared God to be a distinct personage, Jesus Christ a separate and distinct personage from God the Father, and that the Holy Ghost was a distinct personage from God the Father, and that the Holy Ghost was a distinct personage and a Spirit; and these three constitute three distinct personages and three Gods."[53]

Although the origin and nature of God the Father are somewhat straightforward in LDS thought—he is a physical Being who is the God of this world, and at some point in the past he was a man of some sort or another (with all of Millet's caveats)—the origin and nature of God the Son and the Holy Ghost are a bit more mysterious. The former, prior to his Incarnation, was, like all human beings, a premortal spirit child of the Father, though he is unique insofar as he was the Father's firstborn spirit child. He is also unique in another way: unlike all other human beings, Christ's physical existence was directly brought about by God the Father with the Virgin Mary's cooperation.[54] (Whether this divine "siring" involved literal conjugal relations between God the

---

[51] *Catechism of the Catholic Church*, no. 255.

[52] "And then the Lord said: Let us go down. And they went down at the beginning, and they, that is the Gods, organized and formed the heavens and the earth. And the earth, after it was formed, was empty and desolate, because they had not formed anything but the earth; and darkness reigned upon the face of the deep, and the Spirit of the Gods was brooding upon the face of the waters." (Abraham 4:1–2.)

[53] Smith, *History of Latter-day Saints*, 6:474.

[54] As Millet puts it: "Jesus Christ is the Son of God—the firstborn spirit Son of God the Father and the Only Begotten of the Father in the flesh. This expression, declaration, and doctrine of the divine Sonship of Christ is neither mythical nor metaphorical. From Mary, a mortal woman who had never had sexual relations with any man (Luke 1:34), Jesus inherited mortality, including the capacity to die; from God, the immortal man of Holiness, Jesus inherited immortality, the capacity to live forever. He is the Son of God, and he is God the Son." (Robert L. Millet, "Virgin Birth", in Millet et al., *LDS Beliefs*, 653.)

Father and the Virgin Mary is a matter of dispute among contemporary LDS scholars and authorities. Some believe it was literal,[55] while others claim it was shrouded in mystery and one ought not speculate about its precise meaning.[56]) As for the Holy Ghost, his origin and nature are even more mysterious, though we are told that he is "the third member of the Godhead, is a male spirit personage, the minister of the Father and the Son [, and] ... a revelator, a teacher, a converter, a comforter, a sanctifier, and a sealer".[57]

That, in a nutshell, is the Mormon doctrine of deity. It differs radically from classical theism, in its understanding of both ultimate

---

[55] Brigham Young (1801–1877), the church's second president, asserts: "The birth of the Savior was as natural as are the births of our children; it was the result of natural action. He partook of flesh and blood—was begotten of his Father, as we were of our fathers." (Brigham Young, July 8, 1860, *Journal of Discourses*, 26 vols. [London and Liverpool: LDS Booksellers Depot, 1854–1886], 8:115) Apostle Bruce McConkie writes: "Christ was begotten by an Immortal Father in the same way that mortal men are begotten by mortal fathers.... God the Father is a perfected, glorified, holy Man, an immortal Personage. And Christ was born into the world as the literal Son of this Holy Being; he was born in the same personal, real, and literal sense that any mortal son is born to a mortal father. There is nothing figurative about his paternity; he was begotten, conceived and born in the normal and natural course of events, for he is the Son of God, and that designation means what it says.... Our Lord is the only mortal person ever born to a *virgin*, because he is the only person who ever had an immortal Father. Mary, his mother, 'was carried away in the Spirit' (1 Ne. 11:13–21), was 'overshadowed' by the Holy Ghost, and the conception which took place 'by the power of the Holy Ghost' resulted in the bringing forth of the literal and personal Son of God the Father (Alma 7:10; 2 Ne. 17:14; Isa. 7:14; Matt. 1:18–25; Luke 1:26–38.) Christ is not the Son of the Holy Ghost, but of the Father. (*Doctrines of Salvation*, vol. 1, pp. 18–20.) Modernistic teachings denying the *virgin birth* are utterly and completely apostate and false." (Bruce R. McConkie, *Mormon Doctrine*, 2nd ed. [Salt Lake City: Bookcraft, 1966], 547, 742, 822 [emphasis in original])

[56] The LDS church's eleventh president, Harold B. Lee (1899–1973), states: "You asked about the birth of the Savior. Never have I talked about sexual intercourse between Deity and the mother of the Savior. If teachers were wise in speaking of this matter about which the Lord has said but very little, they would rest their discussion on this subject with merely the words which are recorded on this subject in Luke 1:34–35: 'Then said Mary unto the angel, How shall this be, seeing I know not a man? And the angel answered and said unto her, The Holy Ghost shall come upon thee, and the power of the Highest shall overshadow thee: therefore also that holy thing which shall be born of thee shall be called the Son of God.' Remember that the being who was brought about by [Mary's] conception was a divine personage. We need not question His method to accomplish His purposes. Perhaps we would do well to remember the words of Isaiah 55:8–9: 'For my thoughts are not your thoughts, neither are your ways my ways, saith the Lord. For as the heavens are higher than the earth, so are my ways higher than your ways, and my thoughts than your thoughts.' Let the Lord rest His case with this declaration and wait until He sees fit to tell us more." (Harold B. Lee, *The Teachings of Harold B. Lee: Eleventh President of the Church of Jesus Christ of Latter-day Saints*, ed. Clyde J. Williams [Salt Lake City: Bookcraft, 1996], 14)

[57] Robert L. Millet, "Holy Ghost", in Millet et al., *LDS Beliefs*, 307.

reality and the nature of God. We now turn to some of the questions that Elder Roberts raised in his discussion with Father Cyril.

II. Elder Roberts' Concerns

In his seventy-three-page rebuttal to Father Cyril, Elder Roberts covers large swaths of theological real estate. Because I cannot hope to cover all of it here, I will focus on three queries raised by Elder Roberts on the topics of the Incarnation (II.A), the Trinity (II.B), and Greek philosophy and Scripture (II.C).

II.A. The Incarnation

In his reply to Father Cyril, Elder Roberts maintains that classical theists, who believe that God the Son became incarnate in Jesus Christ, cannot also claim that the LDS view of God the Father's corporeality diminishes his deity. Writes Roberts:

> And now I ask, as I did in my discourse, *is Jesus God*? Is he a manifestation of God—a revelation of him? If so, there must be in him an end of controversy; for whatever Jesus Christ was and is God must be, or Jesus Christ is no manifestation, no revelation of God. Is Jesus Christ in form like man? Is he possessed of a body of flesh and bone which is eternally united to him—and now an integral part of him? Does he possess body, parts and passions? There can be but one answer to all these questions, and that is, "Yes; he possessed and now possesses all these things." Then God also possesses them; for even according to both Catholic and orthodox Protestant Christian doctrine, Jesus Christ was and is God, and the complete manifestation and revelation of God the Father.[58]

The classical Christian theist does in fact affirm that Jesus Christ is God, but he does not affirm that Jesus' human nature is his divine nature. For the Catholic, Jesus Christ is both God and man insofar as he has *both* a human nature *and* a divine nature. He is not a mixture of both natures or some strange hybrid. In his divine nature, Jesus has all the attributes of deity that we discussed in section I.A. And in his

---

[58] Roberts, *Mormon Doctrine of Deity*, 95.

human nature, he possesses all the human attributes required to make one human. Thus, when the Catholic says that God the Son became man in Jesus Christ, he is affirming that God assumed a human nature, not that the divine nature changed in any way. Therefore, what is true of the human nature of Christ is not true of his divine nature, the latter of which God the Son possesses in its fullness as does God the Father and God the Holy Spirit. Thus, the Incarnation is possible *precisely because* God is not by nature corporeal. This is evident from the opening verses of the Gospel of Saint John:[59] "In the beginning was the Word, and the Word was with God, and the Word was God. He was in the beginning with God.... And the Word became flesh and dwelt among us, full of grace and truth; we have beheld his glory, glory as of the only-begotten Son from the Father" (1:1–2, 14). The Word was both God and with God, and the Word became incarnate. It bears repeating that this sort of claim can make sense only if in fact the divine nature is not corporeal. After all, Saint John is claiming that the Word, which *became incarnate*, is both identical with God and somehow distinct from God. But to say that the Word was both God and with God reveals a great mystery in the divine nature, implying that there are relations within God that are fundamental to a divine nature that is neither divisible nor composite. Remember, Saint John is writing within the confines of a strictly monotheistic Judaism. So, in order to express both God's oneness as well as the relations within God's nature (i.e., Father, Son, and Holy Spirit) that are now part of divine revelation, Saint John employs the only terminology that can best capture this mystery. In that case, Elder Roberts has it exactly backward: by taking on a human nature, the Word (or God the Son) did not graft on to his divine nature something new, which then became "integral" to it. Rather, the unity of the divine nature and

---

[59] Elder Roberts does address John 1 directly: "The identity between Jesus of Nazareth— 'the Word made flesh'—and the 'Word' that was 'with God from the beginning,' and that 'was God,' is so clear that it cannot possibly be doubted. So the Son is God, as well as the Father is God." (Roberts, *Mormon Doctrine of Deity*, 14.) By itself, this quote is consistent with Catholic doctrine. However, later on in the same book, Elder Roberts offers an account of this and other passages of Scripture that he believes support LDS tritheism, that the Father, Son, and Holy Spirit are three separate Gods. But, as I have already noted in the text, Saint John had written his Gospel within the confines of a strictly monotheistic Jewish culture. This is why the relationship between God and his Word is presented in a fashion that presupposes God's unity while at the same time extending our understanding of that unity to include relations within, and essential to, God's nature.

the relations within it retained their integrity even after the Incarnation. The Incarnation did not change God, though it allowed men to be changed. Now human beings may partake in the divine nature by means of the grace offered to them through the death and Resurrection of Jesus Christ. As the *Catechism of the Catholic Church* states:

> Our justification comes from the grace of God. Grace is *favor*, the *free and undeserved help* that God gives us to respond to his call to become children of God, adoptive sons, partakers of the divine nature and of eternal life (cf. Jn 1:12–18; 17:3; Rom 8:14–17; 2 Pet 1:3–4). Grace is a *participation in the life of God*. It introduces us into the intimacy of Trinitarian life: by Baptism the Christian participates in the grace of Christ, the Head of his Body. As an "adopted son" he can henceforth call God "Father," in union with the only Son. He receives the life of the Spirit who breathes charity into him and who forms the Church.[60]

II.B. The Trinity and Divine Simplicity

As we saw in section I.A.3, essential to classical theism is the idea that God is simple, that he is not a composite being with parts or accidents.[61] On the other hand, Catholics and other non-LDS Christians hold that God is triune. Elder Roberts maintains that holding both beliefs—that God is simple and triune—is inconsistent:

> If the three be conceived as one God—yet each with that about him which distinguishes him from the other—how can God be regarded as "simple," "not compound?" The orthodox creeds of Christendom, moreover, require us to believe that while the Father is a person, the Son a person, and the Holy Ghost a person, yet there are not three persons, but one person. So with each being eternal and almighty. So with each being God: "The Father is God, the Son is God, the Holy Ghost is God: and yet there are not three Gods but one God." No wonder the whole conception is given up as "incomprehensible."[62]

---

[60] *Catechism of the Catholic Church*, nos. 1996–97 (emphasis in original).

[61] An accident is the characteristic of a substance. For example, if I say Mr. Jones is wise, I am ascribing to the substance "Mr. Jones" and the accident "wise". Accidents cannot exist on their own but must inhere in a substance.

[62] Roberts, *Mormon Doctrine of Deity*, 112. Roberts is quoting from the Athanasian Creed, the text of which one can find here: www.newadvent.org/cathen/02033b.htm.

There are several problems with what Elder Roberts is claiming. First, the Catholic doctrine of the Trinity *is not*, as he states, that three Persons are one Person, but rather, as I have already noted, that God is one substance in three Persons. As the *Catechism* teaches: "We do not confess three Gods, but one God in three persons, the 'consubstantial Trinity'."[63]

Second, Elder Roberts is wrong in implying that incomprehensibility is the same as falsity or incoherence. For if that were the case, then the passages of the Bible that claim there are truths beyond our ability to comprehend—for example, that God's wisdom is inscrutable (Rom 11:33)—would mean that LDS theology is false or incoherent, since it accepts the authority of such passages. In fact, in his response to Father Cyril, Elder Roberts appeals to God's incomprehensibility to rebut the charge that it is incoherent for the LDS to claim that God is finite in being but infinite in faculties.[64] Moreover, as a matter of common sense, incomprehensibility is precisely what we should expect in certain contexts. Much of high-level physics is incomprehensible to most people today, and it was to all people five thousand years ago. Yet that would not mean that high-level physics is not rational. For a five-year-old, a parent's instructions may seem incomprehensible, and perhaps even unjust, but that would not mean the child has a right to reject the parent's instructions on the grounds of incomprehensibility.

Third, Elder Roberts misunderstands the nature of divine simplicity. It is not the belief that there cannot be any essential relations within God's being—that is, that God is essentially triune. Rather, it is the belief that God is not a composite being made of parts and accidents. For this reason, when we attribute to God certain qualities—wisdom, omniscience, omnipotence, and so forth—we are not saying

---

[63] *Catechism of the Catholic Church*, no. 253, quoting Council of Constantinople II (553): DS 421.

[64] Roberts writes: "If it is argued that it is illogical and unphilosophical to regard God in his person as finite, but infinite in faculties, that is finite in one respect and infinite in another, my answer is that it is a conception of God made necessary by what the divine wisdom has revealed concerning himself, and it is becoming in man to accept with humility what God has been pleased to reveal concerning his own nature, being assured that in God's infinite knowledge he knows himself, and that which he reveals concerning himself is to be trusted far beyond man's philosophical conception of him." (Roberts, *Mormon Doctrine of Deity*, 120.)

that he has them in addition to his being, as we would when we attribute wisdom to Mr. Jones, who would still remain Mr. Jones even if he lost his wisdom. This means that if God were a composite being like Mr. Jones—having accidents and parts distinct from his substance—then he could not be a First Cause, since anything that is composed requires a cause. As Saint Thomas notes: "Every composite has a cause, for things in themselves cannot unite unless something causes them to unite."[65] So, God must be simple. Consequently, any attributes we ascribe to God—such as wisdom, omniscience, omnipotence, and so forth—cannot literally be parts or accidents of God. Thus, when we say, for example, that God is wise and Mr. Jones is wise, we are using the term "wise" analogically and not univocally. We do this for three reasons: (1) God is infinitely greater than anything in his creation (and thus, the Church teaches that he is incomprehensible), (2) Mr. Jones' wisdom is an accident that inheres in Mr. Jones, and (3) God cannot have any accidents because he is simple. So, when we say that God is wise, we speak truly but not literally. This is why Elder Roberts is mistaken when he claims that Father Cyril's "premise is proven to be unphilosophical and untenable, when coupled with his creed, which ascribes qualities, attributes and personality to God. Either the gentleman must cease to think of God as 'infinite being,' 'most simple,' 'not compound,' or he must surrender the God of his creed."[66] Because the Catholic is not ascribing to God attributes univocally, Elder Roberts' critique misses its mark.

Unlike the simplicity of God, which can be known by philosophical reflection on what it means for something to be the First Cause, the Church teaches that the doctrine of the Trinity is known by divine revelation. (This is why the Catholic Church teaches that Christians, Jews, and Muslims worship the same God, even though the Church maintains that Judaism and Islam, by rejecting the Trinity, are nevertheless mistaken.[67] Another way to put it: Christians,

[65] Saint Thomas Aquinas, *Summa Theologica* I, q. 3, art. 7, trans. Fathers of the English Dominican Province, 2nd and rev. ed. (London: Burns, Oates & Washbourne, 1920), www.newadvent.org/summa/1003.htm#article7.

[66] Roberts, *Mormon Doctrine of Deity*, 114.

[67] Second Vatican Council, Declaration on the Relation of the Church to Non-Christian Religions *Nostra Aetate* (October 28, 1965), www.vatican.va/archive/hist_councils/ii_vatican_council/documents/vat-ii_decl_19651028_nostra-aetate_en.html.

Jews, and Muslims get the divine nature right but disagree on what God has specially revealed about his internal life.)[68] Although God reveals in Scripture that there is only one God by nature—that which is self-existent and the Source of all contingent being (Acts 17:24–28)—we learn that he is Father,[69] Son,[70] and Holy Spirit[71] as well. So, within the simplicity and unity of God, there are three divine Persons, distinct from one another, though each fully God. It is important to note that the Church is not teaching that God has different parts or diverse members, for such a claim would be contrary to God's simplicity and unity, which would contravene the biblical account of God's oneness. On the other hand, the Church does not want to say that the three Persons of the Trinity are simply different masks or modes under which God reveals himself, for this would imply that there are no real relations within God, which would be inconsistent with Scripture's testimony that God is Father, Son, and Holy Spirit.[72] However, as we have already seen, the Church teaches that God is incomprehensible, which means that though we can speak truly of God and his attributes, we cannot speak univocally of them. So, the Church's task cannot be to

[68] See Francis J. Beckwith, "All Worship the Same God: Referring to the Same God", in *Do Christians, Muslims, and Jews Worship the Same God? Four Views*, ed. Ronnie Campbell and Christopher Gnanakan (Grand Rapids, MI: Zondervan Academic, 2019), 65–86; and Francis J. Beckwith, *Never Doubt Thomas: The Catholic Aquinas as Evangelical and Protestant* (Waco, TX: Baylor University Press, 2019), chap. 3.

[69] Several Scripture verses refer to God as Father; see, for example, 1 Cor 1:3; Rom 1:7; 1 Pet 1:17.

[70] For example, in Jn 8:58 Jesus calls himself "I am", equating himself with the God of the Old Testament (Ex 3:14). Christ as Creator necessitates that he is God: Jn 1:3; Col 1:16; cf. Is 44:24. These three passages, when carefully compared with one another, clearly affirm the deity of Christ. The last passage, Is 44:24, states that God *alone* made all things. The first and second passages both affirm that all things were made through Christ. Therefore, if God *alone* made all things, and all things were made through Christ, it logically follows that Christ is in fact God. The text of Scripture, and the force of logic, leaves us with no other option. Saint John calls both God and Jesus "the first and the last" and "the Alpha and the Omega" (Rev 1:17; 22:13), and hence he equates Jesus with God. Other passages of the New Testament that implicitly or explicitly affirm Christ's deity include Mk 2:5–7; Jn 1:1–14; 20:28–29; and Col 2:9.

[71] Take, for example, Jesus' teaching that the Holy Spirit will be sent from the Father (Jn 14:26) and that he and the Father will both send the Holy Spirit (Jn 15:26), and cross-reference that with Saint Peter's claim in Acts 5:3–5 that to lie to the Holy Spirit is in fact to lie to God. One cannot lie to a power or a force.

[72] See notes 69–71.

explain the triune God, for it cannot be done. Rather, it is to show how the doctrine of the Trinity, consistent with divine simplicity, is "thinkable without contradiction".[73] This means that one must make use of analogies from the created order to accomplish this task, with the understanding that this is the best we can do given the ontological gulf between Creator and creation.

Scripture teaches that the Son is the Word generated (or begotten) from God (Jn 3:16), and yet the Word is God (Jn 1:1–2) and there is only one God by nature. How can that be? Consider an analogy. A word or thought is generated by the intellect. So, in a sense one is paternally related to one's thought insofar as one generates it, and one's thought is filially related to oneself insofar as it is generated by oneself. But a thought is not something one generates that is external to oneself, as it would be in the case of one physically generating a child or writing a sentence on a piece of paper. That is, the relation between me and this thought is a relation internal to my being. Nevertheless, there is a real relation, a distinction, between me and the concept of me. Suppose, for example, the thought I generate is a concept of myself. Although this thought is an accident that inheres in me and does not share my nature, it is similar to me because it is a thought about me.

Now let us apply this reasoning to God's internal life. God has a concept of himself. Because he is eternal, simple, and perfect, this thought of himself must be eternally generated, perfect, and not an accident. In contrast, my thought of myself, though inhering in my mind, is generated in time, imperfect, and an accident. Thus, God's thought (or Word) of himself must express the fullness of the divine nature: eternality, simplicity, perfection, etc. But this means that the Word, eternally begotten, is not only internal to God's nature but is God, just as the Father, the eternal begetter, is God. As F.J. Sheed states: "There is a huge difference between God's Idea and any idea we may form. His is Someone, ours is only something."[74] Because God is eternal and simple, there is only one Word, one act of intellect, from which creation derives its order and being. As Saint Paul

---

[73] Brian Davies, *Thomas Aquinas's* Summa Theologiae: *A Guide and Commentary* (New York: Oxford University Press, 2014), 97.

[74] F.J. Sheed, *Theology for Beginners* (New York: Sheed & Ward, 1957), 43.

writes of God the Son in Colossians 1:15–17: "He is the image of the invisible God, the first-born of all creation; for in him all things were created, in heaven and on earth, visible and invisible, whether thrones or dominions or principalities or authorities—all things were created through him and for him. He is before all things, and in him all things hold together."

As I point out in footnote 71, Jesus teaches us that the Holy Spirit proceeds from the Father (Jn 14:26) and from both the Father and the Son (Jn 15:26) and that the Holy Spirit is in fact God. Assuming that God's external relations to the created order—as noted in these passages—model his immutable internal relations, the Holy Spirit eternally proceeds from both the Father and the Son. The Son, as we have seen, is the fullest expression of the divine intellect. So, the Spirit must be the fullest expression of the divine will. It is, as the Church teaches, the eternal and unchanging love that the Father and Son have for each other. But just as God's perfect exercise of intellect, the thought of himself, must be eternally generated, not an accident, and perfect (because God is eternal, simple, and perfect), God's perfect exercise of will, the love that the Father and the Son have for each other, must be eternally spirated,[75] not an accident, and perfect as well. Thus, God's love of himself must express the fullness of the divine nature: eternality, simplicity, perfection, etc. But this means not only that the love eternally proceeding from the Father and the Son is internal to God's nature but also that he is, like the Word, a Divine Someone, just as the Father is a Divine Someone.

---

[75] Why "spirate" rather than "generate"? "Spirate" comes from the Latin verb *spiro*, which means "breathe". The use of the word is to distinguish the eternal origin of the Holy Spirit from that of the Son. As Catholic writer Tim Staples notes: "The Holy Spirit proceeds from the Father and the Son, but not in a generative sense; rather, in a spiration. 'Spiration' comes from the Latin word for 'spirit' or 'breath.' Jesus 'breathed on them, and said to them, "Receive the Holy Spirit ..."' (John 20:22). Scripture reveals the Holy Spirit as pertaining to 'God's love [that] has been poured into our hearts' in Romans 5:5, and as flowing out of and identified with the reciprocating love of the Father for the Son and the Son for the Father (John 15:26; Rev. 22:1–2). Thus, the Holy Spirit's procession is not intellectual and generative, but has its origin in God's will and in the ultimate act of the will, which is love. As an infinite act of love between the Father and Son, this 'act' is so perfect and infinite that 'it' becomes (not in time, of course, but eternally) a 'He' in the third person of the Blessed Trinity. This revelation of God's love personified is the foundation from which Scripture could reveal to us that 'God is love' (1 John 4:8)." (Tim Staples, "Explaining the Trinity", *Catholic Answers* [June 20, 2014], www.catholic.com/magazine/online-edition/explaining-the-trinity.)

Consequently, the distinctions between the Persons of the Trinity are grounded in real relations internal to God, which are eternal and unchanging: the Father begets the Son,[76] the Son is begotten,[77] and the Holy Spirit proceeds from the Father and the Son. Moreover, since there is only one divine nature, and that nature is simple, each Person of the Trinity must *fully* share in the divine nature. Thus, there is a mutual indwelling of the divine Persons that follows from divine simplicity. As the Council of Florence (1438–1445) declared: "Because of this unity the Father is whole in the Son, whole in the holy Spirit; the Son is whole in the Father, whole in the holy Spirit; the holy Spirit is whole in the Father, whole in the Son."[78] It is, to be sure, a mystery, one that goes beyond the ability of the human mind to comprehend fully.[79] But it is not, as Elder Roberts believes, inconsistent with divine simplicity. For when we speak of God's eternal acts of intellect and will, and the processions within God, we are using language analogically and not univocally and thus are not literally talking about different events, acts, or parts of God but trying to express as best we can with inadequate human language what the simple God truly is in his nature. Much more, of course, could be said about this subject, but space constraints prevent us from engaging in any further exploration.[80]

---

[76] For example, "In the beginning was the Word, and the Word was with God, and the Word was God. He was in the beginning with God.... And the Word became flesh and dwelt among us, full of grace and truth; we have beheld his glory, glory as of the only-begotten Son from the Father.... No one has ever seen God; the only-begotten Son, who is in the bosom of the Father, he has made him known." (Jn 1:1–2, 14, 18.)

[77] See ibid.

[78] Council of Florence, Session 11 (February 4, 1442), www.ewtn.com/catholicism/library/ecumenical-council-of-florence-1438-1445-1461.

[79] "The Trinity is a mystery of faith in the strict sense, one of the 'mysteries that are hidden in God, which can never be known unless they are revealed by God' (*Dei Filius* 4). To be sure, God has left traces of his Trinitarian being in his work of creation and in his Revelation throughout the Old Testament. But his inmost Being as Holy Trinity is a mystery that is inaccessible to reason alone or even to Israel's faith before the Incarnation of God's Son and the sending of the Holy Spirit." (*Catechism of the Catholic Church*, no. 237.)

[80] For further reading, I highly recommend Brian Davies, *The Thought of Thomas Aquinas* (New York: Oxford University Press, 1992), 185–206; and James F. Dolezal, "Trinity, Simplicity, and the Status of God's Personal Relations", *International Journal of Systematic Theology* 16, no. 1 (January 2014): 79–98. Dolezal is a Reformed Protestant scholar, though there is nothing in his account of divine simplicity and the Trinity with which a Catholic would disagree.

II.C. Greek Philosophy and Reading Scripture

In response to Father Cyril, Elder Roberts raises a charge to which I
alluded earlier in this chapter: classical theism is the result of the inor-
dinate influence of pagan (or "Greek") philosophy on the development of Christian doctrine. Writes Elder Roberts: "The conception
of God as 'pure being,' 'immaterial,' 'without form,' 'or parts or passions,' as held by orthodox Christianity, has its origin in Pagan philosophy, not in Jewish nor Christian revelation."[81] The assumption behind
this charge is that doctrine can be derived from Scripture without the
benefit of philosophical reflection. But Elder Roberts never defends
that assumption. He just takes it for granted. Nevertheless, as we have
seen, the Bible is rife with passages that can be interpreted to support
classical theism, and, as Elder Roberts points out, there are portions
of Scripture[82]—such as those that present God in anthropomorphic
language[83]—that lend support to LDS theism. So, trying to figure out
how to reconcile these apparently disparate accounts of God found in
Scripture by merely recommending an unphilosophical reading of the
text, as Elder Roberts does, is not only not a solution but also practically impossible. (In fact, at one point in his rebuttal to Father Cyril,
Elder Roberts reveals the poverty of this approach: when confronted
with counterexamples to the LDS reading of Scripture, Elder Roberts
crassly begs the question and resorts to dismissive ridicule.)[84]

[81] Roberts, *Mormon Doctrine of Deity*, 119.

[82] See, e.g., ibid., 84–98.

[83] The Bible, for example, says that God has a face (Ex 33:11), ears (2 Sam 22:7), eyes (Ps
34:15), hands (Ps 95:4–5), a mouth (Deut 8:3), and shoulders (Deut 33:12).

[84] Writes Roberts: "It is well known that the language of the Bible is highly figurative,
almost extravagantly so in places, and much allowance must be made for the inclination to
imagery of prophetic natures, which, like poetic temperaments, are given to imagery; and
hyperbole is the vice of oriental speech. But Mr. V. is not true to this canon of interpretation
he lays down, viz., the same rule of interpretation must be applied to passages that are similar
in character. After laying down this principle of interpretation, he proceeds to depart from it
by placing for comparison very dissimilar passages. What similarity is there, for example,
in the plain, matter of fact statement, 'God created man in his own image, in the image of
God created he him;' and the passage he quotes from Psalms: 'If I take my wings early in the
morning, and dwell in the uttermost part of the sea, even there shall thy hand lead me, and
thy right hand shall hold me'? And this also: 'Whither shall I flee from thy face. If I ascend into
heaven, thou art there; If I descend into hell thou art there?' Has not the Reverend gentleman
placed for comparison here the most dissimilar passages that perhaps could be found in the
whole Bible? Yet he insists that the prosy passage from Genesis must be regarded as equally

As I noted at the beginning of this chapter, classical theism (or some rudimentary form of it) was the assumed framework of the early Church long before the New Testament canon was fixed in the mid-fourth century.[85] This is not surprising, since the Jewish community from which the early apostolic witness arose had long appropriated the categories of Greek philosophy in its understanding of God. As Pope Benedict XVI described it in his 2006 Regensburg address:

> Within the Old Testament, the process which started at the burning bush came to new maturity at the time of the Exile, when the God of Israel, an Israel now deprived of its land and worship, was proclaimed as the God of heaven and earth and described in a simple formula which echoes the words uttered at the burning bush: "I am". This new understanding of God is accompanied by a kind of enlightenment, which finds stark expression in the mockery of gods who are merely the work of human hands (cf. Ps 115). Thus, despite the bitter conflict with those Hellenistic rulers who sought to accommodate it forcibly to the customs and idolatrous cult of the Greeks, biblical faith, in the Hellenistic period, encountered the best of Greek thought at a deep level, resulting in a mutual enrichment evident especially in the later wisdom literature. Today we know that the Greek translation of the Old Testament produced at Alexandria—the Septuagint—is more than a simple (and in that sense really less than satisfactory) translation of the Hebrew text: it is an independent textual witness and a distinct and important step in the history of revelation, one which brought about this encounter in a way that was decisive for the birth and spread of Christianity.[86]

So, it should not surprise us that certain portions of the New Testament employ Greek philosophical categories (e.g., Jn 1; Acts 17:24–28)

---

figurative with David's poetry, and insists that if 'Mormons' believe literally that God made man in his own image and likeness, or that Moses and seventy elders saw the God of Israel, as plainly declared by Moses, then 'They must believe that God had such a very long hand as to extend to the uttermost parts of the sea;' and 'such an extremely long face, reaching from heaven to hell;' and 'conclude that David had wings!' Further remarks on this head are not necessary. One is under no obligation to seriously discuss nonsense." (Roberts, *Mormon Doctrine of Deity*, 91.)

[85] See note 18.

[86] Pope Benedict XVI, "Faith, Reason, and the University: Memories and Reflections" (September 12, 2006), www.vatican.va/holy_father/benedict_xvi/speeches/2006/september /documents/hf_ben-xvi_spe_20060912_university-regensburg_en.html.

and that the early Christian creeds do so as well. On the other hand, as Pope Benedict points out, it was "a mutual enrichment", in the sense that while Jews and Christians appropriated Greek categories to express biblical faith, that appropriation reshaped Greek thought. As church historian J. N. D. Kelly notes: "The classical creeds of Christendom opened with a declaration of belief in one God, maker of heaven and earth. The monotheistic idea, grounded in the religion of Israel, loomed large in the minds of the earliest fathers; though not reflective theologians, they were fully conscious that it marked the dividing line between the Church and paganism." Kelly explains that "the doctrine of one God, the Father and creator, formed the background and indisputable premiss of the Church's faith. Inherited from Judaism, it was her bulwark against pagan polytheism, Gnostic emanationism and Marcionite dualism."[87] Philosopher Etienne Gilson argues that because the Greeks did not think of their ultimate metaphysical principle as the eternal God who is the Source of all contingent being—which is what the Jewish-Christian tradition teaches—Greek metaphysics was transformed by the Jewish-Christian view of God, "whose true name is 'He who is' [Ex 3:14]".[88]

Suppose after reading Elder Roberts' scriptural defense of LDS theism, a critic replies by pointing out that the LDS worldview, because it is bereft of a First Cause, cannot account for itself: How can a universe consisting entirely of a series of *per se* causes not fall prey to the infinite regress objection? Suppose further that the critic points out that certain passages of Scripture have been interpreted by virtually all Jewish and Christian prelates and scholars since ancient times to teach *creatio ex nihilo* as well as the classical theism seemingly entailed by that doctrine. If he were to take these queries seriously, Elder Roberts would have to entertain the possibility that his method of interpreting Scripture could be wrong and that the classical theist reading of Scripture may be right. But in that case, there is no neutral, nonphilosophy-laden text to which Elder Roberts can appeal. He must either read the Bible with the Church (and the synagogue) that gave him (and us) the Bible or provide a sufficiently compelling reason why that presumption should be discarded.

---

[87] Kelly, *Early Christian Doctrines*, 83, 87.
[88] Etienne Gilson, *God and Philosophy* (New Haven, CT: Yale University Press, 1941), 51.

III. Conclusion

The Catholic Church and the LDS church hold radically different concepts of God. This was clearly understood by Elder Roberts and Father Cyril in their historic dispute at the dawn of the twentieth century. Because much of LDS scholarship and popular writings have (in my judgment) uncritically accepted Elder Roberts' account of classical theism (or some variation of Elder Roberts' account), I hope that what I have offered in this chapter not only helps clarify what Catholics (and many other non-Catholic Christians) believe about the nature of God but also better explains to our LDS friends why Catholicism and these other traditions came to accept this understanding of the divine nature as orthodox and biblical.[89]

[89] A special thank you to Shawn Floyd (Malone University) for reading an earlier draft of this chapter and offering some valuable suggestions.

4

James Barker's Case for the Great Apostasy

James Hitchcock

The Apostasy from the Divine Church[1] was perhaps the most ambitious single effort by a Mormon apologist to justify the historical claims of the Church of Jesus Christ of Latter-day Saints. Presumably, it is still widely read in LDS circles,[2] although it is not considered an official publication.

The author was James L. Barker (1880–1958), whom an "Appreciation" by one Daniel A. Keeler identified as a Mormon who graduated from the University of Utah, served a term as a missionary, and studied in various European universities, where he gained a wide knowledge of Christian history and theology. He then studied phonetics in Paris and, according to Keeler, came to be regarded as one of the leading phoneticists in the world. Since 1983, Brigham Young University (BYU) has sponsored the Barker Lectureship, named in his honor. According to the university's website, Barker

---

[1] The title page says it was published by Kate Montgomery Barker in 1960, with no location given. She was Barker's widow. He died in 1958. Page citations of quotes from the book will appear in the text.

[2] See, e.g., Richard L. Bushman, "Faithful History", *Dialogue: A Journal of Mormon Thought* 4 (Winter 1969): 11; Royal Skousen, "Through a Glass Darkly: Trying to Understand the Scriptures", *Brigham Young University Studies* 26, no. 4 (Fall 1986): 3–20; William O. Nelson, "Is the LDS View of God Consistent with the Bible?", *Ensign* (July 1987), www.lds.org/ensign /1987/07/is-the-lds-view-of-god-consistent-with-the-bible?lang=eng; Richard Ouellette, review of *Christianity: A Global History* by David Chidester, *A World History of Christianity* by Adrian Hastings, and *The Next Christendom: The Coming of Global Christianity* by Philip Jenkins, in *Brigham Young University Studies* 41, no. 4 (2002): 129–44; Daniel C. Peterson, " 'Shall They Not Both Fall into the Ditch?' What Certain Baptists Think They Know about the Restored Gospel", *FARMS Review of Books* 10, no. 1 (1998): 12–96.

served as chair of BYU's Department of Modern Language from 1907 to 1914.[3]

Oddly for a linguistic scholar, Barker, in his sweeping criticisms of historic Christian creeds, only rarely analyzed the actual Greek or Latin texts. He appears not to have had a wide knowledge of Christian history and to have relied almost entirely on secondary works—usually general surveys, only rarely specialized monographs. He could be considered ecumenical in the sense that he cited Catholic, Protestant, and secular authors almost indiscriminately. But his method was the rhetorical device of citing a Catholic author if one could be found to make a particular negative point about the Church, Protestant authors if no Catholic was available, and skeptical authors (Edward Gibbon and Will Durant) to show both Catholic and Protestant fallacies.

I. Christian Origins

At the beginning of the book, Barker stated his assumptions, including especially the crucial phrase—easily missed by someone unfamiliar with those assumptions—"after His [Jesus'] death and resurrection He continued to guide them [the apostles] by revelation, in their ministry, in the selection of officers, and in the government of the Church" (3). The key issue is that "all historical churches believe that no revelation has been given to the world since the death of the Apostle John" (4–5), whereas the Latter-day Saint communion alone believes in this modern revelation and is thus itself the return of the "divine church" (5).

Barker turned a universally held Christian principle on its head—modern beliefs are not validated by appeal to the New Testament but the reverse: "If a single quotation [from the Gospels] is confirmed by modern revelation we may be sure of its interpretation" (16–17). The apostolic Fathers were inferior because they were "quite without any new enrichment of revelation" (21). Discrepancies between them and the New Testament could be resolved only by "revelation through the Prophet Joseph Smith" (41). Everything else was lost or distorted.

[3] "James Barker Lectureship", College of Humanities, Brigham Young University, 2020, https://humanities.byu.edu/james-barker-lectureship.

Occasionally, Barker used sleight of hand in such a way as possibly to mislead his readers. Thus, he claimed that "eminent theologians, considered in the main to be orthodox, were carried away by Gnosticism" (154), because Clement of Alexandria and others claimed to possess the true gnosis. (In fact, by themselves claiming to have gnosis, they were opposing Gnosticism, denying it the right to make that claim.)[4]

Prior to tracing the Great Apostasy, Barker quoted *The Catholic Encyclopedia*: "In the case of a Church, such a change in its hierarchical constitution and in its professed faith suffices to make it a different Church from what it was before.... A new Church is formed"[5] (113–14). Readers might suppose the Catholic author was admitting that such had occurred, but in fact he was using a hypothetical example to show that it could not have.

Although Barker's book ranged over eighteen centuries, its history was in a sense irrelevant. Readers were told over and over again that certain things manifested the Great Apostasy, but only gradually did it become clear exactly what that meant—the post-apostolic Christians did not manifest the revelations that would come to Joseph Smith, which were the restoration of the original revelation.

The major errors were seeing God as immaterial and triune, original sin, the need for divine grace, *creatio ex nihilo*, infant baptism, pagan practices in worship, false ideas of church government, and the suppression of religious liberty. Throughout the book there are periodic allusions to the criteria of true orthodoxy but no comprehensive exposition of them, although a first-person account by Smith is appended.

In Barker's account, apostasy began with the Jews, who departed from the covenant of Abraham, until they were sent Moses as a new teacher. Subsequently, they departed also from Moses' law, until in the fullness of time God sent his Son. As Jehovah, Jesus had given the gospel and the priesthood to Adam, and now he restored it.

Barker could accept a somewhat skeptical view of the New Testament because it was destined to be partly superseded by the Book of Mormon. He cited Eusebius of Caesarea, who cited Origen to the

[4] Jaroslav Pelikan, *The Emergence of the Catholic Tradition (100–600)* (Chicago: University of Chicago Press, 1971), 96.

[5] George Joyce, "The Church", *The Catholic Encyclopedia*, vol. 3 (New York: Robert Appleton, 1908), www.newadvent.org/cathen/03744a.htm.

effect that the Gospel of Matthew was originally written in Hebrew. Many New Testament writings were probably lost, Barker thought—it was inconceivable that there were only four accounts of Jesus' life or that Paul wrote only thirteen letters.

But despite the fact that the New Testament did not contain "the fullness of the Gospel", there could be no doubt the apostles were true witnesses to the Resurrection of Jesus, "the Christ, the Son of God", Barker affirmed (15). The power of the gospel itself proved its authenticity because it went against the spirit of the age and of Judaism.

After his return to heaven, Jesus guided his apostles by continuing revelation transmitted through the Spirit, through visions (Peter on the housetop), by messenger (Philip and the Ethiopian prince), and in person (the conversion of Paul). There were no new revelations of doctrine, but there were other necessary kinds of revelation, such as answering the question of the authority of the Mosaic Law for Christians.

The apostles governed the Church during their lifetimes. Barker accepted the claim that Peter and Paul were both at Rome and were martyred around the year 68, but he concluded that while Peter was indeed the chief of the apostles, he was not the "rock" on whom Jesus built his Church (Mt 16:18).[6]

After the deaths of the other apostles, the revelation was entrusted to John, who was given authority over all the local churches. (In fact, his authority seems to have been recognized primarily in Asia Minor.[7]) Barker speculated that John was not given authority to appoint new apostles, possibly because no one was worthy, possibly because the likelihood of speedy martyrdom rendered such appointments useless.

II. After the Apostles

Barker saw the governance of the early Church as consonant with the structure of the modern LDS. The relationship between elders and

[6] For a contrary view, see Stanley Jaki, O.S.B., *And on This Rock* (Notre Dame, IN: Ave Maria Press, 1978).

[7] Leopold Fonck, "St. John the Evangelist", *The Catholic Encyclopedia*, vol. 8 (New York: Robert Appleton, 1910), www.newadvent.org/cathen/08492a.htm.

bishops in the early Church is uncertain and confusing. But, relying on Adolf Harnack and others, Barker speculated that some local churches, including Rome, at first had no bishops and were governed by a council of elders (103 ff.). As in the LDS, the title of priest was probably conferred on every worthy man, none of whom could exercise his ministry without authority from an overseer. The proceedings in Acts 15 were comparable to the letters and reports sent by modern Mormon authorities to their subordinates.

Freedom and authority were perfectly balanced in the early Church. No local church was without a bishop. Candidates for the office were nominated by a higher authority but had to be accepted by the congregation. There was no real distinction between clergy and laity—as in the LDS, a layman could immediately be ordained to the priesthood; all were "saints". (Unlike most Protestants, Barker evidently regarded the modern office of bishop as of divine origin.)

The New Testament contained many predictions of apostasy, which occurred because God allowed freedom for men to grow and develop, a freedom that was essential to the gospel, Barker explained. Heresy began during the apostolic age, and afterward there was no authority competent to hold it in check.

Sources for the immediate postbiblical period are very sparse, Barker noted. But in the second century, the apostolic Fathers (e.g., Ignatius of Antioch, Polycarp, and Clement of Rome) were heroic Christians who witnessed to the faith as it was known to them, although they lacked the authority of the apostles themselves, to whom they were "quite inferior" (21). But however fragmentary the revelation may have been by that time, each person could still understand the divine plan and how it should be followed.

Barker's claims about the corruption of doctrine depended partly on this sparseness of sources, which allowed him to make a series of assumptions. The problem of fidelity occurred when, in contrast to the generation of the apostolic Fathers, the generation of the apologists (e.g., Justin Martyr, Irenaeus, Origen, and Cyprian) made use of pagan philosophy in trying to understand the gospel, emphasizing "doctrines scarcely more than mentioned in the New Testament" (28).

If the gospel had not been lost, Barker proclaimed, "the priesthood would have been transmitted from generation to generation", along with "ordinances, performed with authority" (57). The recurring phenomenon of apparently "novel" teachings was simply a betrayal of the gospel, whereas Mormonism's own claims constituted God's continuing revelation, which was lost through disobedience, then "given again more than once" (to Joseph Smith) (57).

Barker thought the Second Coming of the Savior and his millennial rule on earth were clearly attested to in the gospel, along with divine judgment pronounced on every resurrected human being. But these doctrines were among those lost. In the spirit of pagan philosophy, the New Testament prophecy of the millennium came to be understood allegorically. (In fact, the early Fathers all believed in the Second Coming, a belief universally held in the early Church. The Fathers held a variety of positions concerning the reign of Jesus on earth, a belief that grew out of the Book of Revelation.[8])

Each local church was autonomous, and, lacking apostolic authority, they were reorganized "from the bottom up", Barker claimed, a process that brought abuses, such as worldly ambition and a valuing of worldly attributes like education over spiritual qualities (138). Gradually, bishops formed themselves into provinces and came together to consider important questions under the often-usurped authority of patriarchs and metropolitans. In time the laity were pushed aside, and state officials meddled in episcopal elections.

A major sign of the Great Apostasy was the Church's infidelity with regard to baptism, Barker said. He speculated that the lengthy period of the catechumenate, certain ascetical practices, and belief in the saving power of the sacraments were all adapted from the mystery religions of the Near East. Quoting the Lutheran historian Lars Pedersen Qualben, after Paul's death "a mystical significance began to be attached to the rites, which reflected the influence of pagan philosophy"[9] (121).

Barker did not explain the meaning of the term "mystical significance". It seems already applicable to Paul's teachings concerning baptism and the Eucharist. In the mid-third century, baptism was

[8] Pelikan, Emergence, 124–27.
[9] A History of the Christian Church, 62. There were several editions of the book (e.g., New York: Thomas Nelson, 1936), and Barker did not specify which he used. For the opposite view, see Gunter Wagner, Pauline Baptism and the Pagan Religions, trans. J.P. Smith (Edinburgh: Oliver & Boyd, 1967), and Ronald H. Nash, "Was the New Testament Influenced by the Pagan Religions?", Christian Research Journal (Winter 1994), 8–15.

already believed to confer actual gifts, not merely to signify them.[10] Barker implied that the influence of the mystery cults is also seen in such things as the sign of the cross, the use of oil and salt, and exorcisms in the baptismal ceremony. Paul spoke of the need to subdue the body (1 Cor 9:27), and by the third century, the leading Fathers praised those who lived lives of penance.[11] The period of the catechumenate was probably lengthened because of the onset of severe persecution.[12]

The most serious error, according to Barker, was the decision by the early Church to accept as valid the baptism of those who converted from heretical sects. Here the Roman Church was in error, and Cyprian and the African Church correct in demanding the rebaptism of former heretics, although the African Church later conformed to Roman usage. (The earliest usage required, as did the Eucharist, that a bishop at least be present at baptism. But Tertullian [d. c. 240], who wrote the first treatise on the sacrament, said that laymen had an obligation to administer it in an emergency.[13] Gradually, the principle came to be accepted that baptism properly performed was valid no matter who administered it.)

Barker's argument was simply an assertion: "It is perfectly obvious that whoever baptizes must be authorized of Jesus Christ, must bear His priesthood" (165). By accepting an erroneous idea of baptism, "the divine church became the human church" (174). (Once again in contrast to Protestantism, Barker apparently assumed that the priesthood, like the episcopacy, was divinely ordained.)

Barker called infant baptism "a mockery in the sight of the Lord" (185), a practice for which he thought there was no evidence in the early centuries. (References to "households" in the New Testament did not include infants, he insisted.) This in itself would have been sufficient to rob the Church of her divine character, as would baptism by sprinkling or pouring rather than the required immersion.

---

[10] Pelikan, *Emergence*, 163.

[11] Thomas Campbell, "Asceticism", *The Catholic Encyclopedia*, vol. 1 (New York: Robert Appleton, 1907), www.newadvent.org/cathen/01767c.htm.

[12] Thomas Scannell, "Catechumen", *The Catholic Encyclopedia*, vol. 3, www.newadvent.org /cathen/03430b.htm.

[13] William Fanning, "Baptism", *The Catholic Encyclopedia*, vol. 2 (New York: Robert Appleton, 1907), www.newadvent.org/cathen/02258b.htm.

(Infant baptism is known to have been performed as early as the second century, and various New Testament passages were understood to justify it, although it was controversial.[14] Immersion was generally used in the West until the Middle Ages, and other methods were a kind of innovation.[15])

The practice of infant baptism became especially urgent under the influence of Augustine's doctrine of original sin, Barker thought. Following the Catholic historian Louis Duchesne, he pointed out that Augustine had misunderstood the phrase "*in quo omnes peccaverunt*" in the Vulgate (Rom 5:12) to mean "in whom all have sinned", whereas "because all have sinned" was a better understanding of the Greek text (181–82). Without Augustine's doctrine the practice of infant baptism had no meaning. Requiring that infants be baptized in order to be saved is irreconcilable with God's justice, Barker claimed. (The modern *Catechism of the Catholic Church* states that God's mercy "allow[s] us to hope that there is a way of salvation for children who have died without Baptism".[16])

Since baptism was validly administered throughout the first two centuries, during that time the Church continued to be guided by the Holy Spirit, Barker said. Afterward, lacking that guidance, the Church designated four "notes", or signs, of her alleged divine character—one, holy, catholic, and apostolic—which became the subject of dispute among various groups.

Barker took a consistently reductionist view of early Church history, not acknowledging the possibility of a complex relationship between the gospel and the pagan culture and treating all such encounters as merely the corruption of the gospel.

III. Emperors, Popes, and Councils

Given his "unscrupulous life", it is unlikely that Constantine actually received a vision from God, Barker judged (204). He favored Christianity merely as a way of shoring up the faltering empire. (Although

---

[14] Ibid.
[15] Ibid.
[16] *Catechism of the Catholic Church*, no. 1261.

this is a commonly held opinion, some modern scholarship gives Constantine credit for sincerity in matters of religion.[17])

Barker spent considerable time on the subject of the early papacy, siding with the Eastern Orthodox in his account of the early Church, questioning the line of episcopal succession at Rome, and insisting that the bishop of Rome exercise no particular authority over other bishops.

But, in fact, the historical reality was complex. Disputes were often referred to the bishop of Rome (Barker discounted their significance), and conciliar judgments often confirmed what Rome had previously decided.[18] Barker acknowledged that, beginning with the Council of Chalcedon (451), the see of Rome became "more aggressive" (388). But once again, his claim that Roman authority depended on imperial support missed the crucial point—the popes, with a few ambiguous exceptions, remained steadfast and consistent throughout the great doctrinal quarrels of the era. Some underwent persecution.

The wickedness of some popes proved they did not have the guidance of the Holy Spirit. Based on Mormon beliefs, Barker insisted that papal infallibility would not be possible unless popes periodically received "new revelation". The idea that the Holy Spirit preserves the pope from error reduces him to the level of a mere "machine", Barker said (652).

But Barker found the Orthodox position tenable only with respect to church government. Otherwise, both the Eastern and Western churches—particularly the East—were corrupted by Greek philosophy, especially in the Alexandrian approach to Scripture in terms of allegory. There was an immense and impassable gulf between the original divine revelation and attempts to understand it philosophically. In the absence of authoritative revelation, there were many false theological hypotheses, as philosophical theology attempted to answer questions for which no answers had been given. (Barker quoted the skeptical popularizing historian Will Durant: "There is nothing so foolish but it may be found in the pages of the philosophers" [337].)

Greek philosophy led to the error that God was the Creator and cause of all things, that he created the universe and man out of

<hr />

[17] Timothy Barnes, *Constantine and Eusebius* (Cambridge, MA: Harvard University Press, 1981).

[18] See Margherita Guarducci, *The Primacy of the Church of Rome* (San Francisco: Ignatius Press, 2003).

nothing, and that matter is evil. (In fact, the Christian condemnations of various dualisms—for example, Gnosticism, Manicheanism, and Catharism—demonstrated that matter was not considered evil. Belief in *creatio ex nihilo* was considered necessary to protect the absolute power and freedom of God.[19])

Barker summed up the errors of Platonic philosophy:

> God is not in the form of a man.
> God is immaterial.
> God is the absolute Idea, is the first and final cause of all being.
> There is of (logical) necessity only one God.
> Matter is evil. (231)

By contrast, authentic Christianity taught that the Son is like the Father thus also possesses a material body, Jesus was resurrected with a perfect material body, "God organized the world with preexisting element", and Father, Son, and Holy Ghost are "numerically distinct" (231).

The Gnostic and Manichean heresies, although officially condemned, contributed to "the general modern belief that God is immaterial", Barker said (155), and, despite the condemnations, to the belief that matter is evil. (He was of course mistaken in thinking that the early Church, influenced by Platonism, had declared matter to be evil. Belief in the spiritual nature of God was based on the words of Jesus [Jn 4:24], something that Greek philosophy merely reinforced.)

Barker also attributed the early christological controversies to the influence of Greek philosophy, because it taught that there could be only one God, as the Jews believed. Belief in the divinity of Jesus was an obstacle to that, which various theologians attempted to overcome in various ways, by speculations that led them astray. Those who believed that Father, Son, and Holy Ghost were three "Persons" were not monotheists, Barker said. The Arian controversy occurred because people forgot "the pre-existence of the spirits of men, of whom God was the Father; Jesus (one of the spirits) 'alone remained absolutely faithful to God;' and the world was 'organized with pre-existing material elements' " (242). Neither Arius nor Athanasius was

---

[19] Pelikan, *Emergence*, 36.

orthodox, Barker judged, the latter because he taught that the Son coexisted with the Father from all eternity.

The false belief that God and the Logos were immaterial made it impossible to understand how the spirit of Jesus united with his body, Barker thought. In the spirit world, Jesus and men were brothers, and his union of body and spirit was no different from the same union in human beings. Jesus was different from men only "in advancement, in perfection and in fidelity" (333). The preexistence of spirits—a doctrine that alone could have explained the Incarnation—was denied. "Modern revelation", according to Barker, testifies that human intelligence is eternal, clothed by God with "spiritual bodies", and that human beings are brothers of Jesus (341). On earth Jesus could "lose the memory of His pre-existence, could separate from the body at death and unite with His body when he rose again", just as human beings will (360).

Barker took what might be called a skeptical/rationalist view of these early theological controversies. When speculation led to impasses, as it invariably did, the theologians invoked the claim that these doctrines were "mysteries", mere word plays to conceal their errors, Barker implied, mere confusions arising from the abandonment of the simple terminology of apostolic times. (Apparently, it did not occur to him that finite human attempts to understand the infinite God could scarcely help but be mysteries, although he admitted that "the idea of eternity is, in a sense, beyond human understanding" [341].)

The postapostolic Fathers were "the blind leading the blind", their creeds merely futile attempts to resolve problems deriving from a series of false theological assumptions, one leading to another (340). How could "numerical three" actually be "numerical one" (330)? In the Nicene Creed the claim that the Father and the Son are distinct Persons is incompatible with the assertion that they are of the same substance, which cannot be divided or diminished.

New doctrines were introduced long after the age of revelations had passed, and the Nicene Creed was unscriptural and incompatible with apostolic beliefs. (Barker quotes Church historian F. X. Funk as saying: "Church historians generally agree" [266]. But he quoted him as merely stating the obvious—that not all theologians held Nicene doctrines prior to Nicaea. If they had, no council would have been necessary.)

If Barker in effect sided with the Orthodox concerning the authority of the bishop of Rome, he turned against them—and indeed against almost all later Christians—in condemning the Nicene Creed, which "substituted for the personal God of love and for Jesus of the New Testament an immaterial abstraction" (207). Jesus was treated as merely another philosopher, and the Fathers of the First Council of Nicaea preferred the philosophy of the Greeks. Here was the essence of the Great Apostasy.

Barker cited the Council (Synod) of Arles (313) as the first example of the control of the Church by the state. The council settled a dispute in North Africa by deposing Donatist bishops, and Barker claimed that the emperor simply functioned in place of the apostles, adjudicating Church quarrels on his own authority.

This historical reductionism seriously hampered Barker's understanding. While Constantine convened the gathering at Arles, he did not impose his own solution of the dispute. The council confirmed a previous judgment that had been pronounced by the bishop of Rome and other Western prelates. As Donatism persisted in North Africa, Constantine moved to suppress it, based on the ecclesiastical judgment at Arles.[20] (Barker was also critical of Arles because it affirmed the legitimacy of baptism by heretics.)

He gave a fairly detailed account of the proceedings at the First Council of Nicaea, mainly based on Eusebius of Caesarea and a few modern historians. Constantine summoned a council in order to preserve the unity of the empire, Barker said. But without seeming to understand how it modified his own views, Barker cited Eusebius to the effect that the emperor primarily sought to impose a "spirit of concord" (257), not that he dictated the doctrinal conclusions. If in fact Constantine was primarily concerned with political unity, his very lack of theological convictions allowed the assembled bishops to decide the issues. There was fierce debate, although Constantine ultimately sided with the anti-Arian party. The fanatical passion that fueled these disputes, and the tactics to which they gave rise, testifies to the sincerity of the participants.

In charging that the emperors "made the church a political arm of the state" (498), Barker did not see that, while the bishops of this era

[20] W. H. C. Frend, *The Donatist Church* (Oxford: Clarendon Press, 1952).

were dependent on imperial authority to enforce their decrees, their claims about truth were based on Scripture, entirely independent of the emperor. Barker quoted Duchesne to the effect that the bishops did not object when the emperors supported orthodox teachings, only when they did not, a generalization that, contrary to Barker, shows their essential independence. While many people were undoubtedly opportunists who acceded to the emperor's wishes, many on both sides of these bitter disputes suffered exile and even death rather than compromise their beliefs. To many, at different times and for different reasons, the emperor was a heretic, and when he was orthodox, it was not because of his imperial authority but because he had received divine enlightenment to see the truth.

The First Council of Nicaea was followed by "caesaro-papism", according to Barker (272), in which the half-pagan emperor promoted the Christian faith vigorously. Constantine brutally murdered his son, his second wife, and a number of others in a palace intrigue, then built numerous churches to assuage his conscience, eventually leaving Rome as a hated man. "Such was Constantine, who was made a saint by the Greek Orthodox Church", Barker sneered (277).

Barker narrated in some detail the story of how Arians and semi-Arians fought a partly successful rear-guard action against the formulae of the First Council of Nicaea, with some support from Constantine and his successors. The establishment of the capital of the empire at Constantinople deepened the divisions between the Eastern and Western churches, but the renewed theological struggles following the First Council of Nicaea led to appeals to the authority of the bishop of Rome even in the East, Barker acknowledged. Pope Julius was instrumental in restoring Athanasius to his see at Alexandria, and both Nestorius and his opponents appealed to the see of Rome, the prestige of which grew along with the strength of a reestablished Western Roman Empire, although the Eastern bishops still did not acknowledge Roman primacy.

Barker cited the famous case of Pope Liberius (d. 366), who at one point signed an ambiguous, possibly Arian, formula, after having been severely pressured by the emperor Constantius. For a time "Constantius made the entire official Christian world, Arian" (422), Barker said, and if the Church had not already lost her divine authority over the doctrine of baptism, this heresy would have had the same effect (420–21). (The Church did not formally commit itself to Arian formulae under Constantius. To the contrary, it was still officially committed to Nicaea, a fact that the infidelity of particular popes and bishops did not alter. Eventually, the entire hierarchy, including Liberius' successor Damasus, again subscribed to Nicene formulae, once more with imperial support.)

The councils that followed the First Council of Nicaea extended the same errors and were continuing occasions for conflict and division. No modern Christian doctrine can be traced earlier than 325, Barker asserted.

The theological disputes of the East had to do with the nature of God, while those in the West had to do primarily with the nature of man and his salvation. But the East had forced false doctrines on the West, Barker claimed, so that theological speculation in the West was also fatally corrupted. The principal error was the belief that the souls of men had been created by God out of nothing. But if an all-good God did so, how did evil enter the world?, Barker asked.

IV. The Trouble with Augustine and Monasticism

Both Catholic and Protestant understanding of the nature of sin originated in Augustine rather than in the Scriptures, Barker asserted, repeating the simplistic claim that Augustine's theology was essentially shaped by his Manichean period. He also "contaminated Christianity" by his interest in philosophy (435). (In his discussion of Augustine, Barker relied heavily on secondary surveys, including Will Durant's work.)

Prior to his conversion, Augustine struggled to understand the concept of an "immaterial God", not realizing that it was an error, which made his attempts to understand it lead to further errors. Barker claimed, equally simplistically, that Augustine followed Plato rather than Scripture,[21] as in his belief that the world was made out of nothing. His doctrine of the Trinity, which was the basis of Christian belief for centuries, compounded the error still further.

[21] For a careful account, see A. H. Armstrong, "St. Augustine and Christian Platonism", in *Augustine: A Collection of Critical Essays*, ed. R. A. Markus (Garden City, NY: Doubleday, 1972), 3–37.

Augustine did not explain how an omnipotent immaterial God could create human beings who sin, Barker charged, and the doctrine of original sin is "untenable" (441, quoting Phillip Schaff). Such teachings left no room for the God of love and were the principal cause of atheism. (In fact, Augustine accounted for sin very clearly—man retained free will after he was created. His nature remained good, although it was corrupted. Men were predestined in that the all-powerful God could arrange the conditions of a man's life in such a way as to cause the individual to choose either good or evil. Crucial to each person was the "grace of perseverance".[22])

Barker found Augustine's theology to be similar to the account of Lucifer's in the Pearl of Great Price (PGP),[23] one of the three books the LDS count as Scripture along with the Protestant Bible. Lucifer was the brother of Jesus who, prior to his rebellion, proposed a plan by which all men would be saved, simply by being prevented from doing evil. Pelagius also started from false premises, according to Barker, once again the idea of an all-powerful immaterial God. Whereas Augustine put full responsibility for salvation on God, Pelagius so exalted man that the Savior seemed not to be necessary. (Characteristically, Barker did not cite the PGP but merely recounted the story of Lucifer as though it were generally known by Christians.)

Barker exaggerated Augustine's doctrine of predestination, which Barker claimed reduced "man to a puppet" (455) and God to "an oriental despot" (457). Like many commentators, Barker did identify a real tension in Augustine's theology—while he affirmed free will in his refutation of the Manicheans, he seemed to deny it in his refutation of the Pelagians. As Barker recognized, in the latter controversy Augustine was thought, both in his own time and later, to have overstated his case, so that the official condemnations of Pelagianism did not imply the full acceptance of Augustine's own position, especially his doctrine of predestination.[24]

Monasticism began in the fourth century, its origins lost in antiquity, possibly first arising in India, Barker said. But his knowledge of the actual history of monasticism seems not even to have reached the

---

[22] Pelikan, *Emergence*, 299–301; John M. Rist, "Augustine on Free Will and Predestination", in Markus, *Augustine*, 218–44.

[23] See Moses 4, in PGP.

[24] Pelikan, *Emergence*, 318–19.

level of an elementary textbook, and his strong disapproval allowed him to see nothing in it but insane fanaticism on the one hand and hypocritical worldliness on the other. It was a way of life that Barker apparently thought was devoid of all spiritual value. Those who entered religious orders did not do so "in response to a need of a society or of the church, but they were seeking something for themselves" (528). Religious life was bound to be corrupted because of the essentially selfish motives of its adherents. (Barker made only grudging mention of the educational and missionary work of the religious orders and said nothing about their many martyrs.)

The condemnation of matter was one of its roots, Barker claimed, and its essence was "a desire to save one's soul, by living an ascetic life, devising means of self-torture, thinking by torturing the body to purify the soul" (513). In the monks' "disordered fancy, the desert was fill[ed] with devils" (514). Some became monks to escape slavery, and many were lazy and immoral. But they were often fierce and violent participants in the doctrinal quarrels of the time. Barker said nothing about the rich spirituality of the desert monks.[25] (He appears to have been personally offended by ascetical practices, departing briefly from his historical analysis to condemn as hypocritical a group of English Christians of his own day who had gone on pilgrimage carrying a cross.)

"Caesaro-papism" was a kind of "strangulation" of the Church that determined the doctrine, Church government, monasticism, and intolerance that would characterize the Middle Ages (277). "The influences were human, when not in their cruelty and inhumanity diabolical", Barker charged (277). "'Christian' violence" was worse than that of the pagan emperors (297). Orthodoxy was imposed by force. "Henceforth, throughout the Middle Ages and into modern times, the churches appealed to fear and, when possible, to force", Barker said (318), something that began in the West with Augustine, who sought imperial support against the Donatists.

Barker admitted that the decadence of late Roman society, and of the Church herself, made monasticism appealing to many people, so that with the reforms of Benedict the monastery became "a healing

---

[25] Peter H. Görg, *The Desert Fathers: St. Anthony and the Beginnings of Monasticism*, trans. Michael J. Miller (San Francisco: Ignatius Press, 2011).

refuge" (522). But Barker then passed immediately to the monastic decadence of later centuries, skipping even the conventional account of the civilizing role of monks in the Dark Ages. (Apparently confusing the priesthood with monastic vows, he claimed that marriage among monks did not cease until the eleventh century.) The Cistercians of the twelfth century overcame monastic corruption and were especially successful in carrying the gospel to northern Europe, but from that point Barker's account jumped again—to the briefest account of the Trappist reforms of the seventeenth century.[26]

Barker barely noted the achievements of the mendicant orders, then immediately moved on to the subject of their corruption. Barker cited Durant to the effect that most of Francis of Assisi's followers could not live "the life of almost delirious asceticism that had shortened Francis' life" (527). With apparently no knowledge of the complex history of the split between Conventual and Spiritual Franciscans, Barker also cited Durant's claim that most of Francis' followers were burnt at the stake.

Dominic was mentioned only in connection with the prosecution of heresy, and from that brief mention, Barker skipped three centuries to the Jesuits. Here he relied on the liberal Baptist/Unitarian minister Alfred W. Wishart,[27] who wrote that the Jesuits were sinister agents of the papacy who sought to crush human free will. They schemed against lawful rulers and were eventually suppressed.

V. Sacraments, Church, and State

The simplicity of the early Christian liturgy was, according to Barker, corrupted, largely by the desire to imitate pagan rituals. Once more he relied on general secondary surveys, not on any of the scholarly studies of liturgy available in his time. (His superficial knowledge of the subject was revealed in his listing of the introduction of the Rosary as a change in the liturgy.) In a true understanding of

[26] He noted the establishment in his own day of a Trappist monastery in his home state of Utah (525).

[27] See "Fountain Street Church (Grand Rapids, Mich.) records, 1856–1978", University of Michigan Library, https://findingaids.lib.umich.edu/catalog/umich-bhl-86975. Wishart authored *A Short History of Monks and Monasteries* (Trenton, NJ: A. Brandt, 1900).

"the sacrament" (the Eucharist), worshippers simply expressed gratitude to the Savior and renewed their acceptance of his leadership, according to Barker. It was absurd to think that "this is my body" was meant literally, but that belief gradually developed and was officially sanctioned by the Church (535–36). (The postapostolic Fathers all held to a belief in the Real Presence, neither understanding it as a symbol nor positing a change in substance.[28])

Strict standards of repentance were enforced in the early Church, but because of the laxness of the culture, those standards were continuously lowered, Barker said. (He evidently approved of the original rigor even though it is known only from the postapostolic age that Barker thought already manifested distortions of the gospel.) As with monastic life, the Church transformed the sacrament into a selfish action ("self-forgiveness of sin"), which was a commonly held belief "until the time of Joseph Smith" (539).

Citing prayers for forgiveness in the liturgy, Barker claimed that, especially because of Augustine's doctrine of original sin, the Church taught that sins could be forgiven repeatedly simply by participation in the rites of the Church. The necessity of leading a good life gave way to easy forgiveness. Barker did not seem to understand that, far from being automatically forgiven in the Eucharist, an unshorn sinner committed a grave sin in even approaching the holy table. (Easy forgiveness in the Mass would also have rendered indulgences superfluous.) According to Augustine, "anyone and everyone who resorts to the good offices of the church will be saved", Barker said (553), which was a direct contradiction of Augustine's actual teaching.[29]

Relying primarily on a book by a Baptist historian,[30] Barker claimed that punishment of sins could be avoided with "money payments" (558). He rejected as sophistical the Catholic teaching that indulgences removed the punishment of the sin but not its guilt— they were an easy way of being forgiven. (Barker quoted from historic proclamations of indulgences, such as the first Holy Year [1300], without noticing that they made little mention of money and that what was required of penitents was very difficult.)

---

[28] Pelikan, *Emergence*, 167–68.

[29] See Pelikan, *Emergence*, 299–301; Rist, "Augustine on Free Will", 218–44.

[30] Albert Henry Newman, *A Manual of Church History* (Philadelphia: American Baptist Publication Society, 1903).

Barker noted that in *City of God*, Augustine laid the foundation for subordinating the state to the Church, something that to Will Durant was a "theocratic state" (508). But for the most part, Barker was able to rely on Catholic historians for his account of the Dark Ages. By the time of Gregory the Great (c. 600), the Roman Church was actively extending her authority everywhere in the West, its most notable alliance—long after Gregory's time—being with the Carolingian house in the kingdom of the Franks. But the coronation of Charlemagne, after he had saved the pope from the Lombards, marked the revival of "caesaro-papism", Barker said, which the clergy resisted partly with the forged *Isidorian Decretals* and *Donation of Constantine*.

Force was often applied, as in Charlemagne's massacre of Saxons who had reverted to paganism, a massacre that, Barker noted, some modern Catholic historians justified. Relying on Albert Newman, Barker said that Saxons who had been converted under Augustine of Canterbury once massacred three thousand Celtic Christians. (Bede the Venerable, the source of that report, gave the number as twelve hundred, all of them monks who were killed by the Saxon king because they were praying for his defeat in battle. Either as a threat or a prophecy, Augustine had warned the Celts that if they did not enter into unity with the Saxon Christians, they would perish at the hands of their enemies. He was dead by the time of the massacre.[31])

But after Charlemagne's death, the Italian nobility once again gained control over the papacy and a line of corrupt popes followed, until German emperors once more came to the rescue of the papal office and again exercised imperial control over the Church.

Despite his animosity toward monasticism, Barker acknowledged that the reform of the medieval Church was mainly due to the monks, as in the struggle against lay investiture. But the revival of papal authority also marked the triumph of the principle of coercion, especially the Crusades and the Inquisition, "two of the most incredible anti-Christian events in church history" (585).

For his account of the Crusades, Barker relied again on Albert Newman, positing unrealistically huge numbers of participants (six hundred thousand people in the First Crusade, a million and a half in

---

[31] Bede, *A History of the English Church and People*, trans. Leo Sherley-Price (New York: Penguin Books, 1968), 102–3.

the Second) and characterizing many of them as desperate criminals let out of prison to join the expeditions. (Newman made an elementary error in claiming that indulgences gave their recipients freedom to sin by forgiving their transgressions in advance.[32])

Barker's account of the Crusades was very brief, mentioning practically nothing about the wars except their cruelty and simply ignoring most of what was relevant to evaluating them—that the Muslims were the aggressors in the Near East, the Byzantine emperor had requested Western help, the Crusades were summoned by the pope for religious reasons, and the leaders and most of their followers were probably also motivated by religion and were often very brave. (There is now much better scholarship about the Crusades that was not yet available in Barker's day,[33] but he also ignored the best scholarly work of his own time, even though much of it was critical of the Catholic Church.[34])

Albert Newman provided Barker with his account of the Inquisition as well, although Barker noted that some Catholic historians condemned the institution. (As with the Crusades, modern scholarship presents a far more complex and nuanced view than was available to Barker.[35]) Barker's view of the effects of the Inquisition was simplistic in the extreme. It "deprived the people of the right to investigate and to think" (599). Innocent IV, by specifying the varying degrees of religious knowledge people were expected to have, "gave formal expression to ... the total scorn of the common man" (599). (Barker apparently thought medieval peasants should have been expected to understand subtle and complex doctrines.) Barker quoted Albert Newman to the effect that hatred of the Inquisition led to major revolts against the papacy: "The Christian consciousness was outraged by the Inquisition, and was sure to have its revenge" (599).

[32] William Kent, "Indulgences", *The Catholic Encyclopedia*, vol. 7 (New York: Robert Appleton, 1910), www.newadvent.org/cathen/07783a.htm.

[33] For example, Thomas M. Madden, *A New Concise History of the Crusades* (Lanham, MD: Rowman & Littlefield, 1999).

[34] Steven Runciman, *A History of the Crusades*, 3 vols. (Cambridge: Cambridge University Press, 1951–1954).

[35] For example, Edward N. Peters, *Inquisition* (New York: Free Press, 1988); John A. Tedeschi, *The Prosecution of Heresy* (Binghamton, NY: Medieval and Renaissance Texts and Studies, 1991).

But, as Barker himself noted elsewhere, resentment of papal taxation was a far greater cause of such discontent.

Except for the Crusades and the Inquisition, Barker skipped rather quickly over the Middle Ages, merely stating that Innocent III and other popes overreached themselves and provoked reaction against "papal tyranny" (595). He touched on the East-West schism only briefly and conventionally, repeating his previous arguments against the primacy of the see of Rome. He did not probe the complexity of medieval church-state relations, making no mention of Henry IV and Gregory VII, of Henry II and Thomas Becket, or of Frederick II and Innocent IV. The Avignon papacy was treated in passing, without explanation of why it occurred, and the Great Western Schism was allotted only two paragraphs. Barker paid more attention to conciliarism, which he said the popes eventually overcame largely due to the loyalty of the Jesuits. (In fact, the Society of Jesus was founded more than a century after the high point of conciliarism.)

VI. Reformation

Prior to the Protestant Reformation, Barker claimed: "The bold spirits, who protested against the abuses of the church, although not separating from it, were burnt as heretics" (673). However, most of those whom he cited were either not accused of heresy or were not burnt at the stake.

Peter of Bruys (d. c. 1126) was a diocesan priest who preached against various Catholic doctrines but was killed by a mob because he desecrated crosses.[36] Barker misidentified the man he called Henry of Cluny (d. c. 1148), who he said was a monk of that monastery. More commonly called Henry of Lausanne or Henry of Bruys, he was perhaps a disciple of Peter of Bruys. He was imprisoned for life.[37]

Arnold of Brescia (d. c. 1155) was a monk who preached that the clergy had to practice absolute poverty or were therefore not fit to administer the sacraments. He was hanged as a rebel rather than burnt

[36] Nicholas Weber, "Petrobrusians", *The Catholic Encyclopedia*, vol. 11 (New York: Robert Appleton, 1911), www.newadvent.org/cathen/11781a.htm.

[37] Paul Daniel Alphandéry, "Henry of Lausanne", *Encyclopedia Britannica*, 11th ed., ed. Hugh Chisolm (New York: Encyclopedia Britannica, 1910), 8:298–99.

as a heretic because he helped lead a rebellion against the pope to reestablish the Roman Republic.[38]

The man commonly called Peter Waldo or Valdez (his real name is uncertain) was a wealthy French layman who gave up his riches and became a preacher, especially attacking the wealth of the clergy. He attracted a large following and eventually denied the priesthood itself and the sacramental system. He also arranged to have the Bible translated into the vernacular. At one point he had papal support, but ultimately the movement was condemned. Waldo's fate (c. 1200) is unknown, but many of his followers were burnt as heretics. The movement still survives.[39]

Strangely, Barker included a heading for "Albigensians" but said nothing about their beliefs and merely said that a crusade had been mounted to suppress them. He could hardly have found their radical dualism acceptable.

Also strangely, one of his examples was the Knights Templar (suppressed in 1307), a group that could hardly be said to have protested abuses and that were suppressed largely because they had enormous wealth.[40] (Unknown in Barker's time, the pope actually absolved them of the charge of heresy after many of them had already been burnt at the instigation of the king of France.[41])

Barker's accounts of the English priest John Wycliffe (Wyclif) and the Bohemian priest Jan Hus were essentially accurate. Hus held views similar to Wyclif's and may have been directly influenced by him. Both attacked papal taxation, advocated the independence of the state from the authority of the Church, arranged for the translation of the New Testament into the vernacular, and cast doubts on the priesthood and the sacraments. With strong political support, Wyclif remained unmolested, but some of his followers (Lollards) were burnt.[42] Hus was burnt at the stake after having been promised safe conduct by the German emperor.[43]

---

[38] Elphège Vacandard, "Arnold of Brescia", *The Catholic Encyclopedia*, vol. 1, www.new advent.org/cathen/01747b.htm.

[39] Nicholas Weber, "Waldenses", *The Catholic Encyclopedia*, vol. 15 (New York: Robert Appleton, 1912), www.newadvent.org/cathen/15527b.htm.

[40] Malcolm Barber, *The Trial of the Templars* (Cambridge: Cambridge University Press, 1993).

[41] Barbara Frale, "The Chinon Chart", *Journal of Medieval History* 30, no. 2 (2004): 109–34.

[42] Ian Christopher Levy, ed., *A Companion to John Wyclif* (Leiden: Brill, 2006).

[43] Mathew Spinka, *John Hus: A Biography* (Princeton, NJ: Princeton University Press, 1968).

Relying on the work of a popularizing English historian,[44] Barker offered a caricature of the Renaissance—a good kind of worldliness opposed to the life-denying negativity of the Middle Ages, virtually all that Barker had to say about that brilliant age. He could perhaps be excused because he wrote prior to modern revisionist historiography,[45] but, once again, he ignored Haskins' *Renaissance of the Twelfth Century*, among other things.

Barker was apparently oblivious to the religious richness of the fifteenth century, his only understanding of "reform" being direct rebellion against Church authority. Nowhere in his eight-hundred-page survey did he pay the slightest attention to the visual arts, except to imply that they constituted superstition. He found the Italian Renaissance pagan, and, while the Northern Renaissance encouraged the study of the Bible, he made only brief mention of Erasmus and the movement called Christian Humanism and none at all of the Devotio Moderna, the Rhenish and English mystics, or Girolamo Savonarola.

The essence of the Reformation was "spirit of free examination, personal judgment and responsibility", according to Barker (692), although he quickly backed away from that claim. He spent some time on the wicked and oppressive Pope Alexander VI, although he acknowledged that the pope's sins were not the cause of Luther's discontent. Barker gave a lengthy and essentially accurate account of the indulgence question and of Luther's subsequent history, except for quoting the famous phrase "Here I stand ...", which, in fact, Luther did not utter.[46]

Unfortunately, in Barker's view (and Albert Newman's), Luther exercised freedom of judgment by measuring the Scripture against his own ideas, which were essentially Augustine's, especially his preoccupation with human sinfulness and his belief in predestination. Luther's attachment to his own ideas was especially demonstrated in his disagreement with Ulrich Zwingli over the meaning of the Eucharist. For all the good that Luther did, Barker noted that, "against all evidence", he clung to the Catholic practice of infant baptism and

[44] D. C. Sommervell, *A Short History of Our Religion* (New York: Macmillan, 1922).

[45] For example, Charles Trinkaus, *In Our Image and Likeness*, 2 vols. (Chicago: University of Chicago Press, 1970).

[46] Derek Wilson, *Out of the Storm* (New York: St. Martin's Press, 2007), 153. In Barker's time, the quote was still considered authentic.

"baptism without authority" (by heretics) and accepted the decrees of the early councils (739, 723). In time, his principle of freedom of conscience gave way to a system in which the prince was the ultimate authority in matters of religion and the Church was supported financially by the state.

Ultimately, Luther, too, was part of the Great Apostasy and "contributed little to the religious thought of the world and nothing to church government". But he was "one of the greatest benefactors of mankind" because he made the Bible accessible to the people, and out of his movement came "liberty of conscience and political freedom" (730).

Barker's accounts of Zwingli and John Calvin were also accurate, except for his erroneous claim that Calvin had been ordained a Catholic priest. In Switzerland the authority of the state replaced that of the bishop in matters of religion, albeit "supported by the sentiment of the people" (738).

But Zwingli and Calvin were also part of the Great Apostasy, holding to the untenable belief that divine revelation ceased with the death of the last apostle. Their Catholic opponents saw that it was necessary to interpret revelation but had no divine authority to do so.

Barker judged that neither Luther, Calvin, nor the Council of Trent were able to resolve the tension between grace and free will, which was therefore classified as a "mystery". Zwingli and Calvin, like Luther, held to the errors of Augustine, including infant baptism. Their doctrine of predestination was based on the erroneous belief that God created the universe and man *ex nihilo*. They and Luther persecuted the Anabaptists, who sought a return to a purer church.

Like most people who studied the English Reformation, Barker saw it primarily as an act of state, although Lollardy helped prepare the way. He briefly but accurately traced the history of the Reformation through the reign of Elizabeth I, with passing mention of the Puritans. The crucial issue for Anglicans was the validity of their bishops, which the Catholic Church rejected, although, Barker said, the Catholic Church herself had long ago ceased to possess a valid hierarchy.

Overall, the Reformation broke the power of the Catholic Church but did not restore the authentic gospel, Barker regretted. Too many Catholic dogmas were retained, especially the decrees of the early councils. Despite proclamations of religious liberty, the Reformers sanctioned persecution.

The Council of Trent did not reform the Catholic Church, except to some extent in morals. Rather, it deepened the apostasy by again defining the doctrine of original sin, the need to baptize infants, the sacrifice of the Mass, and prayers for the dead. The popes, too, supported the persecution of heresy.

VII. After the Sixteenth Century

Barker then skipped over the next three centuries, without scrutinizing the rise of the national state and its implications for religion, not mentioning nor attempting to explain the suppression of the Jesuits by the pope, and—most astonishingly—not mentioning the Enlightenment or the French Revolution. He paid no attention to modern liberal Christianity, although it would have added an important chapter to his story of the Great Apostasy. (Possibly, since it unfolded at about the same time as did the Latter-day Saint faith, he did not wish to emphasize how the "new revelations" of liberal Christianity departed from classical orthodoxy.)

His account resumed in the later nineteenth century, when the rise of nationalism deprived the popes of their temporal power, for which, Barker claimed, Pius IX attempted to compensate by the dogmas of the Immaculate Conception and papal infallibility. The former was an innovation of the Jesuits, who controlled clerical education, he said. (While it was by no means universally held, the doctrine of the Immaculate Conception had been believed by many leading theologians throughout history.[47] The Jesuits did not control all clerical education.) He alluded to Pius IX and "1864" (the Syllabus of Errors), without discussing the pope's severe criticisms of modern culture, many of which Mormons would probably agree with. Writing only a few years before the convening of the Second Vatican Council, Barker accurately quoted Catholic authorities of his day justifying coercion in matters of religion.

Vatican I's definition of papal infallibility meant that "after eighteen centuries of quarreling, strife, and the use of force, the papacy was born", Barker announced, thereby bringing his history to a close.

---

[47] Frederick Holweck, "Immaculate Conception", *The Catholic Encyclopedia*, vol. 7, www.newadvent.org/cathen/07674d.htm.

But his apologetic, while it scanned the centuries, was not historical in nature. It revealed nothing that was not already known, and disagreements about that history have always been based much more on the faith than on facts. Barker's apology for Mormonism was the familiar one of seeking less to justify his own creed than to discredit others. Constantine, Alexander VI, and many others were wicked men. But by basing so much of his argument on the wickedness of Catholics and other Christians throughout history, Barker merely invited inspection of his own church, exchanges that ultimately proved nothing except that every church has a disfigured human face. Can Divine Providence be present even in the deeds of evil men?

Barker's apologetic strategy was obviously aimed at reassuring Latter-day Saints. In essence he accepted the most skeptical judgments about the Church in each age, whatever the source of that skepticism, a strategy that might conceivably shake the faith of a Christian in his own church but could scarcely convert such a person to Mormonism, whose truth Barker merely assumed. A reader persuaded by Barker that many of the claims of historic Christianity are untenable must then make an enormous leap of faith, of giving full assent to the testimony of "the Prophet Joseph Smith". Noting the multitude of sects all claiming to have the truth, Barker merely said that such a claim belongs "assuredly, to the divine church" (4). But, as with all such apologetics, he offered no argument as to why the Latter-day Saint claim should not be dismissed as simply another chapter in the history of ongoing theological cacophony.

The key to understanding the Great Apostasy was Barker's denial that the Church received the guidance of the Holy Spirit once the last apostle was gone. Divine Providence protected only the first generation of Christ's followers. God intended to guide his Church by continuing revelation, but "the human church" thwarted that, "all communication with Him [Jesus] having been cut off" (148). Barker made no attempt to explain why the Spirit abandoned the Church, except by vague references to "human freedom". He seemed to make Divine Providence weak almost to the point of nonexistence. God permitted the leaders of the Church to betray the gospel again and again, with almost no one remaining faithful. Only in the nineteenth century, for reasons not explained, did Providence finally intervene to redeem the wreckage. Barker did not even consider the possibility of the development of doctrine, which is obviously the key question with regard to Nicene-Chalcedonian Christianity. To him the history of doctrine was essentially the story of stumbling and prideful mistakes and crude lusting after power.

He gave central importance to "caesaro-papism", which, if it means anything, means dominance of the Church by the state, a condition to which Barker attributed false doctrines like those of the Nicene Creed. But after so defining it, Barker then went on to tell a story that in the West in effect meant almost the opposite—the growth of a powerful papacy that challenged political authority.

Barker identified "freedom of judgment" as one of the greatest religious values, one that had been suppressed by all the historical faiths except (presumably) Mormonism. But since Barker saw all pre-1840 theological discussions as devoid of divine guidance, such freedom must inevitably have led away from the truth. In surveying the various heresies, from Gnosticism to Anabaptism, he found none that had kept the authentic faith. The postapostolic Fathers began the departure from the gospel, but in a sense, it would have made little difference if they had remained faithful, since God always intended to send new revelations. Barker provided no criteria for believing that Joseph Smith—not Athanasius, Augustine, or Luther—was the authentic vessel of those revelations. (When the true faith was finally restored, freedom to dissent was presumably no longer a good.)

Perhaps the ultimate failing of Barker's work as a historian was what might be called his severe spiritual and intellectual tone deafness. His was a rather mechanical kind of fundamentalism that did not appreciate the depth and brilliance of the history of theology but saw only a hostile invasion of the Church by pagan ideas. He ignored the great Christian intellectual achievements during the many centuries of waiting for Joseph Smith. Augustine was simply mired in error; Aquinas was not even mentioned.

Francis of Assisi interested him only to the degree that the Franciscan movement was in opposition to Church authority; its profound spiritual effects were ignored. So also was high art. After 1054, Eastern Orthodoxy disappeared from the story completely. Ignatius Loyola was merely a tyrant who suppressed human freedom in the interests of the papacy. And in all these many pages, where were Dante, John Bunyan, Johann Sebastian Bach, or John Wesley?

5

Deification in Two Traditions

Glenn Olsen

Not long after I had moved to Salt Lake City, in the early 1970s, Jaroslav Pelikan came to the city to speak to its gathered Protestant ministers. He was a Lutheran at that time, and his audience was composed of most of the Protestant clergy in town. But we had served together on the Board of Regents of Saint Mary's College at Notre Dame and enjoyed each other's company, so he suggested we have dinner after he had given his presentation. In giving his talk, he had mentioned the idea of *theosis*, or divinization, and at dinner he amusedly told me that he had had to explain what that word meant. It is the Greek word that a modern scholarly translation of the Bible, such as the Jerusalem translation of 2 Peter 1:4, renders as "you will be able to share the divine nature."

Pelikan's feigned shock at the ministers' ignorance of the presence of *theosis*/divinization in the Bible was a part of the entertainment value of his story. As someone who had taught in the divinity schools at the University of Chicago and Yale, he well knew how little most American Christians understood of their faith. For example, he knew that few could make sense of Harold Bloom's claim, reached in his study *The American Religion*, that America is a fundamentally Gnostic country whose most characteristic religious product is the Church of Jesus Christ of Latter-day Saints.[1] Admittedly, Bloom's interests and conclusions struck many people familiar with the professed theologies

[1] Harold Bloom, *The American Religion: The Emergence of the Post-Christian Nation* (New York: Simon and Schuster, 1992).

of America's major denominations as a trifle eccentric. He was, for instance, much concerned with Metatron, the angel of America, variously thought to be the Enoch of Genesis and the secret soul of the Mormon prophet Joseph Smith. But the point for our purposes is that the Mormons are now attracting the attention of prominent scholars, who are struck according to their interests by various aspects of the religion.

To return to Pelikan, his story about the Salt Lake City clergy had a double humor about it, because the concept of deification or divinization or exaltation is at the heart of the religion above all associated with Salt Lake City, that of the Latter-day Saints.[2] In fact, Mormons and non-Mormon Christians do not have a shared understanding of what deification or divinization entails, although—truth to say—few non-Mormons in the city would be any more able to give a definition of *theosis*, the Greek word used in 2 Peter 1:4 and lying behind all these ideas, whether translated "exaltation", "deification", or "divinization". Fewer still would know that the word has synonyms, specifically that one of the documents of Vatican II, *Lumen Gentium*, spoke of *vitam divinam*, the divine life.[3]

I want first to explain what *theosis* originally meant in Greek and early Christianity and then to show how this meaning, which remains the Catholic understanding, shifts in Mormonism.[4] The argument is that the original understanding of this word is still found in Eastern Orthodoxy and Catholicism today but that Mormon usage embodies a nineteenth-century idea of progress or development imported into

---

[2] Thomas Berg, "Our Divinization: O What a Deal" (fatherberg.com/our-divinization-o -what-a-deal) is a Christmas Day sermon by a Catholic priest on the *admirabile commercium* ("marvelous exchange") by which "God became man, that man might become God", containing a number of the traditional texts on divinization, as by Irenaeus, Athanasius, and Aquinas. See also Antonio Lopez, "'Blessed Is She Who Believed': Mary's Faith and the Form of Christian Existence", *Communio: International Catholic Review* 40 (2013): 680–712 at 682 n. 5 (deification as the goal of Christ's sacrifice).

[3] "The eternal Father, by a free and hidden plan of His own wisdom and goodness, created the whole world. His plan was to raise men to a participation of the divine life." (Vatican Council II, Dogmatic Constitution on the Church *Lumen Gentium* [November 21, 1964], no. 2, www.vatican.va/archive/hist_councils/ii_vatican_council/documents/vat-ii _const_19641121_lumen-gentium_en.html.)

[4] There is a very useful entry on "Divinization" in the *Encyclopedia of the Early Church*, 2 vols., ed. Angelo Di Bernardino, trans. Adrian Walford, with a foreword and bibliographic amendments by W.H.C. Frend (New York: Oxford University Press, 1992), 1:242–43.

that religion at its foundation. The first Mormons lived in a world in which ideas of general progress and the dynamic nature of history dominated. Henry Adams' *Mont-Saint-Michel and Chartres*, originally published in 1904, gives a good idea of this world, especially in its chapters devoted to comparing the Virgin and the Dynamo, the symbols of the Middle Ages and of the dynamism of the nineteenth century, respectively.[5] The one typified the great symbol of the Middle Ages, the cathedral, and the other the great symbol of the nineteenth century, the machine.

When I first moved to Utah, Mormons tended to emphasize how different their religion was from Christianity—that they were not Christians. As the religion has grown in numbers and, so to speak, has had to defend and explain itself on a world stage, it has become increasingly concerned to stress that Mormons are indeed Christians. Their earlier position seems to me more the truth than what they now say. Although the Latter-day Saints clearly are historically descended from especially the early nineteenth-century Evangelical Protestants of the burned-over district in New York State, they nevertheless seem to me far from Christianity not simply on obvious points, such as their rejection of the classical doctrine of the Trinity (and their affirmation of multiple deities), but on what we may call philosophical points, such as *creatio ex nihilo*. Before there ever was a Christianity, the Jews had increasingly come to see that the proper difference between God and man could be articulated only by the assertion that God had made matter itself. There is a great distance philosophically between a Mormon who holds that matter has always existed and that God himself is material, and a Christian who understands that there was once a time when matter itself did not exist but God did. They will, for instance, understand the doctrine of the Incarnation very differently.

I said that for a time Joseph Smith lived in the burned-over district of New York State. This fascinating region, full of the religious fervor and revivalism of the Second Great Awakening and of all kinds of accompanying new religion and religions, is the background against which the birth of Mormonism should be viewed. That is part of

[5] Henry Adams, *Mont-Saint-Michel and Chartres*, ed. Ralph Adams Cram (Boston: Houghton Mifflin, 1904).

the truth of calling Mormonism the most characteristic American religion. It is much more an orthopraxy, a way of life or living, than an orthodoxy, a way of believing or a form of belief. Arguably, with such great exceptions as the Mathers early on and some Reformed Calvinists yet today, disciplined theology is hardly found in America. Maybe in Grand Rapids, but not in America. At all periods of their history, Americans tend to move freely between the denominations, "shopping around" for congregations they like.

One goal of this chapter is to show that Christianity (Catholicism) is quite different from Mormonism. Their compared teachings on *theosis* illustrate this very well. As said above, the word *theosis* occurs only once in the Bible, in 2 Peter 1:4, quoted at the beginning of this essay. In the postbiblical period with the Eastern Fathers, it became the word of choice to describe the process by which man, created by God but then fallen and in some degree alienated from him, returns to God, is restored to his first state.[6] Describing this process was above all the achievement of the greatest of the early Christian theologians and exegetes, Origen, who has been much studied since the time of the two splendid mid-twentieth-century Jesuit scholars Henri de Lubac and Jean Daniélou, each of whom wrote a fine book on Origen.[7] Many followed Origen in a stream of exegetes, including both Alexandrines and the Cappadocian Fathers, especially Saint Gregory of Nazianzus (c. 329–c. 389), Saint Gregory of Nyssa (c. 335–c. 394), Saint Maximus the Confessor (c. 580–662), and Saint Dionysius the Areopagite, whatever century he is to be dated to.[8] The tradition persisted into the Middle Ages and is expressed especially by Saint Thomas Aquinas (1225–1274).[9]

---

[6] Benedict XVI, *Church, Ecumenism, and Politics* (San Francisco: Ignatius Press, 2008), 198, 274. The concept can be seriously misunderstood; see Vigen Guroian, "Godless Theosis", *First Things*, no. 242 (April 2014): 53–55.

[7] Henri de Lubac, *History and Spirit: The Interpretation of the Scriptures according to Origen*, trans. Anne England Nash (San Francisco: Ignatius Press, 2007); Jean Daniélou, *Origène* (Paris, 1948); and see my "Problems with the Contrast between Circular and Linear Views of Time in the Interpretation of Ancient and Early Medieval History", *Fides quaerens intellectum* 1 (2001): 41–65.

[8] On Dionysius, see Paolo Prosperi, "*Novum in Vetere Latet. Vetus in Novo Patet*: Toward a Renewal of Typological Exegesis", *Communio* 37, no. 3 (Fall 2010): 389–424, esp. 391.

[9] Peter M. Candler, "The Logic of Christian Humanism", *Communio* 36, no. 1 (Spring 2009): 69–91, esp. 86, quoting also Benedict XVI.

The enveloping idea, as Benedict XVI (r. 2005–2013) expressed it in our own day, was that the world was fashioned as a sacred space in which the covenant, or love story, between God and man could take place. In the words of Benedict XVI:

> Creation exists for the sake of worship.... The true center, the power that moves and shapes from within in the rhythm of the stars and of our lives, is worship.... The universe exists for worship and for the glorification of God.[10]

Or again:

> Belonging to God ... means losing oneself as the only possible way of finding oneself (Mk 8:35; Mt 10:39). That is why St. Augustine could say that the true "sacrifice" is the *civitas Dei*, that is, love-transformed mankind, the divinization of creation and the surrender of all things to God: God in all (1 Cor 15:28). That is the purpose of the world.... And so we can now say that the goal of worship and the goal of creation as a whole are one and the same—divinization, a world of freedom and love. But this means that the historical makes its appearance in the cosmic. The cosmos is not a kind of closed building, a stationary container in which history may by chance take place. It is itself movement, from its one beginning to its one end. In a sense creation *is* history.[11]

Scott Hahn has it: "Men and women are made to share in the life of God and to cooperate in the accomplishment of this *theiosis* [sic]."[12] Michael Waldstein distinguishes "between nature as created and participated divinization, a distinction the importance of which lies primarily in the need to do justice to the absolutely surpassing glory of

---

[10] Benedict XVI, *In the Beginning: A Catholic Understanding of the Story of Creation and the Fall* (Grand Rapids, MI: Eerdmans, 1995), 27–28, as quoted in Scott Hahn, "The Symphony of the Old and New Testaments in the Biblical Theology of Benedict XVI", *Communio* 37, no. 3 (Fall 2010): 435.

[11] Benedict XVI, *The Spirit of the Liturgy* (San Francisco: Ignatius Press, 2000), 28. For Augustine see David Vincent Meconi, *The One Christ: St. Augustine's Theology of Deification* (Washington, DC: Catholic University of America Press, 2013). See also on "becoming Godlike" for Augustine and Aquinas, Glenn W. Olsen, "The Church in History: *Status Viatoris*", *Communio* 40 (2013): 512–13.

[12] Hahn, "Symphony of the Old and New Testaments", 438.

the gratuitous invitation into the intimacy of love within God's own Trinitarian life".[13]

Christianity is built on the idea that God became incarnate in Christ. This Incarnation moved in two directions. On the one hand, as the Gospel of John says, the Logos or Word or second Person of the Trinity took on flesh. On the other hand, in this act of Incarnation, human flesh "took on God", became divinized. The word for this process of divinization is *theosis*, the "sharing in the divine nature" with which this essay began. It would be misleading to think of this sharing in the divine nature as something static, as some state of life achieved once and for all. The idea is that as creatures, as "not-God", humans may forever imitate God without becoming him. They were meant, before the first sin, to imitate God evermore. Having sinned, they may repent and return to the prospect originally set before them, of ever-increasing *mimesis*, or patterning themselves on God. No matter how much they become like God, they can become more like him.

As the great twentieth-century Catholic theologian Hans Urs von Balthasar states: "The central Word which God speaks and which comprises as their unity and end all the manifold words of God is Jesus Christ, the incarnate God.... His life is a fulfilling of Scripture. Therefore he incorporates the written words into his own life, making it live and there take flesh."[14] The principal means by which the Christian becomes godlike are participation in the Eucharist, where God and man commune, and the reading of Scripture. As to the latter, as Nicholas J. Healy notes: "To read Scripture in the same Spirit it was written is 'to receive Holy Writ as an icon displaying the features of the Incarnate Son—and to receive the impress of those features by the working of the Holy Spirit'."[15] So not only does Christ convey to us an image of the Father, but the Scriptures in turn bring God to us as an icon displaying the features of Christ.

---

[13] Michael Waldstein, "'Constitutive Relations': A Response to David L. Schindler", *Communio* 37, no. 3 (Fall 2010): 514.

[14] Hans Urs von Balthasar, "The Word, Scripture and Tradition", in *Explorations in Theology*, vol. 1, *Word Made Flesh*, trans. A. V. Littledale with Alexander Dru (San Francisco: Ignatius Press, 1989), 13, quoted in Nicholas J. Healy, "Introduction: The Unity of the Scriptures", *Communio* 37, no. 3 (Fall 2010): 371.

[15] Healy, "Introduction", 372, quoting Adrian J. Walker, "Living Water: Reading Scripture in the Body of Christ with Benedict XVI", *Communio* 37, no. 3 (Fall 2010): 383.

Jesus becomes the key by which the physical world itself, that is, matter, can be understood. In the words of Adrian J. Walker: "Jesus' trans-
figuration into a 'life-giving spirit' by the power of the *Spiritus Creator*
does not make him any less physical than he was before [as incarnate or
enfleshed]. On the contrary, it establishes his bodily existence once and
for all as the eternal meaning and pattern of the physical world."[16] This
means that the structure found in the physical world finds its meaning in what Jesus was, that one must examine the enfleshed Jesus to
understand the significance of the structure one meets in matter, and
that there is a correlation between the structure found in matter and in
Jesus. Thus, in the Catholic view, Jesus' very materiality is profoundly
revelatory and is an entrance into grasping why matter exists.

> To read Scripture spiritually, then, is to receive Holy Writ as an
> icon displaying the features of the Incarnate Son—and to receive the
> impress of those features by the working of the Holy Spirit: "All of us,
> mirroring the glory of the Lord with unveiled face, are transformed
> into the same image from glory to glory as by the Lord who is [such
> by the] Spirit" (2 Cor 3:18). To read Scripture spiritually is to share
> in the life of heaven by letting the pattern of sonship Jesus lives out
> before our eyes in the gospels penetrate and transform the whole sub-
> stance of our day-to-day existence in every detail. This is why Paul
> remarks that "all Scripture is inspired by God and is useful for ... the
> training that is to righteousness (2 Tim 3:16)."[17]

Reading Scripture is training in sonship. This is a central aspect of
the Catholic idea of divinization. From the reading of Scripture, the
Christian receives the impress of the Holy Spirit so that through training he comes to mirror the glory of the Lord and is "transformed into
the same image from glory to glory". In Adrienne von Speyr's words,
"Free and open, all giving and receiving, accepting and granting, an
undisturbed flow of riches, eternal life is love."[18] Humans come to

---

[16] Walker, "Living Water", 382.

[17] Ibid., 383. Bracketed insertion in original. I have explored the meaning of the spiritual
sense of Scripture in a number of studies, of which I mention "The Spiritual Sense(s) Today",
in *The Bible and the University*, ed. David Lyle Jeffrey and C. Stephen Evans, Scripture and
Hermeneutics Series, vol. 8 (Grand Rapids, MI: Zondervan, 2007), 116–38.

[18] Adrienne von Speyr, *The Word Made Flesh: Meditations on John 1–5*, trans. Lucia Wie-
denhöver and Alexander Dru (San Francisco: Ignatius Press, 1994), 39, quoted by Antonio
Lopez, "God the Father: A Beginning without Beginning", *Communio* 36 (2009): 242 n. 57,
in a discussion of Hegel.

share in the life of heaven by letting the pattern of sonship manifest in Jesus penetrate and transform their everyday substance. Central is the idea that divinization involves training and transformation (but without any idea that humans become God—they only may become evermore godlike sons of God, changing from "glory to glory"; this is the life of heaven, converting eternally toward God). Humans are made evermore to be generated toward God. This generation is centered in the liturgy, where we learn to read Scripture spiritually.[19]

As the Mormon faith grew in numbers toward the end of the twentieth century, many Mormon teachings that non-Mormons had thought either despicable (such as polygamy) or silly (such as the belief that, various conditions having been met, Mormons will become gods, and males will in the next life receive a planet to rule in the name of the family) received attention from defenders of Mormonism so that they might be formulated in a way that was not off-putting to non-Mormons.[20] This partially inspired the drive to present themselves as Christians, to have Christians see points of similarity between the two religions. The Mormon idea of "exaltation", which had expressed the idea that men would become gods and receive their own planets to rule, was retained but was conveyed as much as possible in line with the language of divinization found in the Bible and in the history of Christianity.[21]

In 1604, King James of England authorized a new translation of the Bible into English, which was completed in 1611. This was the usual

---

[19] As Walker, "Living Water", 384, points out, the great guide here is Scott Hahn, *Letter and Spirit: From Written Text to Living Word in the Liturgy* (New York: Doubleday, 2005). Of Hahn's many other important writings, see "Symphony of the Old and New Testaments". Walker, "Living Water", 385, designates the liturgy "the privileged school of the spiritual reading of Scripture". Especially important is Jean Daniélou, *From Glory to Glory: Texts from Gregory of Nyssa's Mystical Writings*, trans. Herbert Musurillo (New York: Scribner, 1961).

[20] For Mormon belief about the nature and importance of the family, see "Families Are Central to God's Plan", Church of Jesus Christ of Latter-day Saints, www.churchofjesus christ.org/comeuntochrist/believe/life-has-purpose/families-are-central-to-gods-plan. It states: "Families are central to God's plan for His children. They are the fundamental building block of strong societies. Families are where we can feel love and learn how to love others. Life is tough, and we need people we can lean on. Home is a safe haven where we can get love, advice, and support."

[21] The *Salt Lake Tribune* article by Matthew Piper (see note 23) makes it sound like neither its author nor contemporary Mormons know that *theosis* is a belief of Western as well as of Eastern Christianity.

translation of the Bible used by Protestants in Joseph Smith's day, the Authorized King James Version, and Mormons continue to use it. The LDS church has a distribution center in Salt Lake City from which one may obtain a cross-referenced Authorized King James Version with footnotes to the so-called Standard Works, the canon of the LDS church, composed of the Bible, the Book of Mormon, the Doctrine and Covenants, and the Pearl of Great Price. The New King James Version commissioned in 1975 by Thomas Nelson Publishers has no official standing in Mormonism. The Mormon insistence on the retention of the Authorized King James Version parallels some forms of Evangelical Protestantism.[22] However, the LDS attitude to the Bible is somewhat different from the attitude of at least many Evangelicals. For Mormons, the Bible is not free of error, and therefore Mormons will sometimes disagree with it. Their standard of truth is the Mormon prophets, who they believe have from the beginning delivered revelations and messages sometimes correcting the Bible. First Nephi 13:26–27 of the Book of Mormon blames the Catholic Church for the corruption of Scripture.

In 2014, a "Gospel Topics" posting on the LDS website, subsequently picked up by the non-Mormon *Salt Lake Tribune*,[23] took up the question of the nature of LDS teaching on exaltation, or "becoming like God".[24] The *Tribune* story explained the doctrine of exaltation in the manner I have developed here. Thus, we can compare Mormon exaltation and Catholic deification. In sum, the LDS church continues to hold that Mormons may be exalted, become gods, while Catholicism holds that the difference between God the Creator and man the creature is a difference of being, in which the distance between God and man is infinite in the sense

[22] See Grant Adamson, "Luke 22:43–44 and the Mormon Jesus: Protestant Past, KJV-Only Present", *Journal of the Bible and Its Reception* 9.1 (2022): 53–73. See also, by a practicing Latter-day Saint, "Which Bible Should I Use?," Mormon Bible website, http://mormonbible.org /holy-bible/which-bible-should-i-use.

[23] Matthew Piper, "Essay Explains LDS Teaching on 'Becoming like God'", *Salt Lake Tribune*, February 28, 2014, http://archive.sltrib.com/story.php?ref=/sltrib/lifestyle/57597557 -80/god-says-lds-essay.html.csp.

[24] "Becoming like God", Church of Jesus Christ of Latter-day Saints website, accessed June 1, 2024, www.lds.org/topics/becoming-like-god?lang=eng. See also Richard Sherlock, "Becoming Like God: A Critique", in *The LDS Gospel Topics Series: A Scholarly Engagement*, ed. Matthew L. Harris and Newell G. Bringhurst (Salt Lake City: Signature Books, 2020).

that, beginning in this world, humans are called through *theosis* to become evermore godlike, which they are to do without limit, but they are not—and cannot become—gods. To the degree they become like God, even in the present life, they may be spoken of as living eschatologically, living as in heaven; but no degree of change will allow them to "jump species", change from being humans to being gods. Throughout eternity they will become evermore like God without becoming him.

6

Liturgy in Mormonism and Catholicism

Rachel Lu

There is an old Latin adage, *Lex orandi, lex credendi, lex vievendi.* (As we worship, so shall we believe, so shall we live.) This idea has always been central to the ethos of Catholicism, but its application is much broader. It is impossible to understand the ethos of any religion or sect without considering the question of worship.

Worship brings abstract claims into the lives of ordinary believers. In worship, the tenets of a faith find application (or not), of a sort that can sustain it across time and give it relevance in multiple societies and cultures. In a broad sense, worship tests a faith's viability, by measuring its applicability to lived human lives.

For two millennia, Catholics have worshipped God through a liturgical tradition that they can trace back to the time of the apostles. "Liturgy", meaning "public work" or "service done on behalf of the people", is understood by Christians to be the tradition by which God is publicly and communally adored. Through liturgy, Catholics orient themselves and their lives (individually and as a community) toward their Creator. Liturgy brings Catholicism to life.

Because the term "liturgy" is not part of the Mormon lexicon, it is necessary to ask, Do Mormons even have a liturgy? If not, what are the focal points of Mormon worship? Because Mormons reject most of the traditional Christian creeds and set liturgical forms, a fair amount of groundwork must be laid just to make comparison feasible.

At first glance, Mormons seem not to have a recognizable liturgical tradition. Further examination suggests that Mormons do have, if not liturgy per se, at least many similarities to Catholicism of a sort that would enable them to appreciate why liturgy matters. Mormonism is, in a recognizable sense, a historically grounded faith, with an appreciation of high ceremony and ritual. Moreover, Mormon ritual has a significant foundation in Mormon history and theology, and it is integrally connected to the theology and eschatology of the LDS church. So although we probably would not, in the end, say that Latter-day Saints have a liturgical tradition properly speaking, there is good reason to hope that the *subject* of liturgy can be a fertile ground for conversation.

In fact, discussion of worship might be especially useful when considering a faith like Mormonism, which lacks the sort of rarified philosophical tradition that Catholics enjoy. It can be difficult in scholarly discussions of Mormonism to determine who speaks authoritatively for the LDS church and whether particular claims should be considered settled dogma or not. It can be surprisingly difficult to answer the question, What do Mormons really believe about X?

By contrast, it is easy to answer questions about how Mormons spend their Sunday meetings. Where the theological tradition is diffuse, LDS worship is remarkably standardized. This is even a point of pride for many Mormons, who see the LDS church's organization and standardization as a significant accomplishment. And indeed, Mormons do achieve a kind of universality through this standardized template. Weekly Mormon meetings follow the same pattern no matter where in the world they are held.

This is a great advantage from the standpoint of scholarly discussion. The "orandi" element of mainstream Mormonism is quite easy to observe. Of course, there are also certain methodological constraints that arise in scholarly discussion of Mormon worship and ritual, most obviously relating to the secrecy of temple ritual. The most central LDS rituals take place in Mormon temples, which are open only to believers, who are forbidden from discussing the details of what occurs there. Some scholarly discussions of temple ritual do exist,[1] but there is no official or authoritative account of what happens in these ceremonies, or of the appropriate interpretation and

---

[1] David J. Buerger, *The Mysteries of Godliness: A History of Mormon Temple Worship* (Salt Lake City: Signature Book, 2002). This book does not include an account of current temple ceremonies, but extensive historical information is given about their development and the relevant influences.

symbolic significance. Moreover, it would be improper to ask Mormon scholars to comment on analysis that many would regard as sacrilegious or at least irreverent in what it chooses to reveal. We will have to work within the confines of this limitation, but it naturally limits our potential to draw substantive conclusions.

Even without specifics, though, we should still be able to examine larger trends within Mormon worship and then to draw on the Catholic understanding of liturgy by way of raising some probing questions. The first segment of this chapter, then, will examine what *does* occur in Mormon worship services, considering the role of ritual within chapel and temple Mormonism. The next section will consider the Catholic tradition, offering a fuller explanation of the significance liturgy plays within Catholicism. The third segment of this chapter will suggest ways in which the Mormon and Catholic approaches to worship are similar, while the fourth will consider how the differences between them might reflect back on theological differences. Finally, I will suggest some ways in which liturgy might give Catholicism a depth and universality that Mormonism does not obviously have. This might be a useful point of reflection and debate for Mormon and Catholic scholars alike.

I. Ritual in Ordinary Mormon Worship

A visitor to an ordinary Mormon worship service might easily walk away with the impression that Latter-day Saints have no liturgy. The organizing principles of Mormon worship are, in many respects, typically low church, devoid of the type of liturgical structure one would find in a Catholic, Orthodox, or Anglican meeting.

The standard three-hour Sunday meeting includes a congregational segment (known as sacrament meeting) and smaller Sunday school–type gatherings. Sacrament meeting is primarily dedicated to a series of short talks, typically given by members of the congregation on various assigned subjects. Members are scheduled to offer unscripted prayers. Congregational hymn singing rounds out the meeting, occasionally supplemented by a special musical performance of some sort.

The one obvious piece of liturgical action is the weekly distribution of communion, which Mormons refer to simply as "the sacrament".

This typically occurs at the beginning of the congregational meeting and involves two set prayers and the passing of bread and water. It is worth noting that the congregational meeting in which this occurs is called sacrament meeting, suggesting that the ritual is a high priority. Still, within the meeting itself, the sacrament is mostly a *sui generis* event. It is typically preceded by a single solemn hymn; apart from this, there is no preparatory liturgical action and no liturgical postlude. Once the sacrament has been passed, the meeting proceeds without further reference to it. (It is also interesting to note that this ritual occurs *only* in Sunday meetings. Unlike the Catholic Mass, it is never repeated on weekdays or added to weddings, funerals, or other significant occasions.)

Mormons voice many of the standard objections to set liturgical forms and creeds. Joseph Smith was adamantly opposed to the development of a set Mormon creed, suggesting that it would place unnecessary constraints on the consciences of members.[2] Of course Mormons also reject many of the theological claims of the traditional Christian creeds, which would obviously make them unsuitable for use in Mormon worship services. But the Mormon narrative makes much of the claim that mainline Christianity had (by the nineteenth century, when the LDS church was founded) ossified and become corrupt, mainly through unreflective fidelity to set doctrines and creeds.[3] It was precisely because he was dissatisfied with this state of affairs that Joseph Smith sought divine guidance and ultimately ended up as the prophet of the "restored gospel". Unsurprisingly then, Mormons retain a general suspicion of congregational recitation or anything else that might involve too many "vain repetitions".[4]

Mormon meetings are focused primarily on instruction, together with some participatory activities such as hymn singing. Storytelling, group discussion, and personal testimony are very central to Sunday meetings. Mormon worship also includes some activities more specifically targeted for spiritual renewal. In addition to extemporary prayer,

---

[2] See Richard Lyman Bushman, *Joseph Smith: Rough Stone Rolling*, repr. ed. (New York: Vintage, 2007), 275.

[3] Mormons typically refer to Joseph Smith's own account of this. See, e.g., Joseph Smith—History 1:17–19, in Pearl of Great Price (PGP).

[4] This is of course a reference to the Sermon on the Mount concerning prayer when Jesus said, "They think that they will be heard for their many words" (Mt 6:7); but Mormons often use it to refer to prayers that seem too scripted or archaic in language.

some meetings offer time for "bearing testimonies" (what some Protestant denominations refer to as "witnessing"), when members are invited to share personal stories about how God and the LDS church have influenced their lives. On top of this, members sometimes offer preplanned devotional reflections intended to help fellow members "feel the spirit".

The mood of a Mormon meeting is warm and community focused. Congregants discuss their faith, share one another's trials and triumphs, and participate in a kind of narrative tradition that brings the faith to life for most ordinary members. Of course Mormons are known as well for supporting community activities of all kinds, including sports, service projects, and many family-oriented events. In all of this, instruction and community building are high priorities, but ritual has a fairly muted role.

This is not to say that it is nonexistent, nor do Mormons spurn formality in general. Even to the casual visitor, it should be evident immediately that LDS worship is not in every respect low church. For example, Mormons have a clear sense of decorum when it comes to churchgoing. They dress formally, expecting women to wear skirts and encouraging men to wear button-down shirts and ties.[5] Mormons prefer solid, mainline hymnody to popular contemporary music. And even in testimony meetings, the tone is more solemn than charismatic. There is no shouting, fainting, or snake handling at a Mormon worship service.

Mormons also have certain rituals that take place outside the temple, with baptism and confirmation being the most obvious examples. Except in the case of adult converts, they are typically performed together when a child is eight years old. Any Mormon priesthood holder may baptize, so children are most often baptized by their fathers, and converts by the missionaries who taught them. These are not regular events, in that baptism and confirmation are normally experienced only once (though technically Mormons regard baptism as a repeatable sacrament in the case of excommunication). But they happen and are conducted solemnly and in accord with a very definite formula, proving that ritual is not per se inimical to the Mormon ethos.

[5] Christina Sterbenz, "Here's How Mormons Are Supposed to Dress", *Business Insider*, March 3, 2014, www.businessinsider.com/mormon-dress-code-2014-3.

A few other rites can be found in the course of ordinary Mormon life. The "laying on of hands" is still significant, and blessings can be given to the sick, or to anyone else especially in need of grace, by any holder of the Mormon priesthood.[6] (Interestingly, women sometimes gave ritual blessings in the early days of the church, but this is no longer done.[7]) Authorities also use the laying on of hands in a "setting apart" ritual to initiate a member to a particular "calling" (that is, to a position or job within the church). Setting apart happens frequently since it can be done not only for high leadership positions but also for more ordinary jobs like teaching Sunday school. (It is common and expected for active Mormons to hold a number of callings over the course of their adult lives.) Ritual blessing is a fairly ordinary part of mainstream Mormon life.

Other important Mormon rites are less visible, insofar as they ordinarily take place in the context of Mormon temples. Marriage and sealing are ordinarily done in the temple, along with a ritual (normally done in early adulthood) referred to as "the taking of endowments".

Temple ritual is something of a distinctive phenomenon, which is set apart from mainstream Mormon life and more directly connected to more idiosyncratic eschatological views of the Mormon faith. It merits separate consideration.

II. Temple Ritual

As mentioned above, scholarly discussion of temple ritual can be difficult, given that the LDS church asks members not to disclose the details publicly. Happily, we can at least say some general things. In temples, Mormons take oaths and perform rites that are intended to further their spiritual advancement. Mormon marriages take place in temples, and families that convert to the faith at a later stage in life are "sealed" together in temples so that they can (as Mormons believe) be united eternally as families.

---

[6] Some history on the practice of Mormon healing can be found in Jonathan A. Stapley and Kristine Wright, "The Forms and the Power: The Development of Mormon Ritual Healing to 1847", *Journal of Mormon History* 35, no. 3 (July 1, 2009): 42–87.

[7] Jonathan A. Stapley and Kristine Wright, "Female Ritual Healing in Mormonism", *Journal of Mormon History* 37, no. 3 (January 1, 2011): 1–85.

In addition to this, mature Mormons are expected to go through an "endowment" ceremony, which is a kind of initiation to adult Mormon society. (For those raised in the LDS faith, this is most commonly done either prior to one's wedding or before leaving for missionary service.) The term "endowment" comes from the dedication of the first Mormon temple in Kirtland, Ohio, where members reported a Pentecost-like experience in which the Holy Spirit suddenly moved people to prophesy and speak in tongues. Of course this experience cannot be re-created on demand, but the modern endowment ceremony does capture some of the same sense of initiation for Mormon adults, with members being washed and anointed as well as receiving instruction reserved for the initiated.[8]

Mormons believe that these rituals objectively accomplish something for the members who participate in them, enabling them to attain higher levels of postmortem advancement than would otherwise be possible. From its founding in the Second Great Awakening, Mormonism has promised members a path to a particularly exalted realm of heaven that is not accessible to the uninitiated. Temple ritual is integral to that process of salvation; without receiving the necessary rites, members cannot attain the highest available levels of salvation.[9]

This ties into the Mormon valuing of marriage and family, since for Mormons these have eschatological significance as well as this-worldly value. Contemporary Mormons often claim that their temple marriages can last "for time and all eternity" and that "families can be together forever", and Mormons sometimes teach that marriage is a necessary prerequisite to the attainment of the highest level of salvation. Historically, temples were used to integrate people into the Mormon family in more obviously familial ways, for example, through the "adoption" (via temple rite) of adult Mormons by new "parents" who had already been selected among the elite who were to be saved.[10] Polygamy in

---

[8] "The Endowment", 27.2 in "Temple Ordinances for the Living", Church of Jesus Christ of Latter-day Saints website, accessed May 16, 2024, www.churchofjesuschrist.org/study /manual/general-handbook/27-temple-ordinances-for-the-living?lang=eng#title_number11.

[9] Regarding marriage, for example, see President Spencer W. Kimball, "The Importance of Celestial Marriage", *Ensign*, October 1979, available at www.lds.org/ensign/1979/10/the -importance-of-celestial-marriage?lang=eng.

[10] Jonathan A. Stapley, "Adoptive Sealing Ritual in Mormonism", *Journal of Mormon History* 37, no. 3 (2011): 53–117.

the early LDS church was likewise tied to its salvation narrative, with higher levels of exaltation promised to those who were willing to practice it.[11]

After participating in the temple rituals, special clothing is worn to signify the commitments made therein, and members may then (presuming they remain in good standing with the church) return to the temple to perform the same rituals on behalf of the deceased. The Mormon emphasis on genealogy is partly grounded in this belief that the dead may need assistance in order to pass through the spiritual rites they likely were not offered in life. Mormons are often reminded that the dead, including their own relations, are frustrated in their efforts at postmortem development, owing to the lack of baptism and endowments.

Largely for this reason, temple visits are encouraged, and Mormons frequently refer to what happens there as "temple work". There is a clear sense of accomplishment associated with the rituals that are performed, and while temple visits may of course provide occasion for personal reflection, meditative communion with God is not the primary focus or goal.[12]

As in many other areas of life, then, Mormons focus their temple activity on measurable achievement. Temples are a place in which Mormons in good standing can take steps toward higher levels of fulfillment, with the promise that this fulfillment will have an eschatological dimension as well as an earthly one. Temples are special for Mormons, and their specialness is preserved in large part by keeping the knowledge esoteric and reserving the rituals for a proven elite. Objectively advancing the Kingdom of God is the primary justification.

III. What Is Liturgy?

In order to compare Mormon and Catholic approaches to worship, we should now ask, What is Catholic liturgy? How does it function

[11] For an extended discussion of the ideological significance of polygamy in the early LDS church, see Merina Smith, *Revelation, Resistance, and Mormon Polygamy: The Introduction and Implementation of the Principle, 1830–1853* (Logan: Utah State University Press, 2013).

[12] Rachel Bruner, "8 Reasons Why Temples Are Important to Mormons", LearnReligions .com, June 25, 2019, www.learnreligions.com/why-lds-temples-important-to-mormons -2159559.

within Catholic life? Why do Catholics regard this as the most fitting form of worship, and what benefit do they derive from it?

Liturgy is public worship, offered from God's people to their Creator. Its primary purpose is to give honor to God, whom Catholics regard as the Creator of all that exists or will ever exist and as the omnipotent, omnipresent, and entirely benevolent Being that holds all other things in existence at every moment. No further justification is needed for worship than that it is fitting and richly merited. Reality itself demands that we give honor to God.

At the same time, worship is also beneficial to humans. By honoring our Creator, we orient ourselves toward the good and true, and the effects of that right orientation will be seen in every other element of our lives and character. The Catholic tradition continually affirms that God is both the beginning and the proper end of all creation and, more particularly, of human beings. As Saint Augustine famously wrote, "For Thou has made us for Thyself and our hearts are restless till they rest in Thee."[13] Thus, by worshipping God fittingly, we are better able to understand ourselves, and indeed everything else that exists.[14]

How does one worship the true and living God fittingly? This is a deep and mysterious question, since God is far greater than men and also entirely self-sufficient, such that he does not actually need our adoration. There is no reason to expect that we can work out, through mere personal reflection, the sort of activity that would be most pleasing to God. God is infinitely great and mysterious, so it is not generally possible to use personal experience as a reliable source in determining his will.

Fortunately, God has revealed himself to mankind in a variety of ways over the course of history. The Bible is an account of God's self-revelation to the Jews, culminating in the Incarnation and the

[13] Augustine, *Confessions* 1, 1, trans. F.J. Sheed, intro and notes Peter Brown, ed. with notes Michael P. Foley, 2nd ed. (Indianapolis: Hackett Publishing, 2006).

[14] "One must first know, for instance, man's last end and the supremacy of the Divine Majesty; after that, our common duty of submission to our Creator; and, finally, the inexhaustible treasures of love with which God yearns to enrich us, as well as the necessity of supernatural grace for the achievement of our destiny, and that special path marked out for us by divine Providence in virtue of the fact that we have been united, one and all, like members of a body, to Jesus Christ the Head." (Pope Pius XII, Encyclical on the Sacred Liturgy *Mediator Dei* [November 20, 1947], no. 32, www.vatican.va/content/pius-xii/en/encyclicals/documents/hf_p-xii_enc_20111947_mediator-dei.html.)

founding of the Church. Catholics see the history of the Church as a kind of ongoing narrative of God's continued self-revelation to human beings. Although the Church teaches that the Scripture is complete—that is, the Bible is the only written Word of God—"it has not been made completely explicit; it remains for Christian faith gradually to grasp its full significance over the course of the centuries."[15] This includes Christ's revelation to the apostles but goes on to encompass the activity of the Magisterium (the official hierarchy of the Church) and the miracles and inspired words of the Doctors and saints. If we want to gain more perspective on God's relationship to human beings, we should reflect thoughtfully on the ongoing relationship he has forged with us, first through the people of Israel and then through the Church. God has reached out to us, most obviously through the Person of Jesus Christ, but also through this ongoing series of historical interactions. He does this precisely to enable us to orient ourselves toward him, drawing us back toward our final end, which is resting in his presence.[16]

Here we encounter a difficulty. God's salvific work spans centuries of human history, and in an obvious temporal sense, the most important chapter took place two millennia ago with the life (and also death and Resurrection) of Christ. But I am, as a finite human, specially and temporally bound to a particular time and place. What relationship can I realistically have to events that are so far removed from me, and at the same time, so absolutely critical to my own relationship to God (and ultimately my own salvation)? Through the Person of Jesus, God reached out to us by becoming man, but as incredible as that is, it may not really make our approach to the divine so much easier if even the Incarnation is so far removed from us temporally that we are unable to relate or participate in it in a meaningful way.

Catholic liturgy helps us deal with these challenges. It has developed organically over the Church's long life (and also reflects elements of Jewish religiosity from before the time of Christ), and it encompasses and reflects the most important elements of God's

---

[15] *Catechism of the Catholic Church*, no. 66.

[16] Further discussion can be found in Joseph Cardinal Ratzinger, *The Spirit of the Liturgy*, 2nd ed. (San Francisco: Ignatius Press, 2014).

historical self-revelation. The goal is to help mediate the gap between God and man, but that is done in part by mediating distances of time and space.[17]

The centerpiece of Catholic liturgical life is of course the Mass, which is in turn built around the sacrifice of Christ's Body and Blood on the altar.[18] Of course, Catholics believe that this sacrament involves a real, metaphysical transformation of ordinary bread and wine into Christ's own Flesh and Blood. Receiving Communion is not merely a means of remembering Christ's redemptive offering of himself for mankind. It is literally a means of taking Christ into oneself, enabling the believer actually to participate in a small way in this saving event. And because they believe that the one sacrifice of Christ's body is *re-presented* in every Mass,[19] Catholics can see themselves as contemporaries of the salvific act that makes true worship (and their own salvation) possible.

The Mass is a rich collection of images, references, and invocations of important persons and events from throughout history, all of which serve to draw us out of our own particular time and into communion with the whole Church (including both living and dead), with all different points of our salvation history (including those that are yet to come), and finally, with God. Biblical passages are read, saints are invoked, and almost every word and detail connects us to some other era of salvation history. Because God is most clearly seen through the lens of this extended interaction with mankind, this liturgical approach is, as Catholics understand it, the most fitting way to approach him. Although Mass is not literally timeless (in the sense that the clock does keep ticking), it is meant as a kind of removal from the idiosyncrasies of particular times and places, which enables a far more fitting sort of worship than any of us could devise alone.[20]

---

[17] A masterful exploration of this theme of universality can be found in Joseph Cardinal Ratzinger, *The Spirit of the Liturgy*, trans. John Saward, with *The Spirit of the Liturgy*, by Romano Guardini, trans. Ada Lane, commemorative ed. (San Francisco: Ignatius Press, 2020).

[18] A helpful discussion of the symbolic language of the Mass can be found in Romano Guardini, *Sacred Signs*, trans. G. C. H. Pollen, S.J. (London: Sheed & Ward, 1937).

[19] "The Eucharist is thus a sacrifice because it *re-presents* (makes present) the sacrifice of the cross." (*Catechism of the Catholic Church*, no. 1366.)

[20] For more discussion on the history of the Mass, see Adrian Fortescue, *The Mass: A Study of Roman Liturgy* (London: Longmans, Green, 1912).

Obviously, it is essential that Catholic liturgy comes to us through a long-standing tradition, which has been shaped and honed across many centuries. Liturgy changes, but the changes are organic. They should reflect not the revisionist impulse of the reformer but rather the continued unfolding of God's relationship to the Church and to human beings. The organic development of the liturgy actually helps incorporate today's Christians into that ongoing narrative, which will in turn be passed on to future generations until the end of time.

It is telling that critics of liturgy tend to complain that it is both inscrutable and archaic. With a proper understanding of what liturgy actually is, we can see that good liturgy will inevitably inspire those complaints from the ignorant or the uninitiated. If liturgy were always readily comprehensible, it could not draw us out of our worldly concerns and invite us to contemplate the mystery that is God. The Mass does indeed contain far greater riches, symbolically and metaphysically, than even the best-educated worshipper can possibly appreciate. In that sense it is somewhat inscrutable. We can understand elements of it, but no mere mortal understands it completely, because we cannot fully understand tradition, much less God himself.

At the same time, liturgy is not completely beyond the grasp of even a young child. The words and actions are meant to make an impression even—or sometimes especially—on the minds of the simple and the untutored. Those who understand relatively little on the level of intellect are still engaged through sounds, visual images, and even body postures that shape the sensibilities in a salutary way.[21] The Mass is designed precisely for the purpose of setting finite humans on the path toward the ineffable and the infinite, and it offers something of value to people of all ages or levels of education, so long as they enter into it with a real intention to worship God.

Just as the Mass necessarily moves beyond our understanding, so, too, it necessarily moves beyond our particular culture or temporal era. This is why it can easily be dismissed as archaic, ossified, or out

[21] More information on the significance of the details of the Mass can be found in Jimmy Akin, *Mass Appeal: The ABCs of Worship* (San Diego: Catholic Answers, 2003); Jimmy Akin, *Mass Revision: How the Liturgy Is Changing and What It Means for You* (San Diego: Catholic Answers, 2011); George J. Moorman and R. Michael Schmitz, *The Latin Mass Explained: Everything Needed to Understand and Appreciate the Traditional Latin Mass* (Rockford, IL: TAN Books, 2007). Also see Ratzinger, *Spirit of the Liturgy*.

of touch with a given era. It would be more correct to say that it is in touch with so many eras at once that it cannot properly be fit into one alone. If it were recognizably a product of one time, it could not help mediate the temporal gap between a given era and the larger narrative of salvation that it makes present to Christians of every particular age. It spans an enormous stretch of time and thus appears strange and alien to those who are themselves so time-bound that they have little appreciation of that larger history. Nevertheless, true liturgy is one of the few things in the world that can never truly be archaic. It is of very grave and immediate importance to everyone, at all times.

People occasionally ask, What do modern Catholics get from their Mass attendance? Given how precipitously Mass attendance has declined throughout the Western world, many people evidently feel they do not get anything of significance from the Mass. Properly understood, it is inappropriate to begin with this query, because the Mass is for worship. Any benefits that accrue to the worshipper come precisely through the good of honoring God fittingly. And because the Eucharist, as with each of the sacraments, is a cause of grace, it makes us holy. We can see in the Old Testament what happens to the people of Israel when they lose sight of God's greatness and focus instead on their own communal needs. They build idols, become decadent, and fall away from the true God. Worship is fruitless, and often spiritually dangerous, when it is not properly centered on the one Being who is truly worthy of human worship.

At the same time, the Mass is also profoundly human and speaks to the moral and spiritual quandaries of every age. That is because it is attuned to the narrative that is most significant to all human societies, which encompasses mankind's creation, fall, and salvation, as well as our ultimate glorification in the eschatological fulfillment that is to come.

To a great extent, Catholic spiritual life consists in an ongoing effort to be worthy of the goods that are already immediately in our midst. Because it involves Christ's own literal presence at the altar, the Mass is as significant an event as can occur in Catholic life. Of course Catholics still take particular pleasure in events of this-worldly significance, such as nuptial Masses, papal Masses, and so forth. But even a major world event (such as, say, a papal funeral) cannot really upstage the metaphysical significance Catholics attach to every single Mass, whether it is said in St. Peter's Basilica or in a grass-roofed hovel. If Jesus Christ is the guest of honor, what earthly trappings could possibly upstage him?

For a Catholic, then, living up to the bounty of spiritual riches that are constantly in front of us is itself the project of a lifetime. The various requirements the Church imposes on every member, including weekly Mass attendance and at least once-annual confession of serious sins,[22] are intended to help us live the faith more fully.

In the most obvious and immediate sense, then, going to Mass may not seem to accomplish very much. Anyone inclined to argue the point, though, might reflect that the universality of the Mass is itself a remarkable sort of "accomplishment", which tells us much about why Catholicism still exists and claims more than a billion adherents worldwide,[23] while it has watched innumerable other religions and sects (which at various points appeared to have more momentum and energy) collapse into dust.

IV. Liturgy through an LDS Lens

Do Mormons have a liturgy? This question immediately raises an awkward point. Worship reflects underlying theological (and historical) assumptions, the validity of which may affect the authenticity of liturgy. To many Catholics the very term "liturgy" might imply certain sacramental realities that rather obviously cannot be found within Mormonism. In that sense, perhaps no one else has a "real" liturgy, except certain Eastern Rite and Orthodox groups whose sacraments the Catholic Church acknowledges to be valid.[24]

Since Mormons themselves have no attachment to the word, it will be as well to think of liturgy as the sort of long-standing, publicly

[22] The Catholic Church teaches that "after having attained the age of discretion, each of the faithful is bound by an obligation faithfully to confess serious sins at least once a year." (Catechism of the Catholic Church, no. 1457, citing canon 989.)

[23] Vatican News, "New Church Statistics Reveal More Catholics, Fewer Vocations", April 4, 2024, www.vaticannews.va/en/vatican-city/news/2024-04/vatican-central-statistical-office-church-pontifical-yearbook.html.

[24] Pope Paul VI, Decree on the Catholic Churches of the Eastern Rite Orientalium Ecclesiarum (November 21, 1964), www.vatican.va/archive/hist_councils/ii_vatican_council/documents/vat-ii_decree_19641121_orientalium-ecclesiarum_en.html#:~:text=For%20this%20reason%20it%20solemnly,antiquity%2C%20more%20harmonious%20with%20the.

accessible ritual tradition we find within Catholicism and to view Mormonism as a nonliturgical worship tradition that nevertheless includes significant ritual components.

From that standpoint, we can see that Mormons have a number of interesting similarities with Catholics that should enable them to appreciate the value of Catholic liturgy. Both faiths are grounded in a historical narrative, and both regard ritual as a metaphysically efficacious (and not merely commemorative) element of that narrative, which connects believers both to the historical origins of the faith and to its eschatological horizons.[25] Particularly in a society whose religious history is dominated by Protestant influences, this is an interesting point of similarity that might open the door to fruitful discussion.

As explained in the last section, Catholic liturgy serves as a kind of medium through which Catholics of a particular era are connected to the Church as a whole and to a larger narrative about God's ongoing relationship to human beings. Catholicism is a historical religion, but of course it is not *merely* historical; the history is incorporated organically into a living tradition, and liturgy serves as a medium through which members can literally become part of that tradition.

Mormons are in a position to appreciate this, in the first place because their faith is similarly dependent on a historical narrative that plays an essential role in defining their faith and eschatological horizons. There are certain irregularities to the Mormon story (discussed at greater length in the next section), which may make it difficult for them to develop a true liturgical tradition of the sort we find in a Catholic Mass. But the historical component is still significant; despite their assiduous concern for the temporal needs of members, Mormons are not focused exclusively on temporal affairs. They have a strong sense of religious exceptionalism and understand themselves with reference to a narrative that extends both backward (encompassing both Jesus Christ and Joseph Smith) and forward (looking ahead to the final dispensation and glorification in the celestial kingdom). That narrative is essential to their unique sense of identity, and it plays a significant role in motivating high levels of dedication and commitment among members, for which the LDS church is justifiably admired.

---

[25] "Baptism for the Dead", available at www.churchofjesuschrist.org/study/history/topics /baptism-for-the-dead.

To a considerable extent, the uniqueness of the Mormon *identity* depends on the uniqueness of the historical story the church tells. Mormonism claims to correct the mainstream Christian narrative at multiple points and also supplements it with further claims about events that took place on the American continent in the centuries before and immediately after Christ. As a uniquely Mormon story about God's interaction with his people here on the American continent, the Book of Mormon gives Latter-day Saints their own idiosyncratic, historically oriented identity. Of course, the contemporary story of the church's nineteenth-century founding (under the earthly leadership of Joseph Smith), of the persecution of the early Mormons in Ohio and Illinois, and of the eventual journey west to the Salt Lake Valley is also quite important to the Mormon self-understanding.

Mormonism has much to say about the future as well. Mormons tell a somewhat unique apocalyptic story[26] about the end of the world and the prophets of the last days. Initiated members are promised a special kind of exaltation in the world to come in the highest of three heavenly kingdoms (the celestial kingdom), where they may have the opportunity to become gods and create worlds of their own. (Here the Mormon interest in family recurs once again, with even godhood potentially being understood in a literally familial way.)

Mormons regard themselves as the contemporary heirs to the restored gospel, and that claim is plausible to them in large part because they believe they have the full truth that mainstream Christians lack, concerning both the past[27] and the future. Mormonism is in this sense a historically grounded faith, much like Catholicism.

On the level of worship, Mormonism clearly does not reflect this vision with the same level of ritual continuity that we find in Catholicism. Here Mormonism is more fragmented and relies more heavily on a tradition of storytelling and on its strength in community building. There are elements of Mormon spirituality that focus mainly on personal experience and "feeling the spirit", which is unsurprising

---

[26] Dan Wotherspoon, "65: LDS Views on Christ's Second Coming and the End Times", *Mormon Matters* (podcast), December 20, 2011, www.mormonmatters.org/podcast-item/65 -lds-views-on-christs-second-coming-and-the-end-times.

[27] In addition to the Book of Mormon, the LDS church also uses portions of Joseph Smith's corrected version of the King James Version Bible in the Pearl of Great Price. See Moses; Joseph Smith—Matthew, in PGP.

given that Mormonism was born in America's Second Great Awakening. High moral expectations, which are offered together with fairly comprehensive (and sensible) recommended life patterns, fuse together with historical and theological claims to give members a sense of structure and purpose.

At the same time, Mormons are certainly in a position to grasp that God can be better understood in the context of the long-standing relationship he has forged with his own people. Even their lifestyle recommendations are efficacious partly because they are part of the historical and theological narrative. For example, Mormons prohibit the use of alcohol and tobacco, grounding this prohibition in what they take to be direct revelation given to Joseph Smith and recorded in the Doctrine and Covenants. The marriage ceremony, which is performed in the temple, is believed to have metaphysical effects (which in the Mormon view can even extend to the postmortem). A sociologist or a physician could advise us to eat healthy food, avoid smoking, and stay married. For Mormons, though, this advice is bolstered by a more explicit divine sanction.[28]

If Mormonism is, in some sense, a historical faith, it is also one that regards its narrative-grounded rituals as metaphysically efficacious. This point of similarity might easily be missed, given the way Mormon ritual is largely concealed from the general public. But it is significant that Mormons, like Catholics, regard their salutary rituals as metaphysically significant and not merely symbolic. In fact, Mormons care so much about the literal, corporeal performance of temple rituals that they even call for proxies to complete the rites on behalf of the dead. Obviously, Mormons appreciate that ritual can play an important role in mediating man's approach to God.

This is particularly interesting in light of the debates Catholics have often had with Protestants concerning the nature of sacraments. Although it might seem at first glance that mainline Protestants are more liturgical than Mormons (because their worship resembles the Mass more closely), Catholics might consider that in some respects, Mormons have a more similar perspective on worship and ritual. Although

<hr>

[28] A discussion of the influence of religious belief on marriage (with commentary on Christian and Mormon customs) can be found in Loren Marks, "How Does Religion Influence Marriage? Christian, Jewish, Mormon, and Muslim Perspectives", *Marriage & Family Review* 38, no. 1 (December 22, 2005): 85–111, doi:10.1300/J002v38n01_07.

their weekly pattern of worship is more formalized, many Protestants regard their sacramental rituals as merely commemorative. Ritual is seen as a conduit to achieving desired interior dispositions; it is not physically or metaphysically efficacious. Given this tendency to stress interior dispositions over external acts, many Protestants are unable to understand why sacraments and other liturgical actions matter or how they could be real conduits to grace. Why confess to the priest when you can just confess to God in your mind? Why should reverent and respectful non-Catholics not receive Communion in a Catholic Mass?

In many ways, Mormon temple ritual is probably more analogous to Catholic sacraments than to liturgy as a whole (though obviously these are related).[29] Catholics also believe that their sacraments have eschatological significance. It is interesting, though, that Mormon rituals are normally done only once *in behalf of* a given person. This is not absolutely the case since Mormons will repeat baptism and confirmation for those who were previously excommunicated. But there are no rituals equivalent to the sacrament of confession and the reception of Communion, both of which, for Catholics, can be repeated regularly. Mormon ritual has more of the character of a rite of passage; Catholic sacraments are integrated into a process of moral development that is expected to include numerous lapses and the subsequent reception of reparative grace, though confirmation, matrimony, and holy orders are one-time events (except, of course, for widows and widowers who remarry).[30]

Despite these differences, Catholics and Mormons might find fruitful common ground in their shared belief that sacrament or ritual can have more than just a commemorative function. There are many interesting similarities, as, for example, in the significance both attach to marriage (which Catholics, unlike most Protestants, regard as a sacrament, and which Mormons view as a ritually established metaphysical bond extending beyond the grave). Both are concerned to see that rites are performed correctly, mainly because this affects their validity. Both view the body as having a proper and important role

---

[29] See Marcus von Wellnitz, "The Catholic Liturgy and the Mormon Temple", *Brigham Young University Studies* 21, no. 1 (January 1, 1981): 3–35.

[30] Invalid marriages are technically, under Catholic Church law, not real marriages. Thus, someone who "remarries" in the Church after living in an invalid marriage does not technically remarry.

in the process of justification. And both agree that worship and ritual are important in their own right, and not only for establishing the right sort of psychological and spiritual relationship between God and the individual believer; this is why rituals are offered through an authoritative body that connects the individual believer to the greater historical tradition by which those rituals were (divinely) established.

Obviously, Mormons and Catholics will have significant disagreements about the truth of their respective historical narratives and the efficacy of their respective rituals. Still, there are similarities to their perspectives that might make for fruitful discussion.

V. Mormonism through the Lens of Liturgy

Mormonism, despite its robust historical orientation, is a young faith that is still to a nontrivial extent rooted in the same soil where it was originally founded. The culture in which it is most thriving has a great deal of continuity with the one from which it originally came. As Western culture shifts (and perhaps declines), Mormons, together with Catholics, find themselves becoming more countercultural than they were in previous decades, and questions arise about the future of the organization and the faith.

In one way or another, of course, this is bound to happen to any religious movement. History moves onward and culture changes, rendering certain lifestyles obsolete. This inevitably puts pressure on religious people to sift through their creeds and customs and determine which elements are central and unchangeable and which can be adapted. If a religiously grounded culture is unable to adapt appropriately, its membership is likely to dwindle. On the other hand, if it sacrifices too many core elements of the faith for the sake of adaptation, it may become indistinguishable from the mainstream culture. This, too, causes membership to dwindle, eventually spelling the death of the movement.

Mormonism is not completely untested in this regard, and in many respects it appears to be well positioned to withstand a sustained cultural assault. The Latter-day Saints currently have significant financial resources, a significant membership, and a strong family- and community-oriented culture. Many people have found in Mormonism a kind of shelter from the storm of modern dysfunction, since it offers exactly the kind of advice and structure that modern people so desperately need. Catholics look at Mormonism with justifiable envy, considering their success in promoting marriage and curbing addiction, in persuading members to attend church and contribute to the community, and in retaining their own children in the faith.

At the same time, Mormonism is still in many respects a recognizably American faith, steeped in an American ethos of industry and personal perfection. As history and culture shift, how well will it adapt itself to whatever new conditions arise? Catholics may feel more confidence here, precisely because their faith is so thoroughly time-tested and rooted in such well-honed intellectual and liturgical traditions. For Mormons, it might be worthwhile to reflect at least on how liturgy has bridged those cultural and historical gaps within Catholicism, giving rise to a billion Roman Catholics across the world who even today continue to pray using many of the same words as did their coreligionists from centuries past. Are these really "vain repetitions"? If (as the Mormon narrative sometimes suggests) Catholicism is anachronistic and ossified, what has enabled it to survive and adapt in such a remarkable way?

There are many respects in which Mormon worship practices are revealing of a broader Mormon ethos. Mormons reject the notion of original sin and regard earthly life as a kind of school for spiritual development toward the ultimate goal of celestial (perhaps even godly) greatness. Perhaps unsurprisingly, their ordinary services focus on instruction, and their temple rites function as entry points to higher levels of personal advancement. Church services and temple rites are both components of the Mormon "school of life", oriented toward helping members progress.

Mormons are known for being industrious, conscientious, and community minded, and their worship reflects all these goods. Mormons also place a great deal of emphasis (not just communally but also eschatologically) on family, and their temple rites reflect this as well. Couples are married and families are sealed "for time and all eternity",[31] and all Mormon rituals tend to emphasize inclusion in a larger

---

[31] Parley P. Pratt, ed., *Autobiography of Parley P. Pratt* (Salt Lake City: Deseret Book Company, 1938), 260.

celestial family. Performing rites on behalf of the dead makes sense in light of the commitment to family and community and also in light of the focus on spiritual advancement. It helps build the kingdom and assists deceased ancestors by offering them the chance to progress through the same stages of celestial development.

In all these respects, Mormon worship is readily understandable. But it is not as clear whether it can achieve the breadth, depth, and universality of Catholic liturgy. Looking at Mormon services and temple rituals from a Catholic perspective, some questions arise. First, to what extent (and in what way) are Mormon services focused on worshipping God? Second, how effectively does Mormon worship connect members to its larger historical narrative? Third, how do Mormons deal with the realities of human limitation and the fact that man is imperfect, sinful, and bound in space and time?

All three questions really speak to a single larger theme. Worship should be a medium for connecting us to something larger. For Catholics, it connects us first to God, second to a much larger human community (extending across time), and third to truths about ourselves. If a worship tradition is deficient in any or all of these areas, its broader relevance and longevity are likely to be affected.

As mentioned above, liturgy is first and foremost intended to orient Catholics toward God in an act of worship. Mormons also seek to worship God, but because Mormons and Catholics have divergent views about God's nature, we would naturally expect certain differences in their approach to worship.

Catholic worship makes sense in light of the Catholic affirmation of divine simplicity. God is perfection itself, and so orientation toward God (as achieved through the mediation of the liturgy and the Church) is the key to every other virtue. Mormons, by contrast, have no doctrine of divine simplicity and sometimes portray God as a kind of superpowerful but still-finite Being who mentors his human children through a process of maturation that he himself has already experienced. It makes sense, then, that worship would focus less on a final goal of union with God (in something like the Beatific Vision) and more on carrying out God's instructions for navigating the school of life with success.

What does it actually mean to Mormons to acknowledge God as divine? This is a complicated question. Certainly, Mormon church services include prayers of thanks, appeals for divine aid, and so forth.

Mormons also place great emphasis on reading the Bible and talk constantly about Jesus Christ. Pictures of Jesus and of various Bible stories are ubiquitous in Mormon churches and homes. The general attitude of reverence toward God and Jesus Christ seems to qualify as worship.[32]

There are other respects, however, in which the Mormon idea of a "mentoring God" clearly affects their posture with respect to the divine. At the same time, the theme of sacrifice is fairly muted within church services. (Whether this is equally true of temple ritual is obviously hard to assess given the lack of specifics.) Mormons display pictures of Jesus but rarely depict Christ's death, and they do not use crucifixes. The Mormon doctrine of salvation actually deemphasizes Christ's death as such and places greater emphasis on the intercessory prayer offered in the Garden of Gethsemane. In times of distress, Mormon members are encouraged to pray, but the phrase "offer it up" has very little currency within Mormon culture. Mormons sometimes actually refer to Jesus Christ as an "elder brother", suggesting a figure who can offer insight and help to struggling mortals mainly in light of greater experience, rather than ontological superiority.[33]

Again, this makes a certain kind of sense given a "plan of salvation"[34] that is mainly developmental. Sacrifice, however, is generally a critical component of a sort of worship that seeks to bridge the gap between mere mortals and the divine. If Mormon worship minimizes the role of sacrifice, that might reflect a general perspective on God as the sort of being who does not clearly require sacrifice, because the gap between him and his creatures is mostly one of degree.

Returning to the question of universality, this brings us to an important point. In the Mormon conception, God himself is less universal than in the traditional theology of the Catholic Church. The Mormon God is not truth, beauty, and goodness personified, nor is he the single source of all being. Catholics worship God as the

[32] A sympathetic perspective on the Mormon view of God can be found in Terryl Givens and Fiona Givens, *The God Who Weeps: How Mormonism Makes Sense of Life*, 1st ed. (Salt Lake City: Ensign Peak, 2012).

[33] Christ's role within Mormonism is discussed in Douglas J. Davies, *Joseph Smith, Jesus, and Satanic Opposition* (Burlington, VT: Ashgate, 2010).

[34] "Plan of Salvation", Church of Jesus Christ of Latter-day Saints website, accessed May 21, 2024, www.churchofjesuschrist.org/study/manual/gospel-topics/plan-of-salvation?lang=eng.

ultimate, ontologically universal Being, but Mormons regard God more as a very important character in a unique Mormon narrative, and their worship reflects that difference. This in itself may speak to the Mormon potential to translate a particular faith and culture into a universally applicable faith.

This point might become important when we move on to the question of historical connectedness. Catholic liturgy, as previously explained, uses history and tradition as an entry point for bridging the infinite gap between God and man. Mormonism also draws on history and tradition in defining a unique identity and mission, but the need to create a "timeless" entry point into salvation history might be less intense for Mormons, simply because the envisioned gap between humans and God is less daunting. If, as Joseph Smith claimed, God was once as we ourselves are, our own personal experiences in this life might give us some nontrivial insight into God's own nature.

Mormons face a few other challenges when it comes to weaving a universally applicable historical narrative. I will here mention just three questions that all merit attention. First, is the Mormon narrative plausible? Second, can it credibly claim to extend across human history? And third, are Mormons ritually connected to their faith in such a way that the narrative can withstand dramatic cultural change?

The first question is familiar enough to Mormon-interested scholars that it requires little elaboration here. The Book of Mormon in particular raises questions about historical accuracy. The Mormon narrative definitely claims it as a literal, not just allegorical, account of events on the American continent. Can those events reasonably be held to be accurate given other things that we know, from European history, geography, archaeology, and the oral histories of Native American tribes? If not, that is obviously a problem for a faith that views itself as having a foundation in literal historical events.

Concerning the extension of the Mormon narrative across history, we encounter a difficulty in the Mormon doctrine of the Great Apostasy, that period of time in which Christian Europe is said to have lost the true gospel and the authority of the true priesthood. In Mormon lore, the Great Apostasy covers a considerable period of time; by most accounts, this faithless period begins within a century or so after Christ and continues up to the time of the gospel's restoration under the leadership of Joseph Smith. In other words, the great majority of Christian history is, for Mormons, part of the apostasy. While that obviously bolsters the Mormon sense of exceptionalism, it weakens their claim to have a universally applicable historical narrative. Mormons need to answer these questions: What was God doing vis-à-vis human beings during this period? Why was it permitted to go on for so long, and what was accomplished during that time? How should contemporary Mormons relate to the traditions developed by mainstream Christians during those years? Without offering nuanced answers to those questions, sustaining an enduring and historically connected narrative may be difficult.

Finally, there is the question of Mormon ritual and its potential to serve as a vehicle for sustaining Mormon belief and practice. Mormons do have their own robust culture of salvation,[35] which incorporates temple ritual into a broader effort to restore the gospel and induct members into a celestial family. As noted above, there are recognizable similarities to Catholic sacraments, and it is also interesting to note that temple ritual has evolved over time, reflecting an "organic" ideal that is similar to what we see in Catholic liturgy.[36] On the other hand, temple ritual plays a relatively small role in the life of most Mormons. It plays no direct role at all in the formation of young people (who are not permitted to know what happens in the temple), and temple visits are for most adult Mormons a relative rarity. The Mormon tradition and ethos are communicated mainly through story and catechesis, as well as through communal events. Ritual and sacramental action are a relatively minor component in ordinary Mormon life.

An oral (or written) narrative tradition can often be quite effective for communicating an origin story and corresponding sense of purpose within a particular culture.[37] The question to consider is whether they can endure through historical and cultural change without the added element of ritual. "Vain repetitions" can sometimes serve as an effective means of preserving core elements of a religious culture and creed,

---

[35] For a helpful discussion of salvation themes within Mormon culture, see Douglas J. Davies, *The Mormon Culture of Salvation: Force, Grace and Glory* (Aldershot, UK: Ashgate, 2000).

[36] Buerger discusses some of these changes in his *Mysteries of Godliness*.

[37] An admirable discussion of the vitality of Mormon culture can be found in Terryl L. Givens, *People of Paradox: A History of Mormon Culture*, 1st ed. (Oxford; New York: Oxford University Press, 2007).

while allowing more idiosyncratic elements of particular cultural manifestations of the faith to shift over time. This is something to consider when reflecting on the longer-term prospects of the LDS faith.

Finally, we come to the question of liturgy and finitude. An interesting element of Mormonism is its rather optimistic view of human nature and potential. Even leaving aside the question of whether we can become gods, the Mormon "plan of salvation" is relentlessly focused on helping members progress, and their programs and rhetoric all display a certain confidence that people can and will do this. Admittedly, repentance and forgiveness are also recurring themes of some Mormon talks and lessons. Testimony meetings often have an element of "confession" to them as members relate their struggles to live the faith.

Even so, sin and forgiveness are not the focal points either of prayer or of ritual to even remotely the same extent that we see in Catholicism. Whereas every Catholic Mass includes an act of contrition, no portion of Mormon worship is specifically devoted to recalling sin. There is no specific ritual or sacrament for granting forgiveness, apart from, oddly, excommunication and rebaptism.[38] (The Catholic Church reserves excommunication for those who reject the authority of the Church or commit an egregious sin.[39]) Mormons do fast on one Sunday of each month, but they have no penitential seasons (such as Advent or Lent) and obviously no corresponding liturgical action.

All these points are raised for the sake of considering to what extent Mormonism can respond to the human condition in all its remarkable breadth. Does Mormon culture "succeed" at least in part by taking advantage of a kind of self-selection, and if so, how might that affect the faith's universality and longevity?

One of the marks of good liturgy is that it is able to reach people where they are, in all their sin and imperfection, while also moving beyond them, drawing them to greater levels of human perfection. How broad is Mormonism's "range" in this regard? Can it "work"

---

[38] Elder M. Russell Ballard of the Quorum of the Twelve, "A Chance to Start Over: Church Disciplinary Councils and the Restoration of Blessings", Ensign, September 1990, www.lds.org/ensign/1990/09/a-chance-to-start-over-church-disciplinary-councils-and-the -restoration-of-blessings?lang=eng.

[39] For example, according to the Code of Canon Law, someone who procures an abortion incurs latae sententiae, or automatic, excommunication (canon 1397 §2).

for everyone, or is it tailored more to particular types? Most especially, does its characteristically American emphasis on achievement and perfection handicap it when it comes to navigating the realities of human weakness and sin?

VI. Conclusion

Comparing Catholic and Mormon worship is difficult in something like the way it is difficult to compare the life habits of a wizened old grandfather and a healthy young boy. One is a model of activity, brimming with life and energy; the other may seem more stagnant, but there is more to most of his words and habits than immediately meets the eye. How successfully will the boy's habits propel him ahead to a thriving, successful life? We can make certain guesses, but they will all be the stuff of speculation.

Of course the analogy is not perfect, especially insofar as it threatens to relativize the quest for truth that is ultimately the justification for all worship. Even so, it may be helpful in certain respects to think of worship as a religious community's "habits" and to contextualize that within a faith's historical development. Mormons often evaluate themselves using sociological indicators (like marriage and retention rates), and by that standard, the LDS church is in an enviable state of health. But if a true faith is one that will apply yesterday, today, and tomorrow, using that standard of comparison may be more like comparing the blood pressure of the boy to his aged grandfather. It is good, of course, to be healthy in childhood, but that in itself will not enable a person to survive for a century.

Thinking in those terms may prompt a useful sort of self-evaluation. Mormonism should not be dismissed simply because it arose relatively recently, here in the United States. Christ, too, lived in a particular place and time. But does Mormonism have the breadth, depth, and universality to transcend its time and place? Only time will tell for certain, but in the meanwhile, worship may be our richest source of insight.

7

Catholicism, Mormonism, and Eucharistic Realism

Francis J. Beckwith and Alexander Pruss

Does anything *really happen* to the bread and wine at the celebration of the Lord's Supper? Do they remain mere bread and wine, do they become sacred objects of some sort, or are they literally transformed into the Body and Blood of Christ? Although Latter-day Saints and Catholics hold contrary views on this question, each group calls communion a sacrament, and each believes that this sacrament is essential to their worship. In the Doctrine and Covenants (DC), a book in the LDS canon of Scripture, the Mormon prophet Joseph Smith instructs the faithful on the appropriate content of their sacrament meeting:

> The elders or priests are to have a sufficient time to expound all things concerning the church of Christ to their understanding, previous to their partaking of the sacrament [i.e., communion].... It is expedient that the church meet together often to partake of bread and wine in the remembrance of the Lord Jesus; and the elder or priest shall administer it; and after this manner shall he administer it—he shall kneel with the church and call upon the Father in solemn prayer, saying: "O God, the Eternal Father, we ask thee in the

Francis Beckwith is the primary author of this chapter's introductory comments as well as section I and the conclusion. Alexander Pruss is the primary author of section II.

name of thy Son, Jesus Christ, to bless and sanctify this bread to the souls of all those who partake of it, that they may eat in remembrance of the body of thy Son, and witness unto thee, O God, the Eternal Father, that they are willing to take upon them the name of thy Son, and always remember him and keep his commandments which he has given them; that they may always have his Spirit to be with them. Amen."[1]

In her *Catechism*, the Catholic Church offers an account of what happens at her Mass that is not entirely dissimilar from Smith's prescription of the LDS sacrament meeting:

The liturgy of the Eucharist unfolds according to a fundamental structure which has been preserved throughout the centuries down to our own day. It displays two great parts that form a fundamental unity:

- the gathering, the liturgy of the Word, with readings, homily, and general intercessions;
- the liturgy of the Eucharist, with the presentation of the bread and wine, the consecratory thanksgiving, and communion....

The essential signs of the Eucharistic sacrament are wheat bread and grape wine, on which the blessing of the Holy Spirit is invoked and the priest pronounces the words of consecration spoken by Jesus during the Last Supper: "This is my body which will be given up for you.... This is the cup of my blood" [cf. Lk 22:19–20][2]

In order to help our LDS friends better understand the Catholic view of the Eucharist, we will first explain both the Catholic and LDS positions, with an emphasis on the historical and biblical warrant for the Catholic view, and then we will show why the Catholic view makes sense philosophically.

---

[1] DC 20:68, 75–77. In modern LDS sacrament meetings, water has replaced wine and not everyone present at the meeting kneels, just the one offering the sacrament prayer. See "Preparing the Sacrament", 20.4, and "Blessing and Passing the Sacrament", 20.4.3, in *Handbook 2: Administering the Church* (Salt Lake City: Church of Jesus Christ of Latter-day Saints, 2010), www.churchofjesuschrist.org/bc/content/shared/content/english/pdf/language-materials/08702_eng.pdf?lang=eng.
[2] *Catechism of the Catholic Church*, nos. 1346, 1412.

I. Distinguishing the Mormon and Catholic Views of the Eucharist[3]

I.A. The LDS View of the Eucharist

Because non-Mormon Christians disagree on the nature of communion, it is important to see where the Mormon view of the Lord's Supper is situated in the wider Christian world. Catholicism (as well as Orthodoxy) embraces eucharistic realism, the view that the bread and wine at Communion are literally transformed into the Body and Blood of Christ, with his soul and divinity being present as well, when they are consecrated by the priest celebrating the Mass, even though there is no change of appearance. Protestant Christians, on the other hand, hold a range of views about what happens to the bread and wine. Some believe it is not sacramental (as Catholics and many Protestants understand that term) but merely an ordinance that commemorates or memorializes Christ's death.[4] For these Christians, communion is merely symbolic. During the sixteenth-century Protestant Reformation, the leading proponent of this view was the Swiss theologian Huldrych Zwingli (1484–1531), though he was strongly opposed on this matter by Martin Luther (1483–1546) and John Calvin (1509–1564). Nevertheless, Zwingli's eucharistic theology seems to be the dominant view among American Evangelicals, most of whom are members of low-church ecclesial communions that do not have a history of sacramental theology. However, most Protestant churches that are in historical continuity with the Lutheran, Anglican, and Reformed

---

[3] Portions of this section are adapted from Francis J. Beckwith, "A Journey to Catholicism", in *Journeys of Faith: Evangelicalism, Eastern Orthodoxy, Catholicism, and Anglicanism*, ed. Robert L. Plummer (Grand Rapids, MI: Zondervan, 2012), 88, 99–103.

[4] In the Catholic Church, as in Eastern Orthodoxy, there are seven sacraments: baptism, penance, the Eucharist (Holy Communion), confirmation, matrimony, holy orders, and anointing of the sick. According to the Catholic Church, "Sacraments are efficacious signs of grace, instituted by Christ and entrusted to the Church, by which divine life is dispensed to us. The visible rites by which the sacraments are celebrated signify and make present the graces proper to each sacrament. They bear fruit in those who receive them with the required dispositions." (*Catechism of the Catholic Church*, no. 1131.) In many American Evangelical churches, only two are acknowledged—baptism and communion—but they are often called ordinances, since they are not considered means of grace. Rather, they are believed to be activities we should perform out of obedience to the commands of Christ.

(or Calvinist) movements of the Reformation reject the memorialist or symbolic view. They believe that Christ is in some way uniquely and really present in the celebration of the Eucharist,[5] though they do not accept the Catholic view.

The LDS church, though calling communion a sacrament, is in the memorialist camp. The Mormon prophet Joseph Smith taught that the bread and wine are "the *emblems* of the flesh and blood of Christ",[6] but, as one LDS scholar notes, "The emblems are symbolic, and do not physically change into the actual body and blood of Christ, as is believed to be the case with the concept of transubstantiation [which is another name for the Catholic view]."[7] The Mormon church holds that transubstantiation is an invention of the postapostolic Christian community. As one noted Brigham Young University historian puts it:

> The sermon that Jesus delivered on the topic of the "bread of life" in the Gospel of John draws on the symbolism of the Lord himself as "the living bread which came down from heaven." It also prefigures the ordinance of the Sacrament that he initiated later as a reminder to all that salvation comes only through "the living bread" and the "living water" (cf. John 6:48–58). In the postapostolic age, however, theologians transformed the symbolic nature of the Sacrament of the Lord's Supper into the dogma of transubstantiation, thereby introducing the notion that those who partake of the bread and wine miraculously ingest the literal body and blood of Christ, although the outward appearance of the emblems (i.e., the accidentals) remain the same. The LDS Church rejects this dogma and holds that the Sacrament is to help the Saints remember Jesus and that the transformation envisioned is a renovation of the human soul by the Spirit (D&C 20:75–79).[8]

---

[5] There are, of course, real differences between those who reject the memorialist view. However, exploring those differences is outside the scope of this chapter.

[6] DC 20:40 (emphasis added).

[7] Andrew C. Skinner, "Sacrament of the Lord's Supper", in *LDS Beliefs: A Doctrinal Reference*, by Robert L. Millet, Camille Fronk Olson, Andrew C. Skinner, and Brent L. Top (Salt Lake City: Deseret Book, 2011), 549.

[8] Paul B. Paxton, "Sacrament", in *The Encyclopedia of Mormonism*, ed. Daniel H. Ludlow (New York: Macmillan, 1992), 1244.

I.B. The Catholic View of the Eucharist

The Catholic Church affirms what we call eucharistic realism. As we have already noted, it is the belief that at the moment the bread and wine are consecrated by an ordained priest, they are literally transformed into the full Body and Blood of Jesus Christ, with his soul and divinity present by concomitance, even though the bread and wine still appear to be bread and wine. As the Church taught at the Council of Trent (1551):

> The holy council teaches and openly and plainly professes that after the consecration of bread and wine, our Lord Jesus Christ, true God and true man, is truly, really and substantially contained in the august sacrament of the Holy Eucharist under the appearance of those sensible things. For there is no repugnance in this that our Savior sits always at the right hand of the Father in heaven according to the natural mode of existing, and yet is in many other places sacramentally present to us in His own substance by a manner of existence which, though we can scarcely express in words, yet with our understanding illumined by faith, we can conceive and ought most firmly to believe is possible to God.[9]

The Church has a term for this transformation: "transubstantiation". It is a philosophical theory that the Church maintains best accounts for the change of the bread and wine at Consecration. The way the Church explains transubstantiation was influenced by Aristotle's distinction between substance and accident. Aristotle (384–322 B.C.), like many of his ancient contemporaries, wanted to account for how things change and yet remain the same. So, for example, a substance like an oak tree remains the same while undergoing accidental changes. It begins as an acorn and eventually develops roots, a trunk, branches, and leaves. During all these changes, the oak tree remains identical to itself. Its leaves change from green to red and then to brown and eventually fall off. But these accidental changes occur while the substance of the tree remains. On the other

---

[9] *The Canons and Decrees of the Council of Trent*, trans. H.J. Schroeder, O.P. (Rockford, IL: TAN Books, 1978), Session 8, chap. 1 (notes omitted).

hand, if we chopped down the tree and turned it into a desk, that would be a substantial change, since the tree would literally cease to be, and its parts would be turned into something else, a desk. But suppose that rather than turning it into a desk, we take the tree's dead parts and create a replica of the original living tree in such a way that it looks, feels, and smells just like the living one; that is, it would have many of the original tree's accidents—its appearance, feel, and smell—but there would still be a substantial change, as the result would not really be a living tree at all. This might be a case of humanly engineered transubstantiation.

According to the Church, when the bread and wine become the Body and Blood of Christ at Consecration, the accidents of the bread and wine do not change, but the substance of each changes. So it looks, tastes, feels, and smells like bread and wine, both to our unaided senses and to scientific instruments, but it literally has been miraculously changed into the Body and Blood of Christ. This is a case of transubstantiation by divine action.[10] The Church, of course, teaches that we can know this only by faith, informed by Scripture and tradition. As Saint Thomas Aquinas writes, "The presence of Christ's true body and blood in this sacrament cannot be detected by sense, nor understanding, but by faith alone, which rests upon Divine authority. Hence, on Luke 22:19: 'This is My body which shall be delivered up for you,' [Saint] Cyril [of Alexandria] says: 'Doubt not whether this be true; but take rather the Saviour's words with faith; for since He is the Truth, He lieth not.'"[11]

There are several reasons why it would be a mistake to dismiss the Catholic view of the Eucharist simply because of Aristotle's influence on its present formulation. First, Eastern Rite churches in communion

---

[10]The case of humanly engineered transubstantiation is only analogous, for with the human version, you could in principle detect the difference—e.g., one could investigate the new "tree's" molecular structure to show its true substance—whereas with miraculous transubstantiation, no amount of empirical examination could reveal the substance of Christ's Body and Blood in the accidents of bread and wine all the way down to the molecular level.

[11]Saint Thomas Aquinas, *Summa Theologica* III, q. 75, art. 1, trans. Fathers of the English Dominican Province, 2nd and rev. ed. (London: Burns, Oates & Washbourne, 1920), www.newadvent.org/summa/4075.htm. The citation from Saint Cyril of Alexandria (376–444) comes from his *Commentary on Luke* (Sermon 142), which is available online: www.tertullian.org/fathers/cyril_on_luke_13_sermons_135_145.htm#SERMON%20CXLII.

with the Catholic Church rarely employ the Aristotelian language of transubstantiation, and yet the Catholic Church considers their celebration of the Eucharist perfectly valid. Second, the Catholic Church maintains that the Divine Liturgies celebrated in Eastern churches not in communion with Rome (commonly called Eastern Orthodoxy) are perfectly valid as well,[12] even though their theologians very rarely employ the term "transubstantiation". Third, the belief that the bread and wine are literally transformed into Christ's Body and Blood predates Aristotle's influence by over a thousand years. For it was not until the thirteenth century, and the ascendancy of Saint Thomas Aquinas' thought, that Aristotle's categories were employed by the Church in her account of the Eucharist. In fact, when the Fourth Lateran Council employed the language of substantial change in A.D. 1215, Saint Thomas had not even been born!

It should not surprise us, then, that eucharistic realism had been uncontroversially embraced deep in Christian history. This is why Protestant historian J. N. D. Kelly writes, "Eucharistic teaching, it should be understood at the outset, was in general unquestioningly realist, that is, the consecrated bread and wine were taken to be, and were treated and designated as, the Savior's body and blood."[13] Here are a few quotes from some early Church Fathers that make it clear what the Catholic Church has always believed about Holy Communion:

I have no taste for corruptible food nor for the pleasures of this life. I desire the bread of God, which is the flesh of Jesus Christ, who was of the seed of David; and for drink I desire his blood, which is love incorruptible.[14]

Take note of those who hold heterodox opinions on the grace of Jesus Christ which has come to us, and see how contrary their opinions are to the mind of God.... They abstain from the Eucharist and from prayer because they do not confess that the Eucharist is the flesh of our Savior Jesus Christ, flesh which suffered for our sins and that

[12] See *Catechism of the Catholic Church*, no. 1399.
[13] J. N. D. Kelly, *Early Christian Doctrines*, rev. ed. (New York: HarperCollins, 1978), 440.
[14] Saint Ignatius of Antioch, *Letter to the Romans* 7, in *The Fathers Know Best: Your Essential Guide to the Teachings of the Early Church*, ed. Jimmy Akin (San Diego: Catholic Answers, 2010), 293.

the Father, in his goodness, raised up again. They who deny the gift of God are perishing in their disputes.[15]

We call this food Eucharist, and no one else is permitted to partake of it, except one who believes our teaching to be true and who has been washed in the washing which is for the remission of sins and for regeneration [that is, has received baptism] and is thereby living as Christ enjoined. For not as common bread nor common drink do we receive these; but since Jesus Christ our Savior was made incarnate by the word of God and had both flesh and blood for our salvation, so too, as we have been taught, the food which has been made into the Eucharist by the Eucharistic prayer set down by him, and by the change of which our blood and flesh is nurtured, is both the flesh and the blood of that incarnated Jesus.[16]

[Paul] threatens, moreover, the stubborn and forward, and denounces them, saying, "Whosoever eats the bread or drinks the cup of the Lord unworthily, is guilty of profaning the body and blood of the Lord" [1 Cor. 11:27]. All these warnings being scorned and condemned— [lapsed Christians will often take communion] before their sin is expiated, before confession has been made of their crime, before their conscience has been purged by sacrifice and by the hand of the priest, before the offense of an angry and threatening Lord has been appeased, [and so] violence is done to his body and blood; and they sin now against their Lord more with their hand and mouth than when they denied their Lord.[17]

These are, of course, not the only early Church writings that address the nature of the Eucharist,[18] though they are representative. They should, however, not surprise us, given what the Bible says about Communion. When Jesus celebrated the Last Supper with his disciples (Mt 26:17–29; Mk 14:12–25; Lk 22:7–23), which we commemorate at Communion, he referred to it as a Passover meal. He

[15] Saint Ignatius of Antioch, *Letter to the Smyrnaeans* 6–7, in Akin, *Fathers Know Best*, 293.

[16] Saint Justin Martyr, *First Apology* 66, in Akin, *Fathers Know Best*, 293. Bracketed text inserted by Akin.

[17] Saint Cyprian of Carthage, *The Lapsed* (Treatise 3) 15–16, in Akin, *Fathers Know Best*, 295. Bracketed text inserted by Akin.

[18] Akin provides quotes from several other early Church writings. (Akin, *Fathers Know Best*, 292–98.)

called the elements that were present his Body and Blood. In several places, Jesus is called the Lamb of God (Jn 1:29, 36; cf. 1 Pet 1:19; Rev 5:12). Remember, when the lamb is killed for Passover, the meal participants ingest the lamb. Consequently, Saint Paul's severe warnings about partaking in Holy Communion unworthily make sense only in light of eucharistic realism (1 Cor 10:14–22; 11:17–34). He writes, "The cup of blessing which we bless, is it not a participation in the blood of Christ? The bread which we break, is it not a participation in the body of Christ?... Whoever, therefore, eats the bread or drinks the cup of the Lord in an unworthy manner will be guilty of profaning the body and blood of the Lord" (1 Cor 10:16; 11:27).

Moreover, when one combines all these passages with the fact that Jesus called himself the Bread of Life (Jn 6:48) and said his followers must "eat the flesh of the Son of man and drink his blood" (Jn 6:53), the eucharistic realism of the early Church, the Eastern churches (both in and out of communion with Rome), and the pre-Reformation medieval Church (fifth to sixteenth centuries) seems almost unremarkable.

We should note two points here: (1) Some of these early Church Fathers, such as Saint Ignatius, were part of the first generation of Christians who succeeded the original apostles, and thus it seems fair to say that what they wrote about the Eucharist is what they received from the apostles themselves, unless we have very good reasons to believe otherwise; and (2) Because their belief in eucharistic realism predates the fixation of the New Testament canon,[19] and because the subsequent generations of Christians (in both Latin and Eastern churches) in their official ecclesial pronouncements affirmed the same thing about the Eucharist until the time of the Reformation, we should assume that their interpretation of the biblical texts that touch on the Lord's Supper is correct unless we have very good reasons to believe otherwise.

---

[19] See Craig A. Allert, *A High View of Scripture: The Authority of the Bible and the Formation of the New Testament* (Grand Rapids, MI: Baker, 2007), 48–66. D.H. Williams writes, "The means by which the biblical books were regarded as inspired and divinely given for Christian doctrine and practice took place in the postapostolic centuries of the early church. This process was a gradual and untidy one that emerged out of the worship and liturgical practices of the early churches." (D.H. Williams, *Evangelicals and Tradition: The Formative Influence of the Early Church* [Grand Rapids, MI: Baker, 2005], 55.)

There are two central ingredients in the theological view received from the early Church, a view we get by taking literally Jesus' words "This is my body" (Mt 26:26) and "This is my blood" (26:28) together with the invitation to eat and drink this body and blood. The Real Presence is the view that what is present is literally Jesus' Body and Blood. The real absence is the view that bread and wine are absent: what Jesus was pointing to is not bread or wine.[20]

The doctrines of real absence and Real Presence are found in the early Church, but, as we have already noted, they were not conceptualized using the language of "transubstantiation". Nonetheless, the doctrine of transubstantiation encapsulates this faith of the early Church. The bread and wine are absent, but Christ's Body and Blood are present. So the substance of bread and wine has been replaced by that of Christ's Body and Blood. At the same time, it is obvious to the senses that accidents remain. And that is essentially what transubstantiation claims.

II. Making Sense of the Catholic View Philosophically

There are two central philosophical difficulties in the doctrine of transubstantiation, respectively connected with the twin doctrines of Real Presence and real absence. The first is how the very same physical body and blood can be present both in heaven and in many churches on earth at the same time. The second is how it could be that bread and wine are absent, even though there is a continuous appearance of bread and wine, that is, even though the accidents of bread and wine continue to be present.

We will discuss these in turn. But it should be noted that the speculative task of giving philosophical explanation goes beyond the task of explaining what the Church teaches. It would be possible for a faithful Catholic to hold on to belief in transubstantiation while rejecting all these particular explanations. At the same time, the existence of multiple apparently coherent philosophical explanations is strong evidence that the doctrine is noncontradictory.

---

[20] Cf. Pope Paul VI, Apostolic Letter on the Credo of the People of God *Solemni Hac Liturgia* (June 30, 1968), no. 25, http://w2.vatican.va/content/paul-vi/en/motu_proprio /documents/hf_p-vi_motu-proprio_19680630_credo.html.

II.A. Real Presence

If the doctrine of Real Presence is true, then Christ's Body[21] is really present not only in heaven but also in many churches and other places (the Eucharist is often brought to people in hospitals, for instance) at the same time. There is no philosophical difficulty of this sort facing symbolic views of the Eucharist: symbols signifying a person can easily be present in many places at once.

There are two paths out of the difficulty for the defender of Real Presence. The first path is to say that while Christ's presence in the Eucharist is real, it is a *sacramental* way of being present rather than the usual physical presence. If we take this path, we can maintain the intuitive view that no object can be *physically* present in multiple places at once, while allowing for Christ to be really present in heaven and really but not physically present in many places on earth. The second path is to argue that it is possible for an object to be *physically* present in multiple places at once, even if perhaps this never happens in the ordinary course of things.

II.A.1. Multiple Ways of Being Really Present

The Old Testament proclaims that God is everywhere: "If I ascend to heaven, you are there! If I make my bed in Sheol, you are there! If I take the wings of the morning and dwell in the uttermost parts of the sea, even there your hand shall lead me, and your right hand shall hold me" (Ps 139:8–10). But surely God is not *physically* present at all. For either God has a physical body or he does not. If he has a physical body, as Latter-day theology teaches,[22] then surely (unless we accept something like pantheism) that body is physically present only in some places. If, on the other hand, God has no physical body, then he is not physically anywhere. In either case, then, God's omnipresence is not a matter of *physical* presence. But it seems, nonetheless, to be a *real* presence. So, even though God's omnipresence

---

[21] For brevity, we now simply talk of the Body; it is the standard Catholic view that the Body includes Blood and that where the Blood is, the Body is as well.

[22] According to Mormon doctrine, God the Father is a "Man of Holiness" (Moses 6:57, in Pearl of Great Price), who "has a body of flesh and bone as tangible as man's" (DC 130:22a).

may not be a good account for how Christ is present in the Eucharist (God is present *everywhere*, while the eucharistic presence is particular to some places), it gives us good reason to think that it is possible for something to be really present without being physically present.

Saint Thomas Aquinas (1225–1274) had a very Aristotelian metaphysical story. (We briefly covered a bit of Aristotle's metaphysics when we explained transubstantiation in section I.) Ordinary physical presence works as follows: An object has an accident of what we might call its dimensions or its shape and size. Thus, a starfish has an accident of being star shaped with such-and-such size. These dimensions of the object are then located in a place. The starfish, thus, is on the bottom of the ocean because its accident of dimensions occupies a location on the bottom of the ocean. So in the ordinary course of things, an object has its dimensions, and these dimensions are present in a place. In the case of the Eucharist, however, the dimensions of the bread and wine miraculously survive despite the bread and wine ceasing to be present. These dimensions are not the dimensions *of* Christ's Body—Christ's Body is larger than a piece of bread or a cup of wine, and the shape is different—but nonetheless Christ's Body comes to be *in* these dimensions. The usual way for an object to be present in its dimensions is by *having* these dimensions. But Aquinas insists that this is not the only way.[23] Thus, Aquinas maintains that Christ can be present in a nonordinary way on earth by means of dimensions that used to be the dimensions of bread and wine. There are many sets of dimensions in which Christ is present, and each set of dimensions is in a different place. This is not ordinary physical presence, however, because in ordinary physical presence an object is in *its own* dimensions, while here Christ is present by the dimensions of the no-longer-existing bread and wine. Aquinas' account is an example of how one might give a substantive theory about how there can be a nonordinary but nonetheless real kind of presence.

---

[23] See Saint Thomas Aquinas, *Summa Contra Gentiles* 4, 61–67, trans. Charles J. O'Neil, ed. Joseph Kenny, O.P. (New York: Hanover House, 1955–1957), https://isidore.co/aquinas/english/ContraGentiles4.htm; Saint Thomas Aquinas, *Commentary on the First Epistle to the Corinthians* 663–664, trans. Fabian Larcher, O.P. (987–1046 by Daniel Keating), ed. Joseph Kenny, O.P., https://isidore.co/aquinas/SS1Cor.htm, and *Summa Theologica* III, q. 75, art. 1, trans. Fathers of the English Dominican Province, 2nd and rev. ed. (London: Burns, Oates & Washbourne, 1920), www.newadvent.org/summa/4075.htm.

II.A.2. Physical Multilocation

The second strategy we will now explore is to argue that there need not be anything incoherent about an object being *physically* present in multiple places. We will do so in several ways.

Before doing so, let us consider one option that is initially attractive but theologically problematic. If you are standing between two rooms, with one leg in each, it seems correct to say that you are present in the one room and that you are present in the other room. The Protestant (but very ecumenical) philosopher Gottfried Leibniz (1646–1716) famously attempted to account for transubstantiation in such a way, by making the constituent parts ("monads") of the bread and wine become parts of Christ's Body, so that Christ's Body would be partly present on the altar and partly in heaven.[24] However, the Catholic tradition insists that Christ is *wholly* present in the Eucharist, rather than having strange bread- and wine-like parts present there. Thus, we need to work harder and offer a more adequate account.

To that end, first, we'll start with some science fiction. As an adult, Sally invents a time machine, goes back in time, and looks into the window of the house in which she is playing with her electronics kit at age six. As a result, Sally is really and physically present both inside and outside the house. If such time travel is possible, this "multipresence" can be arbitrarily multiplied: she could make a series of trips to that same time and hence be present in many places at once there. There are, of course, paradoxes associated with time travel, but there are also ways to attempt to resolve those paradoxes.[25]

One could try to come up with a theory that uses multiple cases of time travel to account for Christ's Real Presence in the Eucharist. But that is not the point here. Rather, the point is that the apparent coherence of time travel makes it plausible that there need be no *contradiction* in an object's being present in multiple places at once. And that lack of contradiction is what we are defending.

Second, instead of science fiction, consider quantum mechanics. In one historically prominent interpretation, in cases where an event

[24] G.W. Leibniz, *Philosophical Essays*, ed. and trans. R. Ariew and D. Garber (Indianapolis: Hackett, 1989), 197–206.

[25] David Lewis, "The Paradoxes of Time Travel", *American Philosophical Quarterly* 13 (1976): 145–52.

could randomly go one way or another, which way it goes is settled only upon observation. Thus, one can prepare an electron in a mixed up-down spin state and send it through a magnetic field so that if the electron were in a purely up spin state, it would go upward in the field, and if it were purely in a down spin state, it would go downward in the field. But if it is in a mixed state, then whether it has gone up or down in the magnetic field will be settled only once its final position is observed. Until that position is observed, the electron is in a mix of the up and down positional states. And it seems not unreasonable to describe this electron as being really present both in the upper position and in the lower position. This is a real presence, and it is a physical presence, though it is not the ordinary sort of presence. The ordinary sort of presence is restored only upon observation.

One may question whether the mixed positional state really counts as being present in two places at once. Another interpretation of the quantum mechanics is that the electron does not actually have a position until it is observed, at which point it comes to have a position. However, that interpretation is incompatible with the very plausible pair of claims that (a) electrons are material objects and (b) material objects always have a location. Alternately, one might say that the electron in the superposed state has a position, but not a definite one. However, if being indefinitely in a position is still *really* being in that position, albeit in an indefinite way, and the electron is indefinitely in the upper position and indefinitely in the lower position, then it is still *really* in both positions. In any case, we are certainly not claiming that Christ's Body is present in a quantum mechanical superposition, but once we realize how far the location of particles in quantum mechanics departs from our ordinary intuitions, we should be much more open to the possibility that intuitions opposing multilocation are mistaken. We should, however, acknowledge that a minority position in physics is the Bohmian interpretation in which there is no indeterminism and particles always have a single definite position. If that interpretation is right, we get no support for the possibility of multilocation from that quarter.

Third, in a more speculative vein, the physicist John Wheeler has proposed a clever explanation of why all electrons have the same charge and mass: "They are all the same electron",[26] present in many places at once. This may or may not be true, but the fact that such a theory appears coherent to a distinguished physicist is still some evidence that it *is* coherent, and it therefore provides some evidence for the logical possibility of multilocation.

Fourth, philosophers do not have a single generally accepted theory about what it is that makes an ordinary object present in a place. Without such a theory, it seems to be intellectual overreach to claim confidently that it is not possible for the relation that makes an object present in one place to hold between an object and multiple places.

Fifth, consider this line of thought: Reality is four-dimensional, meaning it extends through three spatial dimensions and one temporal dimension. It is, then, a perfectly ordinary occurrence for us to be located in multiple areas of space-time. For instance, when you were younger, you were located in a crib, and you are now located in, say, an armchair. Now, granted, the two areas in this example—the past crib and the present armchair—are found at different temporal coordinates. But it is not clear why that matters to the possibility of multilocation: Why would it be that objects can exist at multiple locations in space-time that share spatial coordinates (perhaps the crib has the same coordinate along some x-axis as the armchair does) but not in locations that share the same temporal coordinate?

This is a controversial line of thought. Many philosophers reject the idea that reality is four-dimensional in favor of a dynamic three-dimensional view. And a number of philosophers who take reality to be four-dimensional deny that we are wholly present in different locations of space-time. Instead, they say, we have different *temporal parts* present at different times. Still, the availability of this line of thought provides further evidence for the coherence of multilocation.

Sixth, we have good reason based on Einstein's general theory of relativity to think that our three-dimensional space is curved, say, like the surface of a balloon—except of course that the surface of a balloon is two-dimensional while space is three-dimensional.

---

[26] Quoted in Richard P. Feynman, "The Development of the Space-Time View of Quantum Electrodynamics", Nobel Lecture, NobelPrize.org, December 11, 1965, www.nobelprize.org/nobel_prizes/physics/laureates/1965/feynman-lecture.html.

Now imagine you have an inflated balloon. Draw two circles, an inch in diameter, on opposite sides, one red and one blue. Put your left thumb in the middle of the red circle and your right thumb in the middle of the blue circle. Press the thumbs toward each other until they meet, with two layers of rubber between them. The balloon now looks kind of like a doughnut, but with no hole all the way through. Imagine now that you press so hard that the two layers of rubber between your thumbs coalesce into a single layer of rubber.

Now the single layer of rubber between your thumbs is at the center of the red circle *and* at the center of the blue circle. We can think of each circle as defining a place, and the coalesced rubber inside it is found in both these places.

Replace the red circle with a drawing of a church and the blue circle with a drawing of heaven. The same coalesced layer of rubber is both inside (a drawing of) a church and inside (a drawing of) heaven. Suppose now that the rubber is infinitely thin and that there is a space that coincides with this rubber and little two-dimensional people, animals, plants, and other objects inhabiting this space, much as in Edwin Abbott's novel *Flatland*.[27] Suppose that the pictures of the church and heaven are replaced with two-dimensional realities. Then the space of the church and the space of heaven literally overlap, so that there is a place that is located in both. An object found in that place will be literally and physically located both in the church and in heaven. In one sense, that object is physically located in two places at once. In another sense, it is located in a single place, but that single place is simultaneously located both in heaven and in the church.

There is no serious additional conceptual difficulty in *three*-dimensional space curving in on itself similarly. The arrangement certainly appears logically possible, and as a result, an all-powerful God could, as it were, pinch together a region of heaven occupied by Christ's Body and a region in a church formerly occupied by a piece of bread so that Christ's Body would be present both in heaven and in church. And while it is harder to imagine it, there is no logical

---

[27] Edwin Abbott, *Flatland: A Romance of Many Dimensions* (Boston: Little, Brown, 1899). A particularly entertaining and more carefully worked-out account of a two-dimensional reality is also found in Alexander Dewdney, *The Planiverse: Computer Contact with a Two-Dimensional World* (New York: Copernicus, 2001).

difficulty about a similar identification between places in multiple churches (and multiple areas of a single church) and a single heaven. On this apparently logically coherent view, Christ is physically present both in heaven and in multiple earthly locations.

We are certainly not claiming that this is how God does transubstantiation; God has not revealed his method. But a philosophical defense of the doctrine does not require us to identify *how* God does it. At most it requires us to show that God *could* do it. Likewise, if one's child claims to have placed a marble on a high shelf but refuses to say how this was done, to accept the child's claim one at most needs to figure out one or two possible ways in which he *could* have done it—perhaps he stood on a step stool or climbed on the lower shelf—rather than to identify the particular way he did.

And there is a bit of a complication to the balloon story. The Catholic tradition holds that the manner in which Christ is present in the Eucharist is not the ordinary manner in which bodies are present,[28] while in the balloon story, Christ ends up present in a way very similar to ordinary physical presence. And indeed, there is an important difference in the manner of presence—one that the story did not mention—between ordinary bodily presence and Christ's presence: Christ is not affected by physical events like chewing, breaking, and drinking that occur at his eucharistic location. But the balloon story could be supplemented to include this: God is, after all, all-powerful and can ensure that Christ is affected physically only by what happens in heaven.

We thus have multiple lines of thought, each yielding the idea that it is possible for the same object to be physically present in multiple locations at once. There is good reason, then, to accept that possibility. And it is easy to explain why a lot of people have the contrary intuition that an object cannot be physically present in multiple locations at once: in the ordinary course of macroscopic events, such multilocation does not happen. But the Eucharist is not an ordinary event.

And, of course, even if it is not possible for an object to be *physically* present in multiple places at once, there is the possibility of a

---

[28] Pope Paul VI, Encyclical on the Holy Eucharist *Mysterium Fidei* (September 3, 1965), no. 46, www.vatican.va/content/paul-vi/en/encyclicals/documents/hf_p-vi_enc_03091965 _mysterium.html. We are grateful to Christopher Tomaszewski for drawing our attention to this text.

different kind of real presence than physical presence, as we discussed in the previous section.

II.B. *Appearances despite Real Absence*

It is an evident fact that the appearances of bread and wine persist. How can this happen if bread and wine are absent?

A simple but theologically inadequate explanation would be that God simply causes everyone in the vicinity to suffer coordinated hallucinations, preventing them from seeing (and feeling, for example) the Body of Jesus and making them see (and feel, for example) bread and wine instead. This explanation would be theologically inadequate, as it does not seem fitting for God to cause hallucinations.

Aquinas had a metaphysically weighty explanation. In his Aristotelian theory, reality divides into (at least) two kinds of things: substances and their accidents. A starfish is a substance, but associated with that starfish is a whole host of real things called "accidents": the starfish's shape and size, the starfish's color, the starfish's texture, etc. Normally, these accidents depend on the starfish's substance for their existence. The starfish's substance can survive many changes in accidents (the starfish can grow, can change color, etc.), but the accidents need the substance.

However, Aquinas argues,[29] whatever a creature has the power to do, God has the power to do as well.[30] If the starfish's substance has the power to keep the accidents of the starfish in existence, God can do it as well—without needing the starfish's substance to help him. So God could, if he so chose, miraculously keep the starfish's accidents in existence after the death of the starfish. In fact, as far as we know, God does not ever do this for a starfish. But according to Aquinas, God does do it for bread and wine in the context of Communion. The substance ceases to exist, and while the accidents would normally stop existing as well, God's power keeps them in existence.

---

[29] *Summa Theologica* III, q. 77, art. 1.

[30] One may argue that God has no power to do evil, while we have the power to do evil. A quick answer would be that while God can never do evil, this is not due to a lack of power but due to his goodness.

This is not a hallucination or a deception. The accidents of color, shape, and taste of the bread and wine that we perceive really are there in Aquinas' picture. The substance, however, is absent.

Aquinas' story has two points of difficulty. The first is his use of the power of God. While God is all-powerful, it is generally acknowledged in the Christian tradition that God's power does not extend to the logically contradictory—God cannot, for instance, create a circle that is a square. But perhaps the existence of an accident without its substance is logically contradictory because it is the very nature of an accident to depend on the existence of its substance. However, if we think the past is real, then we can maintain that the accidents of the bread and wine depend on the *past* existence of the bread and wine, and hence contradiction is avoided.

The second difficulty is Aquinas' Aristotelian metaphysics in which accidents are really existing things. One might wonder whether such things as the size and shape of a starfish literally exist. Nonetheless, this metaphysics is a genuine philosophical possibility, and so a Catholic can be reasonable in accepting it as part of an account of Real Presence and real absence.

One can, further, directly argue for the possibility of the persistence of accidents or appearances in the absence of a substance without depending on Aristotelian metaphysics. The light from distant stars takes many years to reach us. Suppose one of these stars has been destroyed while the light was traveling. Then it seems reasonable to say that the appearance of the star's color and brightness still exists and can be seen, even though the star no longer exists. And there is no hallucination here, any more than there is hallucination in our hearing thunder several seconds after the lightning has run its course.

III. Conclusion

Although Latter-day Saints and Catholics both celebrate communion, and both call it a sacrament, their views are radically different. Like many Protestant groups, the LDS maintain that the sacrament, though important, is symbolic, that the Body, Blood, soul, and divinity of Christ do not become present through a change of the elements. The Catholic Church, on the other hand, believes that the

Eucharist is *both* a symbol of God's love for us *and* a literal presence of Christ: the bread and wine at the Lord's Supper are literally transformed into the Body and Blood of Christ, with his soul and divinity being present as well. To be sure, the Church's philosophical understanding of the Eucharist has developed over time. Nevertheless, as we have argued in this chapter, its roots can be found in the testimony of Scripture as well as the writings of the early Church Fathers. We also showed that there are reasonable answers to some of the philosophical questions raised about the rationality of the Catholic view. Because we believe, as the Church teaches, that the Eucharist is the "fount and apex of the whole Christian life",[31] we would be remiss if we did not conclude by inviting our LDS friends to consider the Catholic perspective prayerfully.

[31] Vatican Council II, Dogmatic Constitution on the Church *Lumen Gentium* (November 21, 1964), no. 11, www.vatican.va/archive/hist_councils/ii_vatican_council/documents /vat-ii_const_19641121_lumen-gentium_en.html.

8

The Papacy:
The Most Real Institution in the World

Ronald Thomas

For Catholics, the papacy is not a magical institution, nor is it linked to various allocutions within the schema of "continuing revelation". This is because it is a *real* institution; that is, the papacy inheres in a larger framework of created reality and of the triune God. In this sense, it is "demystified". Nothing could be more antithetical to the reality of the created order and God's sponsorship *of* and transcendence *beyond* it than a type of open spiritualism that gives humanity the idea that God's life and designs are a kind of "guessing game". It might even be said that human beings are not that important; that is, to concentrate on whether people are "getting" God's messages should be a distant second to the fact that God has written the entire universe as an elaborate analogy of himself. God's Word (Logos) is his creative act and achieves full embodiment in his Son, Jesus Christ. While there is certainly a *discovery* of the will of God in one's life, that will is an immutable, total reality—antecedent in God, "placing" man in the world, until such time as that world is transformed, in an indescribable way, into the Kingdom of our Lord and Christ. God is God, qualitatively different from that which he has made; man never becomes this "Ground of Being". To believe in parallel universes of multiple deities is a sad parody of the life of God, manifesting a great confusion about what it means to believe in God. It might also be said that to be "in Christ" is not to be above him but to be located in his limitless nature, precisely as a creature, nothing more, nothing less, who has been redeemed.

An important aspect of the papacy is that it is meant for this life alone. Since it does not constitute some sort of slip knot between heaven and earth, one rejoices in the fact that the papacy, along with all sacraments, priesthood, apostleship, and the like will one day be completely relativized in the new circumstance of the kingdom. The entire apparatus of the Church Militant simply points to the kingdom to be, although its task of adding souls to that kingdom is of eternal importance.

I. Papacy and the Eucharist

The papacy cannot be understood apart from the Sacrament of the Eucharist, the Body and Blood of Christ. The papacy serves this reality—and "reality" is the best word for it. Jesus, the eternal Word, came in the flesh (see Jn 1:14). He was no mere appearance. He took on flesh to redeem flesh. His continued presence in the Eucharist is like a portal to the world to come, in which flesh and blood will be transformed into the spiritual body (*soma pneumatikon*) of the Risen Christ (see 1 Cor 15:44). Nevertheless, that portal is the most important aspect of religious life in this world. It is no abstraction, no mere idea. So, with respect to this sacrament and the life it brings, the papacy is a tool for stressing the overarching importance of the embodiment of Jesus Christ. We wait upon Christ; the papacy waits upon Christ. The Catholic, any Catholic, ministers to Christ's presence in the Blessed Sacrament. It is that simple. The Body of the Church is animated by the presence of the Holy Spirit, but even the Holy Spirit is the spirit of this Christ—enfleshed, eternally present, real.

If Joseph Smith could have known of the reality of the Blessed Sacrament, how relieved and assured his fevered mind would have been. If the Christianity of his environment could have had the principle of unity that the papacy represents, how much discord, dissention, rivalry, and scandalous party spirit would have spared the souls of that region. At the very least, the doctrine of the Eucharist and the papal unity that serves it spares anyone the search for an "alternate reality" in which to dwell. They remove religion from the realms of science fiction to flesh and blood existence, the reality and limits of time, the goodness and reality of "nature" (essences), and the necessity of a hope that has no need of angelic/demonic correctives. In short, the Body of Christ gives sanity, joy, and release. And in an odd way, the fullness of religion gives a man the ability to think about other things besides religion, and yet to be sure that he is participating in God's will.

II. The Transmission of Authority

The construction of the papacy from Christ's own selection of Peter as head of the apostles has been well examined over the centuries. What emerges as anomalous is the idea, favored by the restorationist movements in America, that the apostolic authority could not possibly have been passed down through the centuries through any of those apostles. Surely, Jesus Christ reckoned with the passage of time in the constitution of his Church. Certainly, he promised or prophesied no great apostasy in the Church, but rather the very opposite: "The gates of Hades shall not prevail against it" (Mt 16:18). He also promised the continued action of the Holy Spirit in preserving the Church in all truth (see Jn 16:13). Saint Paul's career, viewed as a whole, might well be considered a creation of apostolic structures in the Roman world, most of which continue to this day.

It is very odd, with respect to the reality of human sin in the Church, as elsewhere, to conclude that a society that owes its origins exclusively to the divine will could somehow, through human frailty, forfeit its title deeds to the world, the flesh, and the devil. That his disciples could somehow be so easily ripped from his hands would certainly surprise the Jesus whose high priestly prayer in John 17 celebrates the unity of "those who believe" (17:20). For all the inconclusiveness of the modern ecumenical movement, the idea that the Church has somehow been lost along the way, that no one could find salvation except through some restored entity, radically severed from the great drama of Christian history, would strike all the participants of the discussions as bizarre. The plenary salvation is, in fact, *on offer*. As to structures of authority, organization, and mission, there might be an intellectually serious plurality of opinion. But even this plurality unfolds, so the participants believe, against an ineffaceable unity in Christ, for it is his unity before it is ours.

III. Points of Contact and Divergence

A Catholic looking at the LDS church should note right away that the patriarchal authority celebrated in the papacy and elsewhere ultimately devolves upon the *family* in Mormon practice. Here is a real point of contact. The role of the *paterfamilias* is a thing of great antiquity, stability, and success. Why should it not extend to the whole of the Church if, indeed, it is a most agreeable and natural feature of human sociality? The instructed LDS member will, of course, respond that, indeed, it does! The president of the LDS church fills an ineffaceable role in the church. Here again, we see points of contact. The role of the president of the LDS church is irreformable. That is to say, according to the LDS manner of functioning, no further restorationist movements could be allowed to supplant what has been in place now for almost two centuries. But, irrespective of whose patriarchal authority one accepts, Catholic or Mormon, one must conclude that restorationism is something of a fool's errand. No one starts out *de novo* to found a church, unless it be God himself. Since Jesus Christ is God, his founding cannot be said to have failed. This, of course, places the actual history of the Mormon founding in great jeopardy.

It would seem that a substratum of Joseph Smith's founding of the LDS church is great doubt concerning the very figure of Jesus Christ. As the Messiah—the *summum bonum* of all the history of Israel, the Lord of life and death, the image of the invisible God, the firstborn of all creation, he in whom all things in heaven and earth were created and are held together—he it is who holds, directs, and confirms all the acts of his earthly Body until his coming again. One may not gainsay this providence and sovereignty by recourse to supposed tribes of Israel, the unsubstantiated existence and movements of peoples, supposed angelic appearances, supposed secret languages, course corrections by ghostly apostles or prophets, such as John the Baptist, or anything of the sort without falsifying belief in the one whose Incarnation is the sole reason for any sort of assembly in his name.

It is really not important to achieve a verdict on the mind, motivations, activities, and hopes of Joseph Smith other than to say that they suggest insuperable theological contradictions. Supportive evidence for this reposes in the fact that the modern LDS movement is more dedicated to its familial, organizational, sociological, financial, and political aspects than any other. In these elements, it presents an imposing socioreligious edifice. Especially in the face of the fragmentation of modernity, it suggests itself as a stable home for all sorts of homeless moderns—hence, its famously conservative character. Its obvious abandonment of odd theological beliefs and conundrums has given contemporary Mormonism its turbo-charged mainstream status. The self-transformation of the LDS church in these latter days has made it an indisputable success. Nevertheless, no amount of success solves any of the issues of ecclesiology and authority that bedevil the Mormon founding.

IV. Jesus Christ and the Transformation of Judaism

Central to the Book of Mormon is the notion of the lost tribes of Israel having found their way to America. This carries the Mormon restorationism much further than is found in other restorationist groups. The notion also runs afoul of the commitment to Christian apostolic origins, which, be they ever so twisted by later generations (so the story goes), must certainly be in place, unless one wishes to deny that Christ commissioned any apostles whatsoever. Here one would be dealing with *contradictory* revelation as opposed to *continuing* revelation. The heart of the matter has to do with Christ's own transformation of Judaism. Whether or not ten tribes found their way to America, Jesus Christ did not intend for his religion either to be limited to Jews or to replicate an earthly Jerusalem. The apostles, especially through the interventions of Saint Paul, soon became aware that "the Way" (Acts 9:2; 19:9, 23; 22:4; 24:14, 22) was cosmic in scope, placing in abeyance any of the aspects of Judaism not consonant with a higher, more comprehensive divine law.[1] The covenant once delivered to the Jews was now set within the context of a new eon.[2] Additionally, Jesus' disciples would be his witnesses "to the end of the earth" (Acts 1:8; cf. Mt 28:19–20). There is no privileged caste in this new dispensation.

---

[1] Cf. Rom 1–2 on natural law as universally applicable.

[2] Cf. John Reid, "Aeon", in *Hastings' Dictionary of the New Testament*, ed. John Hastings (1906–1918), www.studylight.org/dictionaries/hdn/view.cgi?n=66.

Simply because the Americas and their peoples were not specifically mentioned in the Bible, Mormons and other American Christians of a biblicist bent were forced to augment the revelation of Christ with a mythology of a Hebrew Völkerwanderung. If the actual sociology of human groups was a puzzlement to Joseph Smith and other res-torationists, Catholic figures such as Bartolomé de Las Casas (and a host of other missionaries) had no problem simply accepting the fact of native populations—and their souls—as an extension of the Lord's design to convert the world. Given the fact that the Spanish Catholics had already located the role of native populations within the saving economy of the Church in the early 1500s, one can only bewail the isolation and ignorance of the American biblicists as they attempted theoretical explanations of the peoples of the American continents. In a manner of speaking, the Catholic Church had recovered from a flat earth understanding of things long before these American Protestants, who were additionally blinkered by the idea that America was itself a new eon. In this connection, ironically, Joseph Smith's intuition is correct: Church division is an insane scandal. It has deleterious effects, especially when tradition is impugned or ignored.

V. The Papacy and Dogma

To a Catholic, the figure of the pope is enshrouded with much pious affection, and no one seems to think this a bad thing. Though the pope has "universal jurisdiction" as a matter of his dealings with Church law, the actual conduct of the papacy is highly collaborative. Of course, there are multitudes of things the pope cannot change, nor would he wish to, as he is principally a guardian or servant of the faith once delivered to the saints, not its master.

What, then, is to be said about the gargantuan doctrine of papal infallibility? First, that it is not gargantuan at all, but rather a very nar-row aspect of papal functioning, not necessarily completely applicable to every papal regime. At the heart of papal infallibility is the ability to define a dogma. What does this mean? It means that under the grace of the Holy Spirit, typically with the most extensive collaboration humanly possible with all the apostles (bishops) of the world, the pope declares solemnly (*ex cathedra*) that such and such a theological belief is, and has always been, part of the faith once delivered to the saints.

Reasons are advanced as to why a belief, either explicitly or implicitly, has always been present in the *depositum fidei* (deposit of faith) and as to why it is important to make this official and explicit (the act of definition) at this moment in time, even though it may not have been definitively affirmed prior to its official proclamation. The argument is roughly circular: this new statement makes explicit only what has always been in the deposit, and the deposit is never old, being the truth of God. As T. S. Eliot once said, what is permanent is always urgent. Of course, the power of the dogma comes not from the facts of the collaboration or of the reasoning but from the plenary apostolic power of the successor to Peter when he proclaims the dogma. To twist a common phrase, the buck not only stops with the pope, but it also begins there. Of course, everyone has to be clear on what the buck consists of.

The dogmas defined and promulgated by the pope are related only to faith and morals, those truly theological matters, not merely philosophical, sociological, or empirical ones. Dogmas have to do with the content of faith and revelation that reason cannot supply to itself. Hence, the three "modern" doctrinal definitions that fit the template of papal infallibility concern the Blessed Virgin Mary (two times) and the papacy itself. None of these issues are locatable outside the Christian faith; that is, they are not the province of natural reason. Supernatural grace is involved.

Earlier I said that not every papal regime has such a dealing with infallibility. That is, not every pope goes about the business of solemnly defining a dogma. John XXIII, Paul VI, John Paul I, John Paul II, Benedict XVI, and Francis—all our recent popes—were indeed great men, exercising their apostolic powers to the fullest; yet none of them defined a dogma.

Someone might ask, So, then, do Catholics believe only three things (the Immaculate Conception of Mary, the Assumption of Mary, and papal infallibility), since only three such "defined" dogmas seem to exist? It is a good and provocative question.

The Catholic Church is loaded with dogmas, to be sure: the divinity of Christ or the Trinity, for example. For most of Christian history, the weightiest actions of the weightiest councils, the clear witness of Scripture, and the most ancient, constant, even exceptionless usage were the indicators of dogmas and beliefs to which the faithful needed to be committed if they wished to deem themselves Catholic. The process of the formation of explicit Catholic belief is organic and wholistic, carried on under the supervision of the Holy Spirit.

The defining of dogmas seems to be a relatively recent phenomenon, if the mechanism of the modern definitions is seen apart from the organic and wholistic method of the Catholic Church. As a matter of fact, the defining of dogmas by papal pronouncement is merely an efficient way to do what the Church has always done. Some of this efficiency might be due to the fact that over the long history of the Catholic Church, it has become more and more (in fact, irreversibly) certain that the pope has the duty and authority to declare those things that have been formally revealed by God as part of the "faith which was once for all delivered to the saints" (Jude 1:3).

It will not escape the notice of a perspicacious observer that one of the definitions is the idea that the pope has a right and authority to define! This is what I mean by the increasing, and finally absolute, certainty concerning the office of the successor to Peter. This same observer will also notice that this definition is the second in the line of modern definitions (though it was defined by the First Vatican Council and not the pope!). It is almost as if, after the definition of the Immaculate Conception, the Church said, "Oh, wait a minute; we need to make absolutely clear that this kind of defining authority exists as part of divine revelation." Collaborative, conciliar, and traditional elements were all remaining in the process, but, as we said before, it was necessary to show that the buck began and stopped in the supreme apostolic authority of the pope.

Why was this important? That is, why this particular development in the life of the Church? Could it be that under the guidance of the Holy Spirit, the Church, especially in the form of the defining of the dogma of the infallibility of the pope, was proclaiming that, yes, there is real authority in the world given by God to his chosen people, the Church? That all political authority is merely a shadow of this authority? That all the ages of kings and emperors, and this budding age of democracies and republics, are given their license by the holy and undivided Trinity? As for those who say that real authority has passed away—that it is only the activity of material forces that orders things—these people are sponsoring an antihuman error. Authority is necessary in every aspect of human existence—from the microcosm of the individual, to the family, to the community, to the state. How is it anchored? Toward what is it to be directed? Well, God, through his Son and his Church, has shown us the way. The pope anchors those truths, natural and supernatural, by which we absolutely need to live. Every authority has its real place and its real limits in God. Nor is this merely abstract. The Church, which lives to offer spiritual worship to God, especially in the Holy Eucharist, is a community of covenant and divine power that opens the way for every life-affirming authority and power. The Kingdom of Christ gives every other kingdom its power, its authority, its truth, and its renewal.

These are large claims. In fact, they are the largest of claims. One other detail needs to be added, though. It is important to remember that the pope is not an immortal person. He dies, and another is chosen to take his place. It turns out that the papacy is a perennial institution, an office, but not a perennial person. Therefore, it makes absolutely no sense to speak of the pope as if he were a "prophet, seer, and revelator" in the sense of a Mormon patriarch. No mere human can usurp God's own self-disclosure, that is, divine revelation. Not that the contemporary, living pope of any age is not important; it is just that he has a different threefold office from the one envisioned by Mormonism. It is to this that we now turn.

VI. The Threefold Office

The threefold office of Christ (*munus triplex*) consists of Christ as Prophet, Priest, and King. This is perhaps not so remarkable considering Jesus' fulfillment of the entire covenant tradition. Urgently commanding our attention, however, is the fact that Christ shares this threefold office with the Church at every level.

What are the three elements indicated in this *munus triplex*? First, there is the proclamation of the truth of God, the prophetic office. This truth may be either natural or supernatural in character. Examples of the first might be the intrinsic evil of abortion and contraception. Examples of the second would be found in the great dogmas: the divinity of Christ, his two natures, the reality of the divine presence in the Eucharist, the Assumption of Mary, and all such doctrines.

Second, there is the office of sacrifice, the priestly office. Jesus Christ is the great High Priest. In fact, he is both priest and sacrifice. All the sacrificial traditions find their source and summit in him, and he is the complete new sacrifice to which nothing need be appended.

To accommodate redeemed humanity, as it makes its pilgrimage in the world of time, he has continued his presence and power in the Holy Eucharist. This is Christ's own action in which a bishop or priest may cooperate, as we say, *in Persona Christi*, in the Person of Christ—that is, taking the place of Christ according to a graced ministerial function.

Third, there is the office of king. Kingship has to do with authority, governance, direction, defense, shepherding, and service. These are ineluctable things, and God's anointed is, of course, the fulfillment of them all.

This last office stands in stark contrast to the "prophet, seer, and revelator" notion. Why? Because it is so concrete. A king is a king. He deals with his subjects, who need guidance in the world of time. The office cannot be abstract. Nor does Christ deal with it thus. He appoints one of the apostles as the head of the others because the principle of singular leadership (which is the essence of monarchy or kingship) is necessary in the Church.

In rehearsing this notion of the threefold office, we are not saying the pope is the only "king". It turns out that there are "kings" in several spheres: in the family, in the diocese, in nations (potentially), and so forth. This writer was once acquainted with a man who had to leave graduate studies in the United States because his tribe, back home in Africa, had elected him king, *in absentia*! All this is to say that there is *royal nature in Christ* in which all the baptized partake (see 1 Pet 2:9; Rev 1:6). Still, no abstractions may apply. Even though we live in an age in which monarchy has all but faded away, sociologically and politically, we still find the notion indispensable. It is part of the warp and woof of the world. Collaborate as we will, we still do not find democracy totally adequate to human realities. The Church cannot be a democracy, for instance, nor the family. This is to say that democracy cannot be the sole organ for concerns about the truth. Something must crown the hierarchy of human concerns.

In a moment, we will consider Christ's words related to Peter and the question of the establishment of the papacy in the Church, but for now we can certainly say that if Christ uttered those words as we think he meant them, no real surprise, no real scandal, no, not even any real novelty is indicated in them. Christ appointed a singular head, a *monos arkein*, a monarch for his budding community. It would be absurd to think that Christ indicated that this person should take away *his* kingship. This is not possible. But it would be equally absurd to suppose that Christ would leave his community without a real structure of authority of the sort that figures, interestingly enough, in a great many of his parables (e.g., Mt 18:23–35; 22:1–14; 25:31–46; Lk 14:28–33; 19:12–27).

Clearly, Jesus Christ had a revolutionary notion about how those in hierarchical authority in his New Israel would behave. They would serve. Hence, one of the most solemn titles for the pope is *servus servorum Dei*: servant of the servants of God. As to Jesus' unflattering opinion about the usual conduct of earthly monarchs, we have many of his words (e.g., Mk 10:42); but more eloquently, Jesus *kept silence* before Herod and Pontius Pilate. Over the course of Christian history, interestingly, earthly kings received the example of service from their bishops and popes; thus, they were not as predatory and self-aggrandizing as they might have been if they had been pagans full stop. Some kings, notably, Saint Edward the Confessor and Louis IX of France, were recognized as saints.

Finally, it is worth noting that the opposite number of a servant of the servants of God for the whole world would be the specter of an absolutist *secular* ruler for the whole world who would reject the successor to Peter and all that he represented: this representative of secular political messianism we usually refer to as the antichrist.[3] Could it also be that the antichrist is more likely to emerge from the demands of a mob democracy for safety and comfort than from either papalism or monarchy? This would greatly surprise such severe antipapal thinkers as John Calvin, but that does not diminish the possibility. It is worth noting that nowadays the successor to Peter often serves as the singular target for the fiery darts of secularism.

VII. The Commissioning of Peter

In all four Gospels, in the Acts of the Apostles, in the canonical epistles of Peter (whatever their authorship), in early Christian "apocryphal" literature, in the "Clementine" literature, in Irenaeus and other Church Fathers, and in Jewish legend, Simon Peter is preeminent among the apostles, a spokesman, an appointed leader and

---

[3] *Catechism of the Catholic Church*, nos. 675–76.

much else besides. The sheer weight of testimony, practice, artifacts (such as Peter's tomb), and even opposition to the Christian cause, centered on Peter, led the Anglican F.J. Foakes-Jackson at the end of his magisterial study to conclude, "Of the One United and indivisible Church, which has never yet been truly realized on earth, Peter may be said to be the representative."[4]

One may dispute Foakes-Jackson's claim about the missing "realization" of the true Church on earth, but it is highly significant that such a learned adherent of a church founded in opposition to the papal office (the Church of England) cannot bring himself to dispense with Petrine primacy, except on pains of falsification of every sort of evidence that exists about the Prince of the Apostles and the will of the Lord.

It has long been a staple of those who reject the authority of the papacy to claim that, although it is clear that the Lord promoted Peter to headship over his brethren, the *continuation* of Peter's office in successors is doubtful. This claim is easily overcome, as we shall see. The *other* claim that one hears in various quarters is that Peter, in his person, was not so promoted, but rather his "faith" or some other aspect of his character was being extolled by the Lord in Matthew 16 and passages in other Gospels. Why, then, in other places in the New Testament, is he called Peter at all (or Simon Peter), if the "rock" in question had nothing to do with his person? The Gospel of John proclaims this Simon Cephas straightway: "He brought [Simon] to Jesus. Jesus looked at him, and said, 'So you are Simon the son of John? You shall be called Cephas' (which means Peter)" (Jn 1:42).

Now, some claim that the difference between the Greek words *petros* (the name) and *petra* (the object) is enough to indicate that Jesus did not mean a literal assignation of authority to the person of Peter. The incidental difference in these Greek words, with which the Gospel writer must cope, does not exist in the Aramaic words of the Lord: *kepha* is *kepha*. There is no variant for the person or the object. (Cephas is the common rendering for the Greek-language writer.)

It seems as if the Lord is a great devotee of irony in his designation of Peter as a "rock". This is actually an argument for the attribution of authority to the person of Peter! Peter, from the constitution of his

---

[4] F.J. Foakes-Jackson, *Peter: Prince of the Apostles; A Study in the History and Tradition of Christianity* (New York: George H. Doran, 1927), 287.

character, is a "wannabe" rock. He wants to be brave. He wants to be faithful. He wants to be bold. None of this, sadly, is within his grasp. He fails at all of it, with the partial exception of his confession of the Lord as Messiah. The exception is partial, of course, because he follows Jesus' disclosure of his impending suffering with the ignorant faux bravado that provokes the Lord's wrath (see Mt 16:23). Therefore, if Peter is to be a "rock", he will need to be made so by that same infusion of the Holy Spirit upon which all Christians depend to transcend their weak fallenness. Jesus' kingdom is not of this world, and, as the saying goes, Jesus does not choose the equipped; he equips the chosen: "You did not choose me, but I chose you and appointed you that you should go and bear fruit and that your fruit should abide; so that whatever you ask the Father in my name, he may give it to you" (Jn 15:16).

VIII. Succession

The *Catechism of the Catholic Church* sums up the effect of the selection of Peter as head of the apostles in this way: "Simon Peter holds the first place in the college of the Twelve.... Just as 'by the Lord's institution, St. Peter and the rest of the apostles constitute a single apostolic college, so in like fashion, the Roman Pontiff, Peter's successor, and the bishops, the successors of the apostles, are related with and united to one another.'"[5]

When we enter in on the subject of succession, it must simply be declared that for the idea of an *extinction* of the successors to the apostles through persecution, one of the cornerstones of the idea of the Great Apostasy, there is not one whit of historical evidence.

The only way for the earliest successors to the apostles to have been wiped out would have been the annihilation of every Christian Church of antiquity. The pagan Romans were simply not that effective in persecution, despite their aims. As it stands, there is unbroken membership in the Church among the generations of this planet, and a succession of leadership known to every Church historian, be he friend or foe of Catholicism. One of the premises of a transmutation,

---

[5] *Catechism of the Catholic Church*, nos. 552, 880, quoting Vatican Council II, Dogmatic Constitution on the Church *Lumen Gentium* (November 21, 1964), no. 22.

or even a perversion, of Christian doctrine is that the Christians responsible for it did in fact live and die in Christian communities.

One hopes there are few serious Christians to whom the name of Saint Irenaeus (c. A.D. 130–202), bishop of Lyon, does not bring deep joy and pride in the success of the early Church. Persecuted by Gnostics and imperial powers, Irenaeus' church received powerful teaching from its bishop (*Against Heresies*) concerning the hand-to-hand transmission of the faith, going forth from Rome, from the earliest apostolic activity. Gnosticism was attempting to provide a wholly virtual understanding of the transmission of the faith, lodged in secret teachings, which Irenaeus could easily prove had never been in the hands of any actual Christian up to that time. Significant for our reflections is Irenaeus' assessment of the role of Rome and its succession of bishops for the universal Church of that time:

> Since, however, it would be very tedious, in such a volume as this, to reckon up the successions of all the Churches, we do put to confusion all those who, in whatever manner, whether by an evil self-pleasing, by vainglory, or by blindness and perverse opinion, assemble in unauthorized meetings; [we do this, I say,] by indicating that tradition derived from the apostles, of the very great, the very ancient, and universally known Church founded and organized at Rome by the two most glorious apostles, Peter and Paul; as also [by pointing out] the faith preached to men, which comes down to our time by means of the successions of the bishops. For it is a matter of necessity that every Church should agree with this Church, on account of its pre-eminent authority, that is, the faithful everywhere, inasmuch as the apostolical tradition has been preserved continuously by those [faithful men] who exist everywhere.[6]

For Irenaeus, the guarantee of the proper succession of bishops *anywhere* is the succession of Roman bishops. That Christians *everywhere* should be interested in succession is a given for the bishop of Lyon. There is no apostasy in his day, unless it be the work of those outside the Christian community: the Gnostics and their allies.

---

[6] Saint Irenaeus of Lyons, *Against Heresies* 3, 3, 2, trans. Peter Kirby, Early Christian Writings, accessed July 13, 2024, www.earlychristianwritings.com/text/irenaeus-book3.html. Bracketed words included by the translator.

IX. The Slippery Slope of the Apostasy Theory

The unhistorical restorationist fancy of Joseph Smith has lacked the intellectual mettle of the bulk of the papacy's detractors (in Continental Protestant traditions), who nonetheless saw the Church's ecumenical councils as a way of securing Christian truth *in the flow of time*, responding to the need to *pass on* the gospel to the universal Church. One could affirm these councils and still decide to call the pope by the name of antichrist. But even here, a great apostasy is not foreseen. Given the antiquity of the faith and of some sort of role for the successor to Peter, one must look elsewhere than the subapostolic and patristic periods for the roots of error.

Consequently, a much stronger case for Roman error could be made by those who fingered the *medieval* period as the time for the apostasy. The English king Henry VIII fancied that he saw just such an error present in his day and took action to end the tyranny of the Middle Ages and the pope by ending his marriage to Catherine of Aragon. Snubbing the pope and all his works, Henry countered apostasy by marrying a total of six women in his own sort of succession—more authoritative to him, apparently, than the apostolic one. The pleas of Sir Thomas More and Bishop John Fisher, both saints, were powerless against Henry's self-aggrandizement, and the trashing of the Middle Ages and the papacy gained great new traction in England, not, of course, for any reasons connected with *politics*.

One counterintuitive type of apostasy theory concerns what is called sedevacantism (from the Latin meaning "empty chair"). Here is a theory emanating from *ultraconservative* Catholics that the Church has gone off the rails, quite possibly beginning with Pope John XXIII, who began the Second Vatican Council, which sedevacantists uniformly regard as invalid and heretical. Those who relish conspiracy and obsessive pursuits will certainly love sedevacantism. Some sedevacantists have even determined a new pope for themselves. The other one billion Catholics, presumably lost to the Catholic tradition, labor on under the impression that John Paul II, Benedict XVI, and Pope Francis represent a *true* papal lineage.

Sedevacantists take offense at the fact that God works in *fallible human beings*, missing all the while that in such beings God can work his sovereign will. More's the pity, since they thus miss the breathtaking and encouraging drama of divine action, which they do not seem to understand is for their *own* healing. We should not take scandal where God intends for none to be taken.

In point of fact, the idea of an apostasy is merely a slippery slope coming down to the present. Since the Catholic Church continues as a sort of provocation in the world—a sign of contradiction—new theories about its supposed weaknesses, failures, errors, and flaws will continually emerge. All these theories will claim equal validity, even if they are radically opposed to one another. All are probably equally false. Here one recalls Chesterton's pithy comment: "An historic institution, which never went right, is really quite as much of a miracle as an institution that cannot go wrong. The only explanation which immediately occurred to my mind was that Christianity [and one might add, the papacy] did not come from heaven, but from hell. Really, if Jesus of Nazareth was not Christ, He must have been Antichrist."[7]

Jesus must have been doubly the antichrist, according to the mass of antipapalists, if indeed he conferred on Peter *any* status whatsoever. And it is interesting that no non-Catholic religious group in the world can deal with the Lord's designs for Peter other than to *eliminate his role altogether.*

While it is true that the Church, in her members, including her popes, can demonstrate sin, error, and omission, none of this negates the *promise* given to the Church in Christ *via Peter* that the gates of hell will not prevail against this Church (see Mt 16:18). Nor does the Church *as such* teach error, despite the intellectual or moral condition of her members. As a matter of fact, her teaching is what *corrects* sin and error. To quote Chesterton again: "We do not really want a religion that is right where we are right. What we want is a religion that is right where we are wrong."[8] This, of course, is what the Catholic Church continues to accomplish century after century. This is a grand work of the Holy Spirit, and the only persons who can take offense at this probably are those who resent the fact that God works at all in the world that his sovereignty created.

---

[7] G. K. Chesterton, *Orthodoxy* (New York: John Lane, 1909), 165.

[8] G. K. Chesterton, *The Catholic Church and Conversion* (San Francisco: Ignatius Press, 2006; originally published 1926 by Macmillan [New York]), 115.

X. Conclusion

To conclude this consideration of the papacy, we must come back to the figure of Jesus Christ. The Church in which the papacy exists is called the Body of Christ. By this is meant that the real action of Jesus Christ is traceable in the Church and that the Church, of all structures in the created order, gives human beings a direct participation in his sovereign life and action. The created order needs the figure of Christ to proclaim the meaning and purpose of all things, especially if it concerns the *human* participation in all those things. That God's wisdom is traceable in all things is clear, in spite of the presence of evil and tragedy. But when, where, and how shall human beings experience forgiveness, redemption, eternal life, the vindication of the good, final justice, the defeat of death, and a consummation of bliss? The answers to these questions, as far as human beings will ever be able to receive them, is found in the singular figure of Jesus of Nazareth—the Lord, the Savior, the Son of God, the Eternal Judge. This Christ *is* the Church, especially given that everyone within this Body will share his resurrected humanity in the world to come. The future life of all the elect is in him, even now. He *is* his Body, even as he is the Head. Abstractions concerning salvation and the created order are not the stuff of the Christian religion. This religion is based on a divinized realism that includes concrete things, even as it transcends these created things.

Sometimes, anti-Christian polemics within the ranks of the Latter-day Saint community propagate the idea of a "Hellenistic perversion" of the religion of Jesus within the tradition of the Church. Truth be told, given the revolutionary fullness of the revelation of Christ, if we did not already have Greek metaphysics to help with explanation, we would have had to invent it! Actually, we have *reconstructed* the Hellenistic inheritance for the purposes of the gospel, and the evidence is all around us of the divine unction poured out upon the world through the Spirit in the Catholic Church.

In the kingdom to come, there will be no popes, no priests and deacons, no monks, no Masses, no baptisms, no need for terrestrial human order or for sacraments, including marriage (see Mt 22:30). All that Christ has ordained to guide us from this life to the next will be superseded by the fullness of the vision of him forever. Until that time, he is fulfilling his promise: "I will not leave you desolate" (Jn 14:18). If someone were to ask the question, Why has God done so much, provided so much, taught us so much in the Church?, he would be asking exactly the right question. He would show that he understands the generosity and careful, even exhaustive, providence of God. That is the inner meaning of the complexity of the Catholic faith—a complexity that is often daunting to the uninitiated.

But would God actually leave us with little? Would he be stingy? If a structure of authority, teaching, and sacramental action would help us, would God fail to give it? No. Nor has he failed to give it. Those setting out to contemplate the meaning of the papacy must first understand *their real needs* and, then, the amazing, tangible ways God has set about to meet those needs.

9

Mormon Pelagianism

Joel Barstad

I have been invited to address the topic of Mormon Pelagianism[1] with the aim of showing readers the radical difference between Mormonism and Catholicism. As someone who was raised Lutheran, however, I cannot help but be sensitive to a certain irony here. Many readers—Protestant, Mormon, and even Catholic—may be puzzled: "Isn't that like the pot calling the kettle black?" This volume was proposed because the editors felt that Mormonism contains certain key doctrinal claims that Protestant apologists cannot contest forcefully enough because they themselves hold positions akin to those of Mormonism. Topics such as Petrine primacy, faith and reason, and the Marian dogmas all clearly fit in this category. But if there were one topic on which Catholics might be expected to have more in common with Latter-day Saints than with Protestants, surely that would be the necessary role of meritorious good works in achieving salvation. Or so the conventional wisdom would suggest.

To correct this common misconception, one has only to wander through Denzinger's *Compendium of Creeds, Definitions, and Declarations on Matters of Faith and Morals*,[2] looking for entries on original

---

[1] Pelagianism is named for a fourth- and fifth-century ascetical writer from the British Isles, Pelagius (c. 360–418), who sought to defend the natural freedom and ability of the human will to obey God from any form of determinism, whether in the form of pagan fatalism or Christian doctrines of original sin and predestination.

[2] Heinrich Denzinger, *Compendium of Creeds, Definitions, and Declarations on Matters of Faith and Morals*, ed. Helmut Hoping and Peter Hünermann (original bilingual ed.), ed. Robert Fastiggi and Anne Englund Nash (English ed.), 43rd ed. (San Francisco: Ignatius Press, 2012).

sin, freedom of the will, and predestination. Pelagianism and Semi-Pelagianism were rejected long ago as heresies by the Roman Magisterium when it adopted the propositions and anathemas formulated at the Synod of Carthage in A.D. 418,[3] at the Second Synod of Orange in A.D. 529,[4] and by its promulgation of the decrees made by the Council of Trent at its fifth and sixth sessions in A.D. 1546[5] and A.D. 1547.[6] Nonetheless, the conventional wisdom is not without grounds. Catholics very often do seem to attenuate or ignore the Augustinian elements of their past in favor of a practical concentration on the importance of doing good and avoiding evil. There is a strongly moralistic tendency in popular Catholicism, even when the necessity of grace is acknowledged and affirmed.

In my two decades of teaching at a Roman Catholic seminary, the area of Catholic doctrine that has disturbed more of my students than any other is the Augustinian doctrine of grace as affirmed by the Second Synod of Orange and subsequent councils. All of them instinctively prefer the Semi-Pelagianism of Saint John Cassian (c. 360–435) to the anti-Pelagian rigor of Saint Augustine of Hippo (354–430). Nothing is as fearful to them as falling into an Augustinian view of predestination or a Calvinist doctrine of total depravity. To be sure, Augustine's doctrine of election and predestination led some of his followers to conclusions about predestination that the pro-Augustinian Second Synod of Orange condemned.[7] Yet, even the authentic Catholic doctrine of predestination, carefully articulated and qualified by an eminent authority like Saint Thomas Aquinas (1225–1274), is more than some of my students are willing to bear. Some are so used to reducing predestination to foreknowledge and election to a temporal vocation that they actually misconstrue the Augustinian texts when they read them and misunderstand his doctrine, unable to imagine that such a revered Father of the Church could actually teach what he does.

---

[3] Ibid., 222–30.

[4] Ibid., 370–97.

[5] Ibid., 1510–16.

[6] Ibid., 1520–83.

[7] "Not only do we not believe that some are predestined to evil by the divine power, but if there are any who wish to believe such an enormity, we with great abhorrence anathematize them" (ibid., 397). The doctrine of "double predestination" has been a perennial temptation for Augustinians. As taught by the monk Gottschalk of Orbais (c. 808–867), it was condemned at the Synod of Quiercy in A.D. 853 (ibid., 621–24), along with a version of the later Calvinist doctrine of limited atonement.

When they do finally understand what Augustine and the medieval synods taught, they feel betrayed. When they try to argue out a more acceptable doctrine, reason itself seems to betray them and they find themselves floundering in philosophical quagmires. No wonder they quickly retreat from metaphysical theology to the practical boundaries of moral theology, where they find the firm footing they need for moral decision and resolve. It is with great relief that they welcome the assigned reading from John Cassian, whose thought seems more suitable for nourishing good morals and practical piety.[8] I have had some who are even willing to profess themselves Pelagians, not because they wish to repudiate their Catholic faith but precisely because they see no other way to defend the moral vision they have received as an essential element of their Catholic faith against Protestant views of original sin and justification, not to mention secular versions of determinism.

Nor are they alone. As Rebecca Weaver rightly observes, the orthodox position has always invited dispute, qualification, and equivocation even by those formally committed to it.

The relationship between divine grace and human agency has been the source of recurrent dispute throughout the history of the Western church. The controversies surrounding Pelagius in the early fifth

---

[8] I usually assign John Cassian, "The Third Conference of Abbot Chaeremon", in *Nicene and Post-Nicene Fathers*, series 2, vol. 11 (A.D. 426–429; repr., Peabody, MA: Hendrickson, 1994). Exemplifying Cassian's characteristic moderation, chapter 18 concludes the conference by emphasizing the manifold ways in which God works with men according to their need: "God the Father of all things worketh indifferently all things in all, as the Apostle says, like some most kind father and most benign physician; and that now He puts into us the very beginnings of salvation, and gives to each the zeal of his free will; and now grants the carrying out of the work, and the perfecting of goodness; and now saves men, even against their will and without their knowledge, from ruin that is close at hand, and a headlong fall; and now affords them occasions and opportunities of salvation, and wards off headlong and violent attacks from purposes that would bring death; and assists some who are already willing and running, while He draws others who are unwilling and resisting, and forces them to a good will. But that, when we do not always resist or remain persistently unwilling, everything is granted to us by God, and that the main share in our salvation is to be ascribed not to the merit of our own works but to heavenly grace.... For the God of all must be held to work in all, so as to incite, protect, and strengthen, but not to take away the freedom of the will which He Himself has once given. If however any more subtle inference of man's argumentation and reasoning seems opposed to this interpretation, it should be avoided rather than brought forward to the destruction of the faith ... for how God works all things in us and yet everything can be ascribed to free will, cannot be fully grasped by the mind and reason of man" (434–35).

century, the Semi-Pelagians in the fifth and early sixth centuries, Gott-schalk in the ninth century, the Jesuit Molina and the Dominican Báñez in the De Auxiliis controversies in the sixteenth and early seventeenth centuries, and the Jansenists in the seventeenth and eighteenth centuries are only the most prominent instances of a debate for which the church has never found a satisfactory resolution.[9]

Among Catholics, only a few die-hard Thomists and Augustinians seem to be immune to this dissatisfaction.[10] Among Protestants, the Confessional Lutherans and five-point Calvinists, though often vociferous in their own spheres, are seldom welcome in the polite company of the much larger Evangelical and liberal circles. Of course, no one wants to deny the grace of God. Indeed, until recently, few Christians wanted to be thought to deny the primacy of grace. No matter how much they attenuated the efficacy of grace by insisting upon the cooperative role of the human will or by disconnecting the distribution of grace from the historical ministry of the Church, they retained enough of the historical Christian understanding of the gospel of Jesus Christ as the proclamation and work of God's grace that they were loath to break with that element of the tradition.

I. Pelagianism and the Latter-day Saints

Mormonism, however, is not susceptible to the same inhibitions as other historical Christian traditions. Not only does it regard the Catholic centuries before the Reformation as hopelessly corrupt, as many radical Protestants also do, but it even dismisses the pretensions of those who propose reforming the Church on such a venerable basis as Scripture alone. The Church of Jesus Christ of Latter-day Saints does not propose itself as a reformation; it is a restoration, made necessary by an apostasy so early and so complete that even the Old and New Testaments are useless until supplemented and corrected by the revelations,

[9] Rebecca Harden Weaver, *Divine Grace and Human Agency: A Study of the Semi-Pelagian Controversy*, North American Patristic Society Patristic Monograph Series, vol. 15 (Macon, GA: Mercer University Press, 1996), ix.

[10] The index of the *Catechism of the Catholic Church* has only six references under "predestination" and no entry for "election".

reinstituted priesthoods, and temple ordinances given through Joseph Smith. The restored gospel of Jesus Christ cannot be measured by any part of the Catholic tradition, even the Bible, because the true form of the gospel is impossible to reconstruct from the fragments available to historical memory.

When James E. Talmage (1862–1933) wrote his classic exposition of Joseph Smith's Articles of Faith,[11] he showed no deference to even the most hallowed elements of historical Christian theological tradition. After the Great Apostasy, authentic doctrines were replaced by "numerous theories and dogmas of men, many of which are utterly incomprehensible in their mysticism and inconsistency".[12] This objection applies both to the ecumenical Christian doctrine of the Trinity articulated at the Council of Nicaea (A.D. 325) and to the more widespread philosophical doctrine of God's immateriality and incomprehensibility. "The Church of Jesus Christ of Latter-day Saints proclaims against the incomprehensible God, devoid of 'body, parts, and passions,' as a thing impossible of existence, and asserts its belief in and allegiance to the true and living God of scripture and revelation."[13] There is no lip service to the primacy of grace—there is not even an entry for the word in the index to Talmage's work— and his affirmation of human agency could not be stronger: "Man has inherited among the inalienable rights conferred upon him by his divine Father, absolute freedom to choose the good or the evil in life as he may elect."[14]

When the more recent author of the article on "Grace" in the *Encyclopedia of Mormonism* reviews the history of the doctrine of grace in historical Christian theology, he does so with a condescending sympathy for the plight of those who throughout known Christian history struggled in vain to reconcile the teachings of Paul and James because they lacked the true New Testament understanding restored by the LDS position. Indeed, a sophisticated Mormon writer like Sterling McMurrin (1914–1996) is likely to point out that the perennial difficulty of historical Christian theology to account for human free agency

[11] James E. Talmage, *The Articles of Faith: A Series of Lectures on the Principal Doctrines of the Church of Jesus Christ of Latter-Day Saints* (Salt Lake City: Deseret News, 1899).
[12] Ibid., 47.
[13] Ibid., 48.
[14] Ibid., 54.

and responsibility is simply an unnecessary complication resulting from
the adoption of a Platonic-Aristotelian metaphysics of being, which posits such things as immaterial substances, not to mention the acceptance
of the scripturally unwarranted doctrine of *creatio ex nihilo* (creation out
of nothing). A more literal and anthropomorphic reading of the Old
and New Testaments, even as they have them, he argues, would have
preserved Catholics and Protestants alike from the conundrums they
face when trying to explain how a genuinely free, temporal, bodily,
created agency can be derived from a single, necessarily existent, good,
eternal, all-powerful principle of all being and existence. By all means
keep his moral goodness, but are all the other traditional attributes of
God really necessary? Better to risk imagining God as having a being
too much like our own than to make him so unimaginably different
that we end up calling into question our own capacity for independent
and responsible moral action.[15]

Consequently, alongside the irony of a Catholic criticizing someone else for being too Pelagian, a second difficulty arises, namely,
Why would a Mormon reader of this book care if I, stuck in my
historical mire of apostate orthodoxies and heresies, label him a Pelagian? I have no answer to that, except to notice that, for whatever
reason, there seem to be some Mormons, even the author of the
article on "Grace" mentioned above, who seem to be interested in
entering into dialogue with Christians of the historical traditions and
who seem to express some desire to be accorded the recognition that
they, too, are Christian in a respectable sense and are offended by
simply being cast out into the "kingdom of the cults".[16] At the end
of this chapter, such a Mormon reader may remain as convinced of

---

[15] Sterling M. McMurrin, "Some Distinguishing Characteristics of Mormon Philosophy",
Sunstone, March 1993, 35–46.

[16] *The Kingdom of the Cults*, first published in 1965, by Walter R. Martin has for nearly six
decades provided American Evangelicals with a category into which to put religious groups
that sit on the peripheries of historical Christian confessions by virtue of their denial or radical reinterpretation of historically core beliefs about God and Christ. Compare with Ted
A. Campbell, *Christian Confessions* (Louisville, KY: Westminster John Knox Press, 1996),
286–92. These groups are as disparate as Christian Science, the Church of Jesus Christ of
Latter-day Saints, Jehovah's Witnesses, Armstrongism, Theosophy, the Bahá'í Faith, Uni-
tarian Universalism, Scientology, and the Seventh-day Adventist Church. The word "cult",
however, has associations with brainwashing and forms of repressive social control that make
it an unfairly prejudicial term for such a category.

his Mormon faith as I am of my Catholic faith; but both of us should understand more clearly why I think his Mormon faith belongs to another world than does any historical Christian confession rooted in the Scriptures and the ecumenical creeds of the Catholic Church. And while Pelagianism is a perennial temptation in the Catholic world, it remains a heresy; whereas it is one of the natural elements of the Mormon world.

II. Pelagianism

But what, in any world, do I mean by Pelagianism?

In God all creatures "live and move and have [their] being" (Acts 17:28), each according to its nature, a nature that need not exist but that God has freely brought into existence from nothing and freely sustains in existence and act. Such is the classic Christian doctrine of creation. In rational natures, that movement is one of knowing and willing, interior operations that are free from external compulsion. They act for the good they themselves have known and chosen and are therefore responsible for their actions in ways irrational creatures are not. Knowing reality elicits desire for something lacked; desire leads to inquiry and deliberation about what is possible and discriminations between better and worse, as well as judgments about what ought and ought not to be done. The will may be inclined to the better option or not; choice succeeds judgment but need not follow its dictates, in which case the greater good may be refused and the lesser chosen. After choice, the impulse of the will leads to act, which, if no external force intervenes, achieves its object and possesses what it once lacked. And thus desire ends in enjoyment.[17]

In each of these moments, the will manifests its character, but it is in choice that that character is most clearly asserted and defined. In choosing against the judgment of reason, the individual rational nature chooses against its nature as rational. It chooses not to be the kind of nature it was made to be. And yet this possibility is rooted in

---

[17]John Damascene provides a convenient summary and synthesis of ancient philosophy and early Christian theology on these matters. For the sequence of movements of the will, see *On the Orthodox Faith* 2, 22, trans. Frederic H. Chase, Jr., in *The Fathers of the Church: Saint John of Damascus; Writings*, vol. 37 (Washington, DC: CUA Press, 1958), 249.

the nature itself. Here is the mystery of created freedom. God sustains and moves all individual beings according to their natures, but beings of this nature have as natural the possibility of acting unnaturally. There is, thus, a paradoxical asymmetry between good acts, which are in accord with reason, and evil ones, which are contrary to reason. When the being acts in full accord with its nature, God's sustaining and moving causality is not morally problematic; yet, because the possibility of acting contrary to reason is rooted in the nature, when God sustains and moves the being according to its nature, God may find himself sustaining and moving it while it chooses and acts unnaturally. Is God, then, the willing cause of evil? That is one of the conundrums of the classic Christian doctrine of creation.

Moreover, God can sustain and move a creature not only according to its nature but also according to grace. Thus, by grace God can overcome the negative potential of nature, not by changing the nature, that is, not by taking away its natural freedom to choose against reason, but in some other way ensuring that it will act naturally in accord with reason. Moreover, by grace he can move a being to know and will in ways that exceed its natural ability to know and will, and again this is done without displacing the first nature by means of another, for grace belongs to another order of divine operation than that of creating, sustaining, and moving natures. Now reason is confronted with two kinds of unnaturalness: the less-than-nature unnaturalness of moral evil, and the greater-than-nature unnaturalness of grace. Because it is natural to man to act always by knowing and willing, to be confronted with the possibility, let alone the necessity, of his acting in ways that exceed the natural capacities of knowing and willing can only result in vertigo for natural reason and will—unless it is moved and sustained by grace to that kind of knowing Christians call faith and that kind of willing they call charity. It is indeed possible, confronted with the perplexities of reason alone, to experience a peace that passes all understanding, but that does not make the matter in itself understandable and explicable.

The Church teaches that even before Adam sinned, he needed grace to attain the supernatural end for which human beings were created; and that after sin entered the world, no one can or will be saved unless God first chooses to give him the grace he needs to start the journey and then sustains him with grace at every step of the way. Such a teaching deeply undermines an instinctive human desire to affirm the autonomy of human moral agency. Consequently, when using reason to explain, persuade, exhort, or admonish others or themselves, Christians tend to step down from the vertiginous ledge of grace and stand on the broader ground of natural morality.

Pelagianism is the tendency both to reduce grace to nature and to minimize the impact of original sin on the integrity of human nature, thereby minimizing the scope of the remedial grace needed to restore the human will to its proper natural capacity for obedience to the divine will. But more seriously, Pelagianism is the heretical tendency to deny that human nature in its unfallen state, and perhaps even in its fallen state, needs any sort of interior grace in order to be able to obey the divine law.

A pure Pelagian would deny that human beings need any special internal sustaining and moving beyond what is given in nature. The only kinds of grace he would recognize would be external helps from God, such as laws or living examples that supplement the natural finitude of human knowledge. He might recognize the need for remedial help to overcome the bad habits he has acquired, which have an interior binding effect on his will so that it is difficult to begin and sustain a consistent pattern of good choices and acts; but he is likely to look for those in the form of changed circumstances and progressive programs of self-discipline. He might readily accept the "grace" of the forgiveness of past sins, if he is convinced that the work of reparation is beyond his capacity; but what he is really interested in is a fresh start, a new beginning from which he can advance in moral strength, one choice and one act at a time, until he has achieved the stability and excellence of a will that never chooses anything contrary to his judgment or, better still, to God's judgment, regarding what is good. What he really needs from God is a clear revelation by law and example of what is right to do. That, together with the atonement for sins, is precisely what the "grace" of Christ consists of.[18] Everything else depends on man and his free use of his agency.

Semi-Pelagianism acknowledges the need for interior grace but holds out the possibility that in some human beings the natural endowments of reason and will are sufficiently intact to take the first step in seeking the grace needed for salvation.[19] The orthodox position maintains that man, especially in his fallen condition, would not and could not initiate this search if he were not already being moved interiorly by grace. Catholics, when put to it, are usually willing to concede enough of the principles of the metaphysical monism contained in the dogma of *creatio ex nihilo*, as well as in the doctrines of original sin, election, and predestination, to avoid the heresy of theoretical Pelagianism. They may not be as zealous in their embrace of these doctrines as their separated Confessional Lutheran and five-point Calvinist brethren, but they readily acknowledge the need for the supernatural interior grace given in the sacraments. Nonetheless, the desire to be in control of one's own salvation runs deep in the human heart. There is a tendency even among relatively well-catechized Catholics to talk about grace as if it were a kind of extra power that lies within their power to use or not use. They do not deny the necessity of grace, but they attenuate its otherness so that they can concentrate their natural activities of knowing and willing on what lies within their own power to do or not to do. "Pray as if everything depends on God, but act as though everything depends on you." "The grace has all been given; now it up to us to use it." Such have become the slogans of a practical Pelagianism that may remain theoretically orthodox.

III. Mormon Pelagianism

I have belabored this point because it is important to have some sense of the tensions inherent in a Catholic mentality before comparing it with a Latter-day Saint one. I have tried to indicate that I do not think that practical Pelagianism is an acceptable resting place for the Catholic mind. If one sets human agency within the broader context of the Catholic and Latter-day Saint churches' teachings about the nature of God, the origin of the world, and the destiny of men, one will see why for Catholicism the tendency labeled Pelagianism is a heresy, whereas for Mormonism it is simply an essential element of its religious worldview. It was one of the key elements that unfolded

[19] See note 8.

in stages in the revelations received by Joseph Smith. Its interactions with the prior traditions of Christian orthodoxies can result in apparent similarities and superficial differences. Very traditional principles from the Augustinian tradition may be accepted but combined to produce a functionally Pelagian outcome. Nonetheless, if one faithfully follows the theme through its development, one soon sees the difference in Joseph Smith's overarching vision of the divine plan for human destiny and the place of such notions as nature, grace, and free will within it.

For example, when one reads the second of the Articles of Faith of the Church of Jesus Christ of Latter-day Saints, namely, "We believe that men will be punished for their own sins, and not for Adam's transgression",[20] and understands that, therefore, Latter-day Saints reject the ancient practice of infant baptism, one might infer that Mormonism has simply chosen to side with those, such as the ancient Pelagians, who rejected the traditional Augustinian doctrine of original sin.

The Pelagians seem to have taught that infants ought to be baptized, but not for the remission of sins, or, if they accepted the Church's use of such a formula in the case of infants, they did so with the understanding that it did not technically apply to them because "they derive from Adam no trace of original sin that would have to be removed by the bath of rebirth."[21] In their view, Adam's sin introduced bad customs that in time corrupted the common memory of the law and led to children being reared in ignorance and bad habits. The teaching and example of Christ restores a proper understanding of the law, and his atonement provides for the forgiveness of actual sins that a person commits when he reaches a condition of culpability sufficient to make him personally guilty of such acts; but human nature itself has never lost its capacity for choosing and doing what the law requires. The grace of Christ, the gospel, consists essentially of an external restoration of the law and a forensic forgiveness of past sins, not of the internal gift of a new or restored capacity to choose the good.[22] Pelagians see a maximal continuity between the original state of Adam and the state of every human being. Even death is natural to human nature and not a penalty

---

[20] Articles of Faith 2, in Pearl of Great Price (PGP).
[21] Denzinger, *Compendium*, 223.
[22] Compare with ibid., 225–26.

for sin.[23] Life after death is, thus, the natural place of reward for the deeds done during mortal life.

That Mormonism shares this understanding of the human condition and of the function of the gospel seems to be further confirmed by the third Article of Faith: "We believe that through the atonement of Christ, all mankind may be saved, by obedience to the laws and ordinances of the Gospel."[24] It would seem that for Mormonism as for Pelagianism, salvation is essentially a matter of knowing and doing the right thing; grace is primarily for remediation of ignorance and past sins, not for the internal renovation of a damaged human nature. However, whatever the similarities that may exist between Mormon and Pelagian practical attitudes toward moral and religious life, the configurations of theological principles supporting those attitudes are quite different. Consider, for example, Enoch's account of God's revelation to Adam recorded by Joseph Smith in the restoration of the original revelation given to Moses, which is only partially retained in the Old Testament Book of Genesis:

> Because that Adam fell, we are; and by his fall came death; and we are made partakers of misery and woe. Behold Satan hath come among the children of men, and tempteth them to worship him; and men have become carnal, sensual, and devilish, and are shut out from the presence of God. But God hath made known unto our fathers that all men must repent. And he called upon our father Adam by his own voice, saying: I am God; I made the world, and men before they were in the flesh. And he also said unto him: If thou wilt turn unto me, and hearken unto my voice, and believe, and repent of all thy transgressions, and be baptized, even in water, in the name of mine Only Begotten Son, who is full of grace and truth, which is Jesus Christ, the only name which shall be given under heaven, whereby salvation shall come unto the children of men, ye shall receive the gift of the Holy Ghost, asking all things in his name, and whatsoever ye shall ask, it shall be given you. And our father Adam spake unto the Lord, and said: Why is it that men must repent and be baptized in water? And the Lord said unto Adam: Behold I have forgiven thee thy transgression in the Garden of Eden.

[23] Ibid., 222.
[24] Articles of Faith 3.

Hence came the saying abroad among the people, that the Son of God hath atoned for original guilt, wherein the sins of the parents cannot be answered upon the heads of the children, for they are whole from the foundation of the world. And the Lord spake unto Adam, saying: Inasmuch as thy children are conceived in sin, even so when they begin to grow up, sin conceiveth in their hearts, and they taste the bitter, that they may know to prize the good. And it is given unto them to know good from evil; wherefore they are agents unto themselves, and I have given unto you another law and commandment.[25]

This passage does not directly contradict the Catholic understanding of original sin and its effects on the descendants of Adam; rather, in the last two verses it interposes the doctrine of the atonement in such a way as to mitigate the effects of original sin so that infant baptism is no longer necessary and adult baptism is for the remission of personal sins only. The result is a synthesis that implies that the Augustinian doctrine of inherited guilt and bondage to sin may be legitimate in principle, while positing an actual post-Fall status quo that is practically, though not theoretically, equivalent to the Pelagian view. This view of the status quo even posits that thus remediated, the human predicament and the solution to the predicament now lie at the level of knowledge and tradition.

Every spirit of man was innocent in the beginning; and God having redeemed man from the fall, men became again, in their infant state, innocent before God. And that wicked one cometh and taketh away light and truth, through disobedience, from the children of men, and because of the tradition of their fathers. But I have commanded you to bring up your children in light and truth.[26]

The atonement of Christ not only serves to preserve individual accountability and moral agency from the effects of sin but also makes the new susceptibility to temptation and sin a benefit rather than a liability. When, in an earlier chapter of the Book of Moses, Adam and Eve were taught the meaning of animal sacrifice, which God had

---

[25] Moses 6:48–56, in PGP.
[26] Doctrine and Covenants (DC) 93:38–40.

commanded them to keep, namely, that it "is a similitude of the sacrifice of the Only Begotten of the Father, which is full of grace and
truth",[27] they rejoiced that by virtue of the atonement they were now,
even in this life, in a better condition than before they ate of the forbidden tree.

> And in that day Adam blessed God and was filled, and began to
> prophesy concerning all the families of the earth, saying: Blessed be
> the name of God, for because of my transgression my eyes are opened,
> and in this life I shall have joy, and again in the flesh I shall see God.
> And Eve, his wife, heard all these things and was glad, saying: Were
> it not for our transgression we never should have had seed, and never
> should have known good and evil, and the joy of our redemption, and
> the eternal life which God giveth unto all the obedient.[28]

By means of such passages, Latter-day Saint teachers are able to
paint a picture of the actual state of infants and man that is remarkably
consistent with the historical Pelagian optimism about the capacity
of human agency: whatever damages Adam's sin might have caused
to human nature were immediately mitigated by the universal preve-
nient grace of the foreseen atonement of Christ, so that now human
beings are in an even better position to differentiate themselves by
their own free will and obedience than Adam and Eve were before
the Fall, provided, of course, they have true knowledge of the divine
laws and ordinances.

So far the revelations of Joseph Smith cited here have shown an
affinity only with Arminian Evangelical theology. But there are other
passages in which something new and distinctly Mormon comes into
view.[29] The Book of Moses and the Book of Abraham both contain
retellings of the creation accounts of Genesis. Those in the Book of
Moses involve speculative insertions and clarifications that, while dis-
concerting for non-Mormons when read as insertions into a familiar

---

[27] Moses 5:7.

[28] Moses 5:10–11.

[29] Charles R. Harrell, "This Is My Doctrine": The Development of Mormon Theology (Draper,
UT: Greg Kofford Books, 2011), 263. Harrell's work is fascinating not only for the light it
sheds on the development of Mormon theology but also for the perspective in which it allows
one to view the theological landscape of the time.

biblical text, are not in content so different from the speculations about the text that one can find in the commentaries of Saint Augustine or the poetic extrapolations of John Milton.

And it came to pass that the Lord spake unto Moses, saying: Behold, I reveal unto you concerning this heaven, and this earth; write the words which I speak. I am the Beginning and the End, the Almighty God; by mine Only Begotten I created these things; yea, in the beginning I created the heaven, and the earth upon which thou standest. And the earth was without a form, and void; and I caused darkness to come up upon the face of the deep; and my Spirit moved upon the face of the water; for I am God. And I, God, said: Let there be light; and there was light....

And I, God, said unto mine Only Begotten, which was with me from the beginning: Let us make man in our image, after our likeness; and it was so. And I, God, said: Let them have dominion over the fishes of the sea, and over the fowl of the air, and over the cattle, and over all the earth, and over every creeping thing that creepeth upon the earth. And I, God, created man in mine own image, in the image of mine Only Begotten created I him; male and female created I them....

And now, behold, I say unto you, that these are the generations of the heaven and of the earth, when they were created, in the day that I, the Lord God, made the heaven and the earth, And every plant of the field before it was in the earth, and every herb of the field before it grew. For I, the Lord God, created all things, of which I have spoken, spiritually, before they were naturally upon the face of the earth. For I, the Lord God, had not caused it to rain upon the face of the earth.

And I, the Lord God, had created all the children of men; and not yet a man to till the ground; for in heaven created I them; and there was not yet flesh upon the earth, neither in the water, neither in the air; But I, the Lord God, spake, and there went up a mist from the earth, and watered the whole face of the ground. And I, the Lord God, formed man from the dust of the ground, and breathed into his nostrils the breath of life; and man became a living soul, the first flesh upon the earth, the first man also; nevertheless, all things were before created; but spiritually were they created and made according to my word....

And I, the Lord God, spake unto Moses, saying: That Satan, whom thou hast commanded in the name of mine Only Begotten, is the same which was from the beginning, and he came before me, saying—Behold, here am I, send me, I will be thy son, and I will redeem all mankind, that one soul shall not be lost, and surely I will do it; wherefore give me thine honor. But, behold, my Beloved Son, which was my Beloved and Chosen from the beginning, said unto me—Father, thy will be done, and the glory be thine forever. Wherefore, because that Satan rebelled against me, and sought to destroy the agency of man, which I, the Lord God, had given him, and also, that I should give unto him mine own power; by the power of mine Only Begotten, I caused that he should be cast down; And he became Satan, yea, even the devil, the father of all lies, to deceive and to blind men, and to lead them captive at his will, even as many as would not hearken unto my voice. And now the serpent was more subtle than any beast of the field which I, the Lord God, had made. And Satan put it into the heart of the serpent, (for he had drawn away many after him,) and he sought also to beguile Eve, for he knew not the mind of God, wherefore he sought to destroy the world.[30]

When we turn to the Book of Abraham, however, the narrative has taken on a new character.

Howbeit that he made the greater star; as, also, if there be two spirits, and one shall be more intelligent than the other, yet these two spirits, notwithstanding one is more intelligent than the other, have no beginning; they existed before, they shall have no end, they shall exist after, for they are gnolaum, or eternal.

And the Lord said unto me: These two facts do exist, that there are two spirits, one being more intelligent than the other; there shall be another more intelligent than they; I am the Lord thy God, I am more intelligent than they all.

The Lord thy God sent his angel to deliver thee from the hands of the priest of Elkenah. I dwell in the midst of them all; I now, therefore, have come down unto thee to declare unto thee the works which my hands have made, wherein my wisdom excelleth them all, for I rule in the heavens above, and in the earth beneath, in all wisdom and prudence, over all the intelligences thine eyes have seen from the beginning; I came down in the beginning in the midst of all the intelligences thou hast seen.

Now the Lord had shown unto me, Abraham, the intelligences that were organized before the world was; and among all these there were many of the noble and great ones;

[30] Moses 2:1–3, 26–27; 3:4–7; 4:1–6.

And God saw these souls that they were good, and he stood in the midst of them, and he said: These I will make my rulers; for he stood among those that were spirits, and he saw that they were good; and he said unto me: Abraham, thou art one of them; thou wast chosen before thou wast born. And there stood one among them that was like unto God, and he said unto those who were with him: We will go down, for there is space there, and we will take of these materials, and we will make an earth whereon these may dwell; And we will prove them herewith, to see if they will do all things whatsoever the Lord their God shall command them; And they who keep their first estate shall be added upon; and they who keep not their first estate shall not have glory in the same kingdom with those who keep their first estate; and they who keep their second estate shall have glory added upon their heads for ever and ever. And the Lord said: Whom shall I send? And one answered like unto the Son of Man: Here am I, send me. And another answered and said: Here am I, send me. And the Lord said: I will send the first. And the second was angry, and kept not his first estate; and, at that day, many followed after him.

The Gods plan the creation of the earth and all life thereon—Their plans for the six days of creation are set forth.

And then the Lord said: Let us go down. And they went down at the beginning, and they, that is the Gods, organized and formed the heavens and the earth. And the earth, after it was formed, was empty and desolate, because they had not formed anything but the earth; and darkness reigned upon the face of the deep, and the Spirit of the Gods was brooding upon the face of the waters. And they (the Gods) said: Let there be light; and there was light. . . .

And the Gods took counsel among themselves and said: Let us go down and form man in our image, after our likeness; and we will give them dominion over the fish of the sea, and over the fowl of the air, and over the cattle, and over all the earth, and over every creeping thing that creepeth upon the earth. So the Gods went down to organize man in their own image, in the image of the Gods to form they him, male and female to form they them. . . .

And the Gods concluded upon the seventh time, because that on the seventh time they would rest from all their works which they (the Gods) counseled among themselves to form; and sanctified it. And thus were their decisions at the time that they counseled among themselves to form the heavens and the earth. And the Gods came down and formed these the generations of the heavens and of the earth, when they were formed in the day that the Gods formed the earth and the heavens, According to all that which they had said concerning every plant of the field before it was in the earth, and every herb of the field before it grew; for the Gods had not caused it to rain upon the earth when they counseled to do them, and had not formed a man to till the ground. But there went up a mist from the earth, and watered the whole face of the ground. And the Gods formed man from the dust of the ground, and took his spirit (that is, the man's spirit), and put it into him; and breathed into his nostrils the breath of life, and man became a living soul. And the Gods planted a garden, eastward in Eden, and there they put the man, whose spirit they had put into the body which they had formed.[31]

Here we have left the world of traditional monotheism. Even a tritheist account of the Trinitarian doctrine of the Godhead is not very evident; notice how the Spirit of God has become the Spirit of the "Gods" in a realm of eternal intelligences, differing one among the others according to power but not in kind. The "Lord thy God" is merely the greatest of them all and undertakes the task of "organizing" them. In fact, "created" has yielded to "organized" throughout the text, which emphasizes the use of preexistent material. Metaphysical monism, that is, the view that all of reality derives from a single, ultimate source of being, is gone and with it, the doctrine of *creatio ex nihilo*. Human souls are among the intelligences that antedate the creation of heaven and earth, preexisting the bodies formed for them. The material creation has become a second stage—subsequent to the purely spiritual one—added on so that obedience may be tested and glory earned or lost.

In the subsequent history of Latter-day Saint doctrine, different authorities have held widely divergent views about the origin and nature of God. Some, like Lorenzo Snow (1814–1901), echoed later statements by Joseph Smith that contain an image of God as having had a history like our own: "As man now is, God once was: As God now is, man may be."[32] Others, like Bruce R. McConkie (1915–1985), appealing to other, usually early, statements, emphasize that whatever

---

[31] Abraham 3:18–28; 4:1–3, 26–27; 5:3–8, in PGP.
[32] Quoted in *Teachings of the Presidents of the Church: Lorenzo Snow* (Salt Lake City: Church of Jesus Christ of Latter-day Saints, 2012), 83.

the past progress of God or the Gods, he or they are in full possession of divinity now.[33] What is interesting about this varied history of the Mormon doctrine of God is that by the end of the prophet's life, it had become completely detached from the synthesis of biblical and Hellenic monotheism that formed the bedrock of historical Christian theology. Mormon theology in the strict sense, that is, the doctrine of God, harmonizes with its anthropology, the doctrine of man. The anthropomorphisms of the Scriptures are not put through the metaphysical grinder but accepted at face value.

> The greatest truth known to man is that there is a God in heaven who is infinite and eternal; that he is the creator, upholder, and preserver of all things; that he created us and the sidereal heavens and ordained and established a plan of salvation whereby we might advance and progress and become like him. The truth pertaining to him is that he is our Father in heaven, that he has a body of flesh and bones as tangible as man's, that he is a literal person, and that if we believe and obey his laws we can gain the exaltation that he possesses. Now that is the greatest truth and the most glorious concept known to the human mind, and the reverse of it is the greatest heresy in all Christendom.
>
> The Christian heresy, where God is concerned, is that Deity is a spirit essence that fills the immensity of space; that he is three beings in one; that he is uncreated, incorporeal, and incomprehensible; that he is without body, parts, or passions; that he is a spirit nothingness that is everywhere and nowhere in particular present. These are concepts written in the creeds had in the churches of the world.[34]

Theology need not be the tortured intellectual affair that Catholic dogmatic tradition has made of it, a Latter-day Saint teacher might argue. If you want to imagine God and your relationship to him, start with your own father. He brought you into being, but not *ex nihilo*; for one thing, he needed the woman who would be your mother. Nor does he have to hold you in being once you

---

[33] Compare entries on "God" and "Godhood" in his *Mormon Doctrine* (Salt Lake City: Bookcraft, 1966), 264, and his speech "The Seven Deadly Heresies" (Brigham Young University, Salt Lake City, June 1, 1980), https://speeches.byu.edu/talks/bruce-r-mcconkie _seven-deadly-heresies.

[34] McConkie, "Seven Deadly Heresies".

have come to be, giving you existence in every moment. You were dependent on him, of course, when you were young. Without the provident care of your parents, or someone who took the place of your parents, you would not have survived very long. If your father was a good father, he provided for your physical needs, protected you from harm, and stopped you when you were about to do something that would harm you or others. If he was wise, he educated you, disciplined you, gave you rules, made promises, threatened you, punished you, and rewarded you. Sometimes he gave you gifts out of the blue, not because you deserved them but because he knew they would make you happy—but never so often that you would become spoiled. He did not want you to remain in childish dependence. He wanted you to know the joys of self-reliance and the enjoyment of rewards given in response to your own moral advancement and achievement.

Nonetheless, there was no way he could be sure you would turn out well. He could control you outwardly, at least while you were small and not as strong as him, but he could not make you want to do what was right. You had to be willing to learn from him and obey him, to let him teach you what was good and evil; or, if you disobeyed, you had to learn the difference between good and evil from the consequences of your actions. He hoped you would choose the good. He did everything he could to encourage and reward your good choices, but he could not take away your choice. He set you more and more difficult tasks and gave you greater and greater rewards for succeeding at them. As you advanced in goodness and moral character, you became stronger and more like him. Finally, you were ready for a family of your own: a wife and the children you would have with her. You would raise them as your father had raised you. And they would be the greatest reward of all.

Now you are ready to understand that not only do you have an earthly, mortal father but you and every other human being on earth also have the same Heavenly Father, who is as much greater, stronger, wiser, and purer than your earthly father as the heavens and everlasting life are greater than this earth and this mortal life. And he is training you to be like him. But you must choose to be like him and keep on choosing until the day you die. As you choose in this life, so will be your reward in the next. You are free to speculate about the metaphysical nature of God, but do not let your speculations be the sort that distract or confuse you about the meaning of life. Stay focused on the plan of salvation, the true gospel of Jesus, restored through Joseph Smith and practiced in the Church of the Latter-day Saints; stay focused on the rewards promised to those who fulfill the ordinances of the gospel. Here is how LDS materials currently describe the plan of salvation:

> God is the Father of our Spirits. We are literally His children, and He loves us. We lived as spirit children of our Father in Heaven before we were born on this earth. We were not, however, like our Heavenly Father, nor could we ever become like Him and enjoy all the blessings that He enjoys without the experience of living in mortality with a physical body.
>
> God's whole purpose—His work and His glory—is to enable each of us to enjoy all His blessings. He has provided a perfect plan to accomplish His purpose. We understood and accepted this plan before we came to the earth. In the scriptures God's plan is called a merciful plan, the plan of happiness, the plan of redemption, and the plan of salvation.
>
> Jesus Christ is central to God's plan. Through His Atonement, Jesus Christ fulfilled His Father's purpose and made it possible for each of us to enjoy immortality and exaltation. Satan, or the devil, is an enemy to God's plan.
>
> Agency, or the ability to choose, is one of God's greatest gifts to His children. Our eternal progression depends on how we use this gift. We must choose whether to follow Jesus Christ or follow Satan.
>
> We are physically separated from God during life on earth, but He wants every one of His children to find peace in this life and a fulness of joy in His presence after this life. He wants us to become like Him.[35]

As we have seen, the Fall of Adam and Eve is not quite the catastrophe that traditional Christian theology makes it. Although it brought spiritual and physical death to them and their children, those

[35] "The Plan of Salvation", lesson 2, chap. 3, in *Preach My Gospel: A Guide to Missionary Service* (Salt Lake City: Church of Jesus Christ of Latter-day Saints, 2019), www.churchofjesuschrist.org/study/manual/preach-my-gospel-a-guide-to-missionary-service/lesson-2-the-plan-of-salvation.

negative effects were neutralized by the Atonement and Resurrection of Jesus Christ, in whose name Adam and Eve were baptized after their expulsion from paradise. This was the plan agreed upon in the Grand Council of spirits before the creation of the world.[36]

The positive effects of the Fall were that now Adam and Eve could have children, giving the rest of God's faithful spirit children entrance into the mortal earthly life, where they would be able to use their agency to progress—or not, according to how they would choose—until they were capable and worthy of enjoying the full blessings that God himself already enjoyed. The presence of hardships, evil, and temptation was a boon, for it gave agency a scope for action; only through the inevitable experience of sin and its constant possibility could they learn to know good and evil and, by choosing the former, progress to be like God. The risk of sin made possible the varying degrees of glory they could achieve. God rewards each one in the next life according to what they do in this life.

> Those who have repented of their sins, received the ordinances of the gospel, and kept the associated covenants will be cleansed by the Atonement of Christ. They will be saved in the celestial kingdom. In the scriptures this kingdom is compared to the glory or brightness of the sun. . . .
>
> People who do not accept the fulness of the gospel of Jesus Christ in this life or in the world to come but live honorable lives will receive a place in the terrestrial kingdom. This kingdom is compared to the glory of the moon.
>
> Those who continued in their sins and did not repent in this life or accept the gospel in the world to come will receive their reward in the lowest kingdom, which is called the telestial kingdom. This kingdom is compared to the glory of the stars.[37]

Only the sons of perdition—Satan and the minority of spirits who rejected the Father's plan in the preearthly council in Heaven, together with those mortals who commit the unpardonable sin—will be truly damned, having no degree of glory in the next life.[38]

---

[36] John L. Lund, "Council in Heaven", in Ludlow, *Encyclopedia of Mormonism*, 217–18.

[37] "Plan of Salvation".

[38] Rodney Turner, "Sons of Perdition", in Ludlow, *Encyclopedia of Mormonism*, 1391–92.

In the council, Satan had proposed an alternative plan in which he would ensure that no spirit would be lost in the adventure of earthly life, thereby, in effect, seeking to destroy the agency of man.[39] Whatever the means by which he proposed to achieve this were, they would have contradicted the whole purpose of earthly life, which was to provide a field in which each spirit could achieve its own glory through the exercise of its free agency. The gospel is a set of ordinances, to be accepted, obeyed, and used, by which agency is exercised and glory achieved. The third and fourth Articles of Faith are as follows:

> We believe that through the Atonement of Christ, all mankind may be saved, by obedience to the laws and ordinances of the Gospel.
> We believe that the first principles and ordinances of the Gospel are: first, Faith in the Lord Jesus Christ; second, Repentance; third, Baptism by immersion for the remission of sins; fourth, Laying on of hands for the gift of the Holy Spirit.[40]

After these first ordinances come the temple ordinances and covenants that provide the means for achieving the various degrees of exaltation in the afterlife, including the rituals that seal marriages and parent-child relationships for all eternity, as well as vicarious ministrations for the dead who did not live in earthly times and places where the full ordinances of the gospel were known, thus giving everyone the same opportunities for salvation and exaltation as those now living. The family is at the center of the Mormon restoration of the gospel. "The saintly life is not in renunciation but in glorification of the family. The quest for happiness and completeness within the marital state is transformed from the banal and temporary toward the divine and eternal."[41] The "grace" of the gospel of Jesus Christ is simply the fullness of the law, or plan of salvation, set out before the earthly creation, obedience to which brings spirits from the immaturity of their primordial innocence to the full blessed condition of their Heavenly Father by the exercise of their own moral agency.

[39] Moses 4:1, 3.
[40] Articles of Faith 3–4.
[41] Allen Claire Rozsa, "Temple Ordinances", in Ludlow, *Encyclopedia of Mormonism*, 1445.

IV. Catholic Pelagianism and Mormon Pelagianism

Although the Latter-day Saint plan of salvation can be justly classed as "Pelagian" owing to its reduction of grace to law and its glorification of natural human agency, it is a distinctly Mormon form of this religious tendency. It is similar to historical Pelagianism in some respects and quite different in others.

To make clear both the similarity and the difference, I would like to consider Pelagius' *Letter to Demetrias*,[42] written to a young noblewoman who, as she approached marriageable age, was baptized a Christian and embraced the ascetical, monastic life of virginity. Her upbringing amid great wealth and luxury would inevitably ensnare her with all the pleasures of life in this world, binding her with the strongest of chains. "Suddenly," however, "she broke free and by her soul's virtue set aside all these bodily goods at once. Like the sword of faith, her will clipped off the flower of the age she was just entering."[43] Like Christ, she crucified the flesh and renounced not only the pleasures of luxury but also "a posterity of the noblest blood".[44] Now, no longer attracted by the worldly achievements of wealth and reputation, her ambition is set on seeking something higher. "Noble in the world, she wants to be noble before God."[45] She sets her sights on something extraordinary. "She searches for something new and untried; she demands something singular and outstanding."[46] Hers is not to be the life of ordinary people; she is devoted to an excelling achievement. Behind this extraordinary young woman stands a mother who has fostered the conversion and dedication of her daughter and has now written Pelagius for advice that will encourage and sustain such an ambitious beginning.

---

[42] In the following pages, I use the abbreviated translation in *Theological Anthropology*, ed. J. Patout Burns, S.J., *Sources of Early Christian Thought* (Philadelphia: Fortress Press, 1981). This anthology is a good introduction to the Pelagian controversy of the fifth century for the general reader. In other places, however, I have made reference to the full translation provided by B.R. Rees, *Pelagius: Life and Letters*, 2 vols. in 1 ed. (Woodbridge, Suffolk, UK: Boydell Press, 1998).

[43] Pelagius, *Letter to Demetrias* 39, in Burns, *Theological Anthropology*.

[44] Ibid., 40.

[45] Ibid.

[46] Ibid.

Such is Pelagius' task in this letter. The foundation upon which he builds, however, is not some extraordinary grace such a person might have received but the foundation of universal human nature, the strengths and characteristics of which provide the possibility and reasonableness of the ambition he seeks to encourage. He says that whenever he discusses "the principles of right conduct and the leading of a holy life", this is where he begins: "To call a person to something he considers impossible does him no good. Hope must serve as guide and companion if we are to set out on the way to virtue; otherwise, despair of success will kill every effort to acquire the impossible."[47] This is all the more necessary when the form of life to which a person aspires is the highest. "Where a more perfect form of life is to be established, the explanation of nature's goodness should be correspondingly fuller."[48] There is a proportion between one's estimation of the capacity of human nature and the zeal with which one pursues the goods that are possible for it to achieve. "Showing a person that he can actually achieve what he desires provides the most effective incentives for the soul."[49] Moreover, implicit in the possibility of some goal is the obligation to pursue. "Once something has been shown possible, it ought to be accomplished."[50]

With the advent of modern science, many people associate "nature" and "laws of nature" with what happens always and everywhere without exception; but for classical and medieval thinkers, what is naturally possible is not inevitably actualized, even among nonhuman natures. Even so, Pelagius feels obliged to address the problem of the widespread failure of human beings to achieve their natural potential. The empirical fact of so much human evil in the world, he argues, should not undermine one's confidence in the fundamental goodness and power of human nature. "You should not think that humanity was not created truly good because it is capable of evil."[51] A deeper consideration shows that what distinguishes human nature, making it superior to other kinds of nature—and what is truly universal about it—is the freedom to choose between good and evil. "I contend that

[47] Ibid.
[48] Ibid., 41.
[49] Ibid.
[50] Ibid.
[51] Ibid.

the dignity of our nature consists entirely in this: this is the source of honor, of reward, of the praise merited by the best people."[52]

This indeterminacy in human nature makes it possible for human beings to have something—indeed, to be the very source of something—that is truly and properly their own. "By making a person naturally capable of good and evil, so that he could do both and would direct his own will to either, God arranged that what an individual actually chose would be properly his own."[53] An individual may be beholden to God for his existence and nature, but he has the honor or dishonor of being the source of his own choices. "Every other creature has only the goodness which comes from its nature and condition; the reasonable being excels them all in having the goodness of its own will."[54]

Being the source of one's own good or evil choices is a good, but if it were the only good, the actual content of one's choices would not matter. One person's choice would be as good as another's. The real value of the freedom to choose, however, lies within the fact that the choice is made within a field of possibilities that are themselves distinguished by being good or evil, or rather, by being more or less good and more or less evil. For Pelagius the glory of human nature is that an individual can choose, but the glory of an individual human being lies precisely in choosing good—and among goods, the highest good—rather than evil. The Creator made us capable of both good and evil, but not out of any desire that we should actually choose the evil. "Actually, of course, he intended and commanded that we should do what is good. His only purpose in giving the capacity for evil was that we accomplish his will by our own will."[55]

If the possibility of choosing evil "makes the capacity for doing good, better",[56] then a fortiori, the difficulty of persevering in the good, makes the merit of doing so all the greater. The example of Noah is particularly instructive because it shows that no amount of social pressure and bad example can overcome the natural power to do good; "when the whole world had deserted justice he alone remained

[52] Ibid., 42.
[53] Ibid.
[54] Ibid., 43.
[55] Ibid., 42.
[56] Ibid.

upright. Rather than looking to anyone else, he provided an example of holiness."[57]

Difficult does not mean impossible. Wicked people cannot use the weakness of human nature as an excuse for doing evil. Such people "pretend that they do a good job of using what they were given and complain that they were not created differently. Instead of amending their lives, they want an improvement of their nature."[58] The existence of virtuous pagans, who do not even know or worship God, shows that the universal strength and characteristics of human nature are always sufficient for doing good. The pagan philosophers, especially, were "chaste, patient, temperate, generous, restrained, and kind";[59] they rejected human honors and worldly pleasure; they pursued justice and wisdom. "Why are these virtues attractive to people who are themselves separated from God? Where did they get these good qualities if not from the goodness of nature?"[60]

The actuality of goodness under such circumstances proves that such goodness is possible in any circumstance. The particular virtues practiced by individuals singly as well as all the virtues found in the whole group "could actually all be found, each and all, in every one",[61] because each one has the same nature as the others. The will is always free to do good or evil; this is the foundation for all moral judgment. Freedom of the will is responsible for "willing and refusing, choosing and rejecting, not the forces of nature.... We do either good or evil only by our own will; since we always remain capable of both, we are always free to do either."[62] And on the basis of this freedom we judge and are judged.

The universal experience of conscience, among both the good and the wicked, is further evidence of the deep goodness and integrity of nature. To know the field of good and evil in which human agency operates and to make judgments about the value of particular acts, one does not need an external command from God. "Our souls possess what might be called a sort of natural integrity which

[57] Ibid., 45.
[58] Ibid.
[59] Ibid.
[60] Ibid., 43.
[61] Ibid.
[62] Ibid., 49.

presides in the depths of the soul and passes judgments of good and evil.... Everyone who lived well and pleased God between the time of Adam and that of Moses actually made use of this law."[63]

If such is the case, however, why did God add anything to nature by giving the law or by providing the grace of Christ's example? Do Moses and then Christ bring new goods and evils into the field of possible choices, or do they simply reaffirm and make easier the choosing of goods from the field of nature? Pelagius implies the latter, for when he explains the purpose of the law, he does so as acknowledgment that there are conditions that make it harder to do good and easier to do evil and that these conditions accumulate with time. "As long as the exercise of the recently created nature continued to thrive and the long practice of sinning had not shrouded human reason like a fog, nature was left without a law."[64] He compares the law to a file with which one cleans and polishes metal that has become corroded by rust. This corruption, though adhering closely to nature, should not be confused with it. To nature has been added bad "customs".[65]

For the word "custom" we might substitute "habit", were it not for the fact that "custom" implies a social dimension that emphasizes its mode of transmission. "Habit", as well as "virtue" and "vice", that is, good and bad habits, usually appear in the context of individual moral life. But it is to these habits in their social operation rather than a merely individual acquisition that Pelagius attributes the corruption of nature. "Doing good has become difficult for us only because of the long custom of sinning, which begins to infect us even in our childhood."[66] Reared and trained in bad habits, we find it difficult to break free of them. They are not part of human nature, but they hold us "bound with what seems like the force of nature itself".[67] The building of new customs requires hard work.

The law with its promises and threats is given as a spur and aid to this labor. It is God's way of counteracting these evil habits and their social transmission to succeeding generations by establishing customs that accord with the good preserved deep down in human nature. The

[63] Ibid., 44.
[64] Ibid.
[65] Ibid., 50.
[66] Ibid., 49.
[67] Ibid., 50.

coming of Christ has the same purpose. "Christ's grace has taught us and regenerated us as better persons. His blood has purged and cleansed us; his example spurred us to righteousness. We should be better than people who lived before the law, therefore, and better than people who lived under the law."[68] Christians, "whose nature has been restored to a better condition by Christ and who are assisted by divine grace",[69] have no excuse not to excel in virtue.

The grace specific to Christ seems to consist in at least two things, the forgiveness of sins and his personal example, but the purging and cleansing that comes through his blood might also include some relief from the nature-like force of habit, so that one experiences once again the natural freedom that people enjoyed when human nature was first created. Perhaps this is what he means by "regeneration". His earlier description of Demetrias speaks of a sudden break with the past. Although he emphasizes the role of her will in her conversion, he does liken its action to "the sword of faith",[70] which may imply an additional dimension of grace.

Be that as it may, once one has converted to Christ and embarked on the ascetical path of the monastic life, the most important thing is to lay a good beginning of new customs. "Custom will nourish either vice or virtue, and its power is greatest when it develops in people from their early years. For establishing a way of life, therefore, the initial years are most important."[71] He develops this point at length with examples from seedlings, animals, and education of the young. Youth, and perhaps also the second youth after conversion—it is hard to tell because both apply in the case of Demetrias—is a privileged time for establishing new customs. "As long as your age makes you flexible and your soul responds easily to guidance, good custom should be practiced and established by bearing the yoke."[72] By setting one's mind on the highest things and allowing the habits of a holy life to sink deep into the soul, "the soul will climb to the very pinnacle of perfection and will exercise a facility in good living which is grounded in well-established custom."[73]

---

[68] Ibid., 50–51.
[69] Ibid., 43.
[70] Ibid., 39.
[71] Ibid., 51.
[72] Ibid.
[73] Ibid., 51–52.

Pelagius therefore directs his reader to observe all the commands of God even in lesser matters. Even if the commands seem impossible to bear, we should never think they exceed our ability; to do so is to accuse God of wickedness. "What insane stupidity! What impious arrogance! We accuse the Lord of all knowledge of being doubly ignorant. We assert that he does not understand what he made and does not realize what he commands."[74] Nature may appear weak to us, but the Creator of humanity knows all about such weakness and never "imposes precepts which a human being cannot bear". Indeed, "no one understands what we can do better than the one who endowed us with the capacity for virtue. The just one did not choose to command the impossible; nor did the loving one plan to condemn a person for what he could not avoid."[75]

Nothing, therefore, holds one back from seeking the highest purity of which human nature is capable. As if this confidence in nature's capacity were not enough, the Scriptures assure us that what we achieve in this life will receive its corresponding reward in the King-dom of God. God even goes so far as to give us "the strongest exhor-tation possible, for Scripture to call us the children of God. Who would not be embarrassed and ashamed to do something unworthy of such a father, to turn someone called a child of God into a slave of vice?"[76] By bearing in mind this heavenly birth, one can overcome the pressure of "an infinite multitude of sinners surround[ing] you and innumerable examples of the vices".[77]

"A life corresponds to its reward."[78] The children of the Heavenly Father each receive an inheritance in the kingdom of their Father suitable to what they have achieved on earth. "The many mansions in the kingdom of heaven differ according to the merits of individ-uals. As good works differ, so do their rewards. Thus a person will shine there in glory as he has shone here in holiness."[79] He there-fore exhorts Demetrias to give "the strength of your whole mind to achieving a full perfection of life now"[80] and so by a heavenly life

[74] Ibid., 53.
[75] Ibid.
[76] Ibid., 54.
[77] Ibid.
[78] Ibid.
[79] Ibid.
[80] Ibid.

prepare for a heavenly reward. Nothing should hold her back from
this holy ambition, especially since she is young and unencumbered
by vices. If those whose sinfulness of life has nearly eclipsed the inherent goodness of nature can be changed by penance, "if they can
change the direction of their lives and destroy one custom with
another, if they can go from being the worst to being among the
best, then how much more can you overcome the evils that have
never overcome you."[81]

The remainder of the letter turns to warnings about particular evil
thoughts and vices that she may encounter in the course of her chosen life and gives advice on how to deal with them.[82] It is a rich text,
standing within the tradition of ascetical texts that garner and hand
on the practical experience and wisdom of the early Christian ascetics. But this first part of the letter is sufficient to illustrate Pelagius'
general moral worldview, one in which heroic moral ambition is
possible because however encrusted human nature may have become
with bad habits, it never loses its inherent goodness and capacity for
choosing the good and perfect. Moreover, God has provided an anti-
dote for the corrupting influence of evil customs by providing the
law with its commands and promises, as well as the gracious example
of Christ and the cleansing power of his blood.

When we consider the similarities and differences between the
historical Pelagius' vision of morality and religion and the Mormon
plan of salvation, the similarities are obvious, but the difference is
equally striking. Earlier I pointed to the fact that the glory of a man
does not lie in merely making choices but in the particular choices
he makes within a field of possible goods. Pelagius describes two
pairs of distinctions. The first is between things forbidden and things
enjoined; the second, between things allowed and things advised.
The latter sorts of things "have been left under our control, so that
we may either enjoy what is allowed and be satisfied with less honour
as a result or reject even what is permitted for the sake of a greater
reward".[83] Marriage, for example, is allowed, while virginity, being

[81] Ibid., 55.

[82] Patout Burns' translation ends with chapter 17. For chapters 18 to 30, the reader can use
Pelagius, "To Demetrias", in B.R. Rees, *Pelagius: Life and Letters*, 2 vols. in 1 ed. (Woodbridge, Suffolk, UK: Boydell Press, 1998).

[83] Pelagius, "To Demetrias", 46, in Rees, *Pelagius: Life and Letters*.

more perfect, brings the greater reward.[84] This way of characterizing the field of human goods is completely alien to Mormonism, for which the glorification of parenthood, both human and divine, holds center stage.

Here we touch on the essential difference between Catholic Pelagianism and Mormonism. Catholic Pelagianism may have a gravely deficient understanding of grace and an unwarranted confidence in the capacity of nature, but it still has a Catholic awareness of the fact that Christ calls man to a life radically different from the natural goods of his empirical existence. Man is called to live a divine life in Christ that transcends human nature and to do so with a perfection that is exemplified in the exaltation of virginity over marriage. Marriage, too, is a symbol of the supernatural life of grace, but to be that it must take a special form, the form of the espousal of a soul, or more properly the Church herself, to the divine Bridegroom, Christ, which requires of the soul/Church a virginal transcendence of the ordinary horizontal human plain from which the analogy is drawn. When parenthood is glorified, it is the unique maternity of the Virgin Mary.

The Catholic Pelagius still knew the immaterial transcendent Catholic God, the One that Talmage and McConkie would later decry. Pelagius underestimated the gap between the human and the divine, and, as a consequence, he undervalued the grace of Christ— but he was not drawn to the materialistic, anthropomorphic God of the LDS church. For Pelagius, Christ need only reveal the law, set a good example, and atone for sins, while for the full Catholic vision, the Word-made-flesh unites the infinite, incomprehensible, uncircumscribable divinity with finite human nature in such a way as to be the conduit of the divine life for mortals. Catholic salvation is a participation in the theandric life of Jesus, not a mere imitation of it. In sum, Catholic divinization, or *theosis*, is as different from Mormon exaltation as the Catholic God is from the LDS God. I am sorry if Talmage found the Catholic teachings about God "utterly incomprehensible in their mysticism and inconsistency"[85] and that McConkie regards our faith as the greatest of heresies. Like the Sadducees of old, who did not believe in man's resurrection (see Mt 22:23–30), these

[84] Pelagius, *Letter to Demetrias* 39–46, in Burns, *Theological Anthropology.*
[85] Talmage, *Articles of Faith*, 47.

two men seem to have suffered a tragic failure of imagination, limiting the real to what they could see and touch in the current condition of their animal, bodily existence.

The life of the resurrection is more than this life cleaned up and extended indefinitely. It is as different from this mortal life as virginity is from marriage. To achieve the glory of that resurrection can be only the work of grace, not of any created nature. It is God's power at work in us, a God whose essence is incomprehensible to bodily sense. Talmage wrote: "Admitting the personality of God, we are compelled to accept the fact of His materiality; indeed an 'immaterial being,' under which meaningless name some have sought to designate the condition of God, cannot exist, for the very expression is a contradiction in terms."[86]

If materiality and position in space and time are the necessary concomitants of existence, then there is fundamentally only one kind of reality. But Catholic faith sustains an intellectual vision that penetrates deeper and higher, exceeding the native boundaries of reason, but not of the real. Again from Talmage:

A statement of this doctrine, supposedly as announced by Athanasius, is as follows:—"We worship one God in trinity, and trinity in unity; neither confounding the persons nor dividing the substance. For there is one person of the Father, another of the Son, and another of the Holy Ghost. But the Godhead of the Father, Son, and Holy Ghost, is all one; the glory equal, the majesty co-eternal. Such as the Father is, such is the Son, and such is the Holy Ghost. The Father uncreated, the Son uncreated, and the Holy Ghost uncreated. The Father incomprehensible, the Son incomprehensible, and the Holy Ghost incomprehensible. The Father eternal, the Son eternal, and the Holy Ghost eternal. And yet there are not three eternals, but one eternal. As also there are not three incomprehensibles, nor three uncreated; but one uncreated, and one incomprehensible. So likewise the Father is almighty, the Son almighty, and the Holy Ghost almighty, and yet there are not three Almighties, but one Almighty. So the Father is God, the Son is God, and the Holy Ghost is God, and yet there are not three Gods but one God." It would be difficult to conceive of a greater number of inconsistencies and contradictions, expressed in as few words.[87]

[86] Talmage, *Articles of Faith*, 42.
[87] Ibid., 47–48.

How is a Catholic to respond except to imitate the Lord? Perhaps respond as Jesus did when questioned by the Sadducees: "You are wrong, because you know neither the Scriptures nor the power of God" (22:29).

The difference, then, between Latter-day Saint Pelagianism and Catholic Pelagianism lies principally in their different understandings of the divine nature and of the divine life for which human beings are destined.

Be that as it may, Pelagianism in itself already involves a diminished appreciation of the difference between divine and human agency. That is the first problem it poses, and that problem tends to take the form of an intellectual, theological problem.

Only God can cause a free act in another precisely as a free act, which makes the divine agency incomprehensible by creaturely standards, even in the case of purely natural acts. This is all the more so in the case of the acts produced by grace, the kind of acts necessary for salvation. Whereas the divine causality of natural acts operates invariably in accordance with the nature given once and for all, in the order of grace, the initiative belongs entirely to God such that whether the grace is given or not, the integrity of nature and its attendant freedom and responsibility remain intact. Moreover, the acts it effects are not merely superimposed on top of a free creaturely act but are genuinely the free acts of the cooperating creaturely agent, and in such a way that the created agency participates relatively in the merit of the acts. Grace produces in the created agent an act that it could never perform apart from grace, and yet it really is that agent's act.

If, like McConkie and Talmage, we imagine God to be a material being with an existence fundamentally like our own, the previous paragraph will be as incomprehensible as the Athanasian Creed. The understanding of causal relations derived from observing the interactions of created things does not equip reason to handle divine causality with any confidence, especially when it comes to its causal relationship to natures endowed with a rational will. Free will means that the acts of which the will is the source can never be produced necessarily and infallibly by another created cause. No created agency can effect a free voluntary act in another. It may be able to overpower physically and psychologically another by intimidation, manipulation, or deception, but doing so reduces or eliminates altogether the voluntary, responsible character of the action it elicits. Only the incomprehensible God can do such an incomprehensible thing as produce a free act in a created nature. But only thus can we become partakers in his divine nature. We are saved by grace.

Grace, however, cannot be reduced to a peculiar piece of metaphysical machinery. It involves an encounter between persons that begins as a preference, a choice. The primary choice is God's, not ours, and in Christ it no longer comes to us as a law or an ordinance but as a gratuitous gift of his Person, drawing us into participation in the divine life of the incomprehensible divinity. Insofar as that gift expresses his will for us, we might be said to "obey" it, but such obedience is no longer the response of a rational nature to a divine command but is instead the graced acquiescence to a vocation by which nature does no more than allow itself to be taken up into another kind of life for which nature knows itself to have no capacity except that which grace gives it.

The Magnificat of Mary (see Lk 1:46–55) is not the song of a spirit exulting in its moral progress by means of obedience to a set of laws and ordinances. It is the song of one who knows that in herself she is still poor but that she has been made rich by Another, of one who knows that in herself she is still powerless but that she has been lifted up to sit with Another on his throne. It has more in common with the penitential cry of the tax collector than with the prayer of the Pharisee who, rejoicing in his progress and achievement in keeping the law and ordinances of Moses, thanks God that he is not like other men who stand below him in lesser degrees of glory (see 18:10–14).

Much of the Catholic polemic against its own historical Pelagianism, documented in summary form in the pages of Denzinger, focuses on human nature's need for grace, either because of the guilty, wounded condition in which Adam's sin has left it or because of the supernatural end for which it has been created and redeemed. The anathemas are true enough, but I do not believe one has really felt "the horrendous and hidden poison"[88] of the Pelagian error until one confronts and renounces the titanic, even satanic, spiritual

[88] Augustine, *Contra Iulianum* 2, 146, in *Patrologia Latina*, ed. J. P. Migne (Paris, 1841–1855), 45, 1202.

ambition for excellence that lies at its core—and in the depths of the human heart, where pride cloaks itself as virtue.

Mormonism exalts human agency at the cost of a diminished divinity. Perhaps it would be better to forget about the advancement of our own agency and lose ourselves in wonder at the beauty of the divine nature and agency; then we would be able to say with Mary, "Behold, I am the handmaid of the Lord; let it be to me according to your word" (1:38). In the end, such a "Let it be" is the only act that makes our agency worthwhile. To achieve that, one does not need an elaborate scaffolding of ordinances, but only faith, hope, and love— the very same faith, hope, and love that has given the Church saints in every age since that day when Gabriel brought his tidings to Mary.

Only when one has accepted an authentic doctrine of election and predestination can one have a proper attitude toward the pursuit of holiness. Mary has a unique place at the summit of creaturely sanctity, "more honorable than the Cherubim and beyond compare more glorious than the Seraphim";[89] but that place was given to her by a unique predestined election and gift of grace. The Catholic doctrine of election finds one of its most powerful expressions in the dogma of the Immaculate Conception.

Nonetheless, the doctrines of election and predestination constitute a theological minefield where a false step can have disastrous consequences. The *Catechism of the Catholic Church*'s scanty references to predestination walk this ground gingerly and do not provide a systematic account of the matter. What they do provide are markers to keep specialists and simple believers alike safe in transit. Whether, how, and why grace is given is completely up to God and can never be reduced to a correspondence to natural merit. Moreover, without grace man cannot attain beatitude. This is perhaps the essence of the Catholic doctrine of grace formulated by Saint Augustine.[90]

But there are other elements in Augustine's doctrine that the Catholic Church has all but repudiated. Augustine accepted as obvious that out of the whole mass of fallen humanity, tainted by Adam's sin, only

---

[89] A phrase from a Byzantine Christian hymn.

[90] See Augustine, *On the Free Choice of the Will, On Grace and Free Choice, and Other Writings*, ed. and trans. Peter King (New York: Cambridge University Press, 2010). This anthology consists of excerpts from Saint Augustine's writings on free will and grace that he worked on from the 380s through the 420s.

a few will be saved; therefore, only a few are predestined to glory. Augustine's speculations about the plan by which God apportions his grace to men run in a direction contrary to the Church's proclamation of a gospel, a good news, that reveals a divine love reaching out to include all men.

The magisterial teachings of the Catholic Church have never repudiated the absolute necessity of grace for salvation, nor have they yielded to Pelagian and Semi-Pelagian compromises regarding the primacy of the divine initiative, but they clearly wish to eliminate any speculations about the divine plan that would cause anyone to doubt the sincerity with which God has announced his love for all in Christ Jesus. The Church has always maintained that the universal salvific will of God is real and not an illusion. But if God wants everyone to be saved, why do human beings seem to have such disparate destinies within the horizon of history? If God truly loves all, why does he seem to dole out grace so unequally? But perhaps we do not see the whole story. If we do not need to follow Augustine's belief that few will be saved, dare we hope, as one reputable theologian asks, that in the end all will be saved?[91]

Saint Thérèse of Lisieux (1873–1897), the Little Flower, whom Pope Saint John Paul II made a Doctor of the Church in 1997, saw clearly that the foundation of all sanctity is God's election and predestination. Human perfection itself consists in the loving acceptance, not the autonomous achievement, of God's will for one's life. The plan of salvation is not an obstacle course on which souls strive to be the best that they can be and thereby merit the greatest degree of glory possible for themselves, but a garden in which the sun reveals its glory in the wide variety of great and little flowers on which it shines.[92]

V. Conclusion

One of my dear Lutheran relatives, now departed, could never receive a kindness from a Catholic without questioning the motive.

[91] Hans Urs von Balthasar, *Dare We Hope "That All Men Be Saved"?* (San Francisco: Ignatius Press, 1988).

[92] See *The Autobiography of St. Thérèse of Lisieux: The Story of a Soul*, trans. John Beevers (Garden City, NY: Image Books, 1957), 2–3.

"They are only doing it to earn points for heaven", she would say. Occasionally, I do encounter Catholic circles that spend more time talking and worrying about merit than the usual crowds I run with. Perhaps their way of thinking was more common in the past, but the *Catechism of the Catholic Church*'s section on merit reminds us that merit comes from grace and that grace is really not about us but about Christ. Not surprisingly, it ends with a quotation from the Little Flower:

> *The charity of Christ is the source in us of all our merits* before God. Grace, by uniting us to Christ in active love, ensures the supernatural quality of our acts and consequently their merit before God and before men. The saints have always had a lively awareness that their merits were pure grace.
>
> "After earth's exile, I hope to go and enjoy you in the fatherland, but I do not want to lay up merits for heaven. I want to work for your *love alone*.... In the evening of this life, I shall appear before you with empty hands, for I do not ask you, Lord, to count my works. All our justice is blemished in your eyes. I wish, then, to be clothed in your own *justice* and to receive from your *love* the eternal possession of *yourself*."[93]

I fear for all Pelagians, whether Catholic or Mormon, that if they—if we—have spent a lifetime seeking our own moral and spiritual advancement, if all our works of religion, all our acts of kindness, all our love for mother and father and spouse and children have been tainted by spiritual ambition and acquisitiveness, by the desire for our own exaltation and celestial glory, we may find ourselves poorly prepared to enjoy the kind of beatitude that the Lord has actually prepared for us, beautifully described here in a Middle English text for women ascetics.

> Such joy they have of God that the sum of their joy is so great that no mouth may recall nor speech present it. Because each one loves another as himself, each one has of another's good as much joy as of his own. By this you can see and perceive that each one has individually

---

[93] *Catechism of the Catholic Church*, no. 2011, quoting Saint Thérèse of Lisieux, "Act of Offering", in *Story of a Soul*, trans. John Clarke (Washington, DC: ICS, 1981), 277 (emphasis in original).

as many varieties of felicity as is the number of them all, and each of the same felicities is to every single one as great a cause of happiness as is his own separately. Yet over and above all the others, he has in God more joy beyond reckoning than he has in his own rejoicing and in that of all the others.

Now therefore give thought to this. If no one's heart can ever find room in itself for its own joy, so immeasurably great is the single individual bliss that it receives, how does it receive into itself ones so numerous and so great? For this reason Our Lord said to those that had pleased Him: *Intra in gaudium Domini Tui.* "Go," He said, "into the joy of thy Lord." Thou must enter wholly therein, and be all drenched therein, for into thee it can in no wise be taken.[94]

---

[94] From the Middle English *Sawles Warde*, modern English translation attributed to J. R. R. Tolkien, procured from a LISTSERV in the early days of the Internet. Unfortunately, the original email was deleted long ago, and I have so far been unable to track down and verify the attribution.

AFTERWORD

On Being a Catholic in Utah

Brad S. Gregory

When I graduated from high school four years ago, there was only one meaning of "the Church", naturally—*the* Church, the Roman Catholic Church. The crossroads of the West meant Rome, perhaps Paris or even New York. Hence my surprise when I came to Utah State University from Marian Central Catholic High School in Woodstock, Illinois, and learned that here "the Church" meant the Church of Jesus Christ of Latter-day Saints, and the crossroads of the West (the western United States, that is) was Salt Lake City. Four years ago, being religious meant going to Mass on Sunday, receiving the sacraments regularly, praying, thinking about God, and attempting to lead a good life. It still involves all that, but at the same time, being a Catholic in Utah has changed what it means for me to be a religious person.

The problem with the topic for this paper is how to walk through such a potential minefield. I see little point in offering my opinion about any of "those" topics: the notion of a true Church, the allegation of a great apostasy, controversy over Joseph Smith or the Book of Mormon or prophecy or divine revelation or conception of God, etc., ad nauseum. The challenge is to write meaningfully about my experience as a Catholic in Utah in a way at once inoffensive to my many Mormon friends, yet consistent with who I am.

I am indeed quite Catholic, in all facets of my approach to God; I find my faith immensely satisfying and rewarding, and I constantly

Delivered as a valedictorian address at the 1985 commencement for the College of Humanities and Social Sciences, Utah State University, Logan, Utah.

strive to live it. My contact with Mormonism has played an important role in motivating me to grow in my faith and my understanding
of it, as has happened over the past four years. If "collective thanks"
makes any sense, I would like to thank Mormonism for that.

These four years demanded that I seek out the most fundamental
strata of my faith, the true core of what being human means to me.
There is a great power, a transcendent power, in the simplicity and
directness of the Christian message that accounts for its survival and vitality through twenty centuries, despite so much bumbling and so
many setbacks. This power is not blindingly manifest in the entire
history of Christianity; it sometimes harms and threatens to undermine the very goal for which it strives: it is not and can never be
ensconced in a "perfect institution".

Religion is not the great exception to our otherwise human activities; it is rather the eminent human activity by which human beings
show themselves in their totality, in strength and weakness, in good
and evil. Through it all the Christian message remains; *it is simply and
radically that we love.* So long as the message retains its power—that is,
so long as human beings remain human—Christianity will endure.
It will have its problems, as it always has, ever since Saint Paul tried
to reconcile differences in the very earliest communities of faith. But
the message is out, and there is no taking it back. So long as men and
women recognize what God was up to in that man from Nazareth,
Christianity will survive in spite of all setbacks, in those who are at
once foolish and courageous enough to love.

That basic strata of my faith—the power of the Christian message—
compelled me to focus on ecumenism in this paper. Without a serious commitment to ecumenism, my Catholic faith is a sham; indeed,
the two are inseparable. Ecumenism does not mean attempting to
"bring others around" to see "how right we really are", nor is it a
grudging tolerance we manage to squeeze out for those who pursue
an avenue to God different from our own. *Ecumenism is rather radical
ecumenism.* As a friend in Louvain, Belgium, said to me last year: "If
our religious differences prevent us from sitting down and breaking
bread together, then we're missing the whole point." I think this
is dead right, with all its far-reaching implications. Religion is supposed to be that which above all unites us, yet more often than not
it succeeds in dividing us. Oh sure, we're "nice" to those who don't

believe as we believe, but are we able to treat them precisely as we would "if only" they were of the same faith as us? This is the challenge of radical ecumenism. It is nothing less than an application of the Sermon on the Mount to the pluralistic twentieth century. The challenge is not to simply tolerate others, to "be a nice guy"—it is to love them fully and unconditionally *regardless of their religious affiliation or lack thereof.*

When religion becomes a barrier between two people, it has turned on its own object; it has canceled and distorted itself, put out of reach the end for which it allegedly exists. If differences in religious doctrine prevent us from loving another person as much as we would have without those differences, then there is a problem; doctrine is not more important than people. If interpretation of Scripture creates a gulf between ourselves and others, then we are to put interpretation of Scripture in its place: below the imperative for human solidarity. If a conception of God inhibits us in loving another with a different conception of God, then let us recognize such conceptions for what they are: significant insofar as they help us love others in a more authentic way. I don't think God cares about religion; he cares about the world and about people in the world. When religion unites people in love and justice, it is a successful means to an end. When it does not, dividing them in bitterness instead, it is the paradigm of perversion, the ultimate irony.[1]

At the most fundamental level, the question of religious authority is this simple: if we love, we have authority, and if we don't, we don't have authority. This is what Christ is all about. The atheist who loves

---

[1] The twenty-two-year old Brad Gregory was not saying in this paragraph that one should acquiesce on matters of doctrine in order to appease or get along with critics of the faith. Rather, he was saying that one's love of doctrinal truth ought never to diminish one's love for those who reject that truth. What he was expressing, as a very young man, is the anguish we all face when we are called upon to love those who come from religious traditions whose doctrines and understanding of Sacred Scripture challenge what we Catholics believe to be true about the nature of revelation, tradition, and the Church. This posture is echoed in the Second Vatican Council's Decree on Ecumenism *Unitatis Redintegratio* (4, 11): "When ... actions [for and in ecumenical dialogue] are undertaken prudently and patiently by the Catholic faithful, with the attentive guidance of their bishops, they promote justice and truth, concord and collaboration, as well as the spirit of brotherly love and unity.... Moreover, in ecumenical dialogue, Catholic theologians standing fast by the teaching of the Church and investigating the divine mysteries with the separated brethren must proceed with love for the truth, with charity, and with humility."—EDS.

others out of his humanism has more authority than the most pious
Catholic who can't quite bring himself to fully love a Mormon; than
the most devout Mormon who can't manage to love a Protestant
without reservation; than the most ardent Protestant who refuses to
embrace a Catholic in love. Ecumenism means we not only must
love those in our parish or ward or Church or nation but also must
open our arms to all others. As Teilhard de Chardin has said, we
must "embrace the universe". If our religious beliefs are a barrier to
our ability to love others, then let us adjust our religious beliefs or
become atheists. Better to be a nonbeliever who can love without
restriction than a believer who cannot.

It's funny—I sound like someone who has mastered that about
which he writes. I am the first to admit the extent to which I struggle
with my own ecumenical standards, especially as a Catholic here in
Utah. Rarely am I able to come close to practicing what I know to be
the ideal, particularly with my personal barriers of intellectual pride
and enthusiasm about Catholicism.

The Catholic University of Louvain is the oldest Catholic university in the world and an internationally recognized center for Catholic thought. When I was there last year, I was "so ecumenical"—how
easy it is when you're dealing only with other Catholics. But back
in Utah this year has been the challenge. I have not met it very
well. It is extremely difficult for me to keep things in perspective.
Although more often than not I fail to some extent in my ecumenical endeavor, which bothers me, my goal never wavers. Meeting it
will always be a struggle, but that does not lessen the importance of
the ideal.

I've spent a great deal of time thinking about ecumenism because
of my general and specific experience of being a Catholic here in
Utah. It is not merely a theoretical issue, peripheral to my religiosity—
it is and has been a daily, lived reality. It's like this: I fell in love
with a Mormon girl here at Utah State, and she fell in love with me.
Never had I met anyone who touched me the way Connie did; never
were any and all words so crude in attempting to express a relationship. Without any rules to follow, we invented our love as we went
along—that's the way it is when Catholic boy meets Mormon girl. Of
course, it's not a good idea to date people outside your own faith; how
many times have we all been told that? Yet compared to the concrete

person, the sheer beauty of who Connie Madson is, that warning melted away like the snow from the Wellsvilles.

Do you know what tragedy is? Sin is where you turn away from God and hurt because of it, but tragedy is where you turn *toward* him and still hurt. God forgives sin, but he cannot "forgive" tragedy, because there is nothing to forgive—no wrong has been done. I am not so naive as to think Connie would be anything like the person she is without the LDS faith, which is at the center of her being— likewise for Brad and his Catholic faith. A non-Mormon Connie and a non-Catholic Brad are two imaginary people, not two people who fell in love with each other here in Logan. And yet that very religiosity, without which we would not have been attracted to each other, prevented what would almost certainly have been a permanent union. That is tragedy. Neither Sophocles nor Shakespeare could have done any better.

I would like to relate here a poem from last fall dedicated to Connie. Appropriately, it is entitled "Ecumenism".

> There are moments
> when I am able to go beyond
> those green eyes and proud chin
> and see you and I as we really are
> When I am filled only to overflow
> When I can climb inside you
> and hug you from within
> When Joseph and Thomas, Spencer and John Paul
> are no more than the names of people we've never met
>
> In the embrace of our souls
> Two droplets of God become one.

I love and I will always love Connie Madson. What else can be done? Dear God, how I despise religion sometimes! But even though it prevented a marriage, here and now, it could not prevent love. We proved that. Nothing can ever take that away, and neither of us would trade it for anything.

Being a Catholic in Utah has been eye-opening, challenging, meaningful: I have no doubt it has made me a better human being. My embrace is wider now than it was when I came to live among the Mormons four years ago. When I recall my years at Utah State, I won't think first about the courses I took, the good times I had, or the extracurricular activities in which I was involved. I'll think instead about my few moments of ecumenical success—of when I managed to go beyond those green eyes and that proud chin, and of the girl who showed me that was possible.

CONTRIBUTORS

Francis J. Beckwith is a professor of philosophy and church-state studies and associate director of the graduate program in philosophy at Baylor University.

Richard Sherlock is a professor emeritus of philosophy at Utah State University.

Rachel Lu is an associate editor at *Law & Liberty* and a contributing writer at *America* magazine and *National Review*.

Ronald Thomas is an associate professor of theology at Belmont Abbey College.

Alexander Pruss is a professor of philosophy and the director of the graduate program in philosophy at Baylor University.

The Reverend Joel Barstad is the director of Human Formation at Byzantine Catholic Seminary of Saints Cyril and Methodius.

Matthew Levering holds the James N. and Mary D. Perry Jr. Chair of Theology at Mundelein Seminary at the University of Saint Mary of the Lake.

James Hitchcock is a professor emeritus of history at Saint Louis University.

Glenn Olsen is a Distinguished Fellow of the St. Paul Center for Biblical Theology and a professor emeritus of history at the University of Utah.

Brad S. Gregory holds the Dorothy G. Griffin Collegiate Chair in European History at the University of Notre Dame.

INDEX

Protestantism (*continued*)
  Reformation, 10
  Second Great Awakening, 123,
    137, 147

Qualben, Lars Pedersen, 98
Qur'an, 29, 30, 38

Reformation, 10, 57, 113–17, 159–60,
  165
restorationism, 9, 10, 13, 14, 95, 153,
  179–82, 191, 198, 205, 206, 217
Revelation, Book of, 98
revelation(s)
  absence of authoritative revelation,
    101
  on alcohol and tobacco
    prohibition, 147
  apostolic Fathers and, 97
  approach to special revelation, 77
  augmentation of, 182
  Barker on modern revelation,
    94–96, 103, 117, 118, 119
  continuing, 181
  contradictory, 181
  divine revelation ceasing after
    apostles, 116
  dogma and, 183–85
  on God's purposes, 45
  God's self-revelation to the Jews,
    139–41
  interpretation of, 116
  on Jesus Christ as God, 80
  Jesus' continuing revelation to
    apostles, 94, 96
  of Joseph Smith, 205, 206, 208
  of Mormon prophets, 129
  Mormonism's claims to continuing
    revelations, 98
  to Muhammad, 29–30
  on origin and nature of God, 23–24
  original revelation restoration, 95
  papacy and continuing revelation,
    177
  Pelagianism and, 203

philosophical theology on, 101
popes' infallibility as, 101
Scripture and, 198, 199
from Septuagint, 90
sharing of fullness of God's, 34
Smith claim to further, 9
on Trinity, 81, 84–86
Roberts, B.H., 12–13, 58–59. *See also*
  classical theism
Rowe, William, 42

sacraments
  baptism, 98–100, 105–106, 115–16
  debates over nature of, 147–48
  Eastern Orthodox churches and,
    144
  Eucharist, 110, 143
  grace and, 143, 204
  Mormon ritual and, 154
  Protestantism and, 113, 114
  salvation and, 100
salvation
  baptism and, 100
  Catholic doctrine of, 218, 225, 226,
    231
  confidence in God's salvation, 41,
    43
  economy of, 18, 32
  Eucharist and, 143, 164
  good works as essential to, 195–96,
    214–16, 224–25, 228
  grace and, 143, 203–4, 206, 228, 231
  Incarnation and, 39–40, 51, 107,
    140
  liturgy and, 140–41, 143
  logos theology and, 51
  Mormon doctrine of, 15–16, 25,
    152–55, 160, 206, 213, 215, 217
  temple ritual and, 137–38
Scriptures
  Catholic reading of, 61–64
  corruption of, 129
  translations of, 26
Second Great Awakening, 123, 137,
  147